Chronicles of a Soul

A Journey of Remembrance

John Steven Albin

Copyright © 2011 by John Steven Albin.

Cover photos of Lotus Copyright 2011 Subbotina Anna. Image from Bigstock.com
Cover enhancements courtesy of Xlibris Design Team

Library of Congress Control Number:		2011913566
ISBN:	Hardcover	978-1-4653-4528-8
	Softcover	978-1-4653-4527-1
	Ebook	978-1-4653-4529-5

All rights reserved. No part of this book may be reproduced or transmitted in any form or by any means, electronic or mechanical, including photocopying, recording, or by any information storage and retrieval system, without permission in writing from the copyright owner.

This book was printed in the United States of America.

To order additional copies of this book, contact:
Xlibris Corporation
1-888-795-4274
www.Xlibris.com
Orders@Xlibris.com
Book ID # 103486

I dedicate this book to all who have chosen to walk the spiritual path

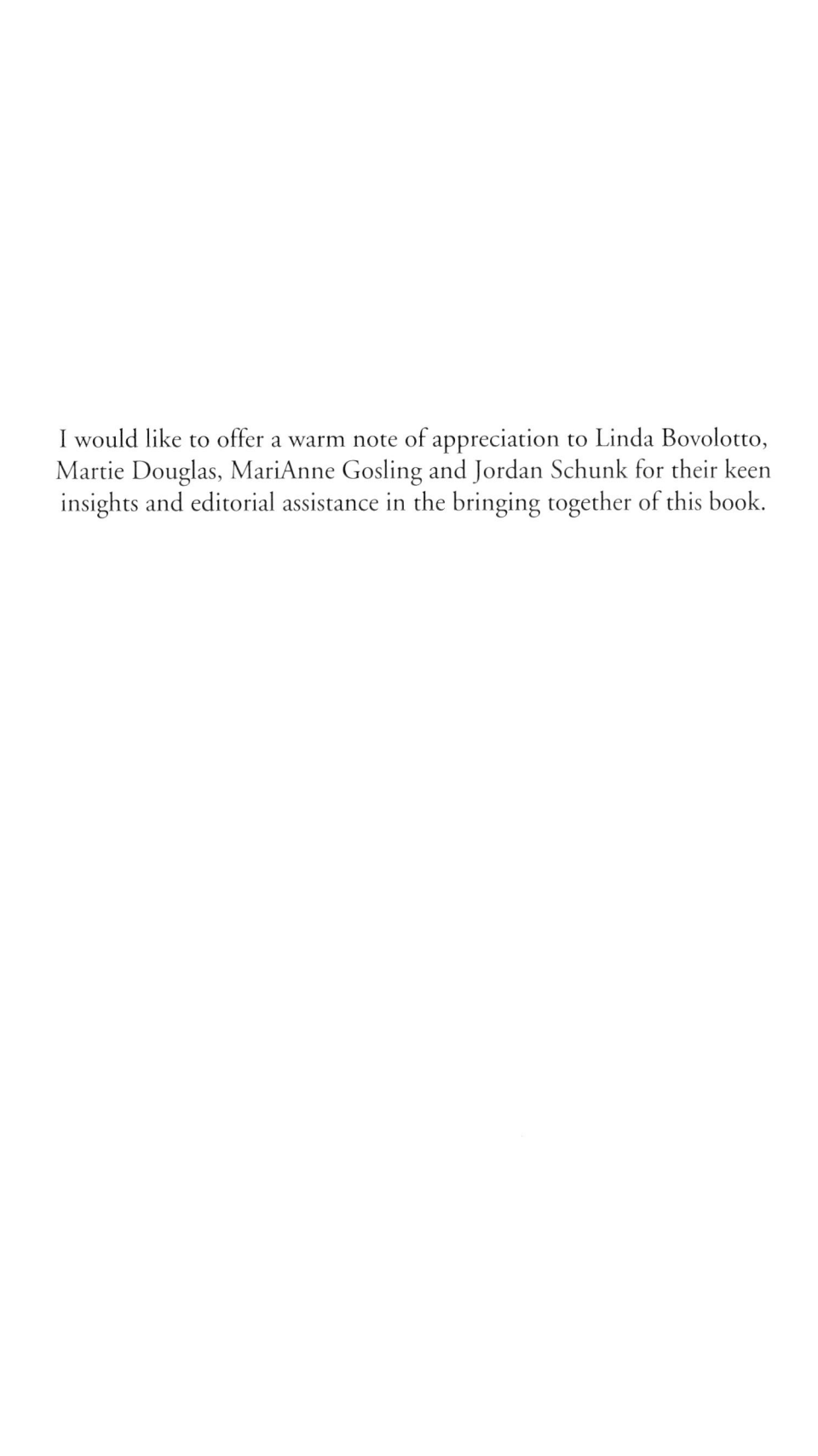

I would like to offer a warm note of appreciation to Linda Bovolotto, Martie Douglas, MariAnne Gosling and Jordan Schunk for their keen insights and editorial assistance in the bringing together of this book.

Author's Preface

Imagine a depth of inner peace and love that may transcend your most secret imaginings and yearnings. Imagine unveiling the joy and beauty of the Divine that lies within you. Imagine coming to a place, an intimately profound state of being, where all you feel is the loving encompassment of God flowing through you. I marvel with wonder and gratitude at how my own journey unfolded.

Chronicles of a Soul . . . A Journey of Remembrance is a written account of what became for me, a deeply spiritual odyssey. I experienced the potential of humanity as a whole to lift our selves into the Light and find our selves within God. I experienced the realization that humanity is truly part of a bigger whole, and that we ourselves are much more than we realize.

In setting out to write this book, I started with the idea that I would write a story of my journey; a story written in the hopes that through the writing of it, it would offer support, validation, or guidance to those on their own healing and spiritual journeys, but as it flowed through its many incarnations it became much more. It grew as I grew, and it has become whole unto itself and carries its own message. I have written it in a way that is part memoir, part observations and insights, and part learnings. I was gifted with much along the way, much more than I would have originally known possible, and it was through the writing of this book that I came to realize that my whole life has been a gift and a Divine blessing. It did not always feel that way though, and throughout the pages that follow you will be able to experience this journey as I did, by looking through a window into my heart.

Though this book has been written as a reflection of my life, there may be much within these pages that can assist anyone who is searching for a deeper meaning to their own life, searching for a deeper sense of whom they truly are, or who is searching for a deeper sense of spiritual connection. This book has been written for anyone who feels an inner yearning to fully connect to something deeply intimate, personal, or meaningful within their lives. It was through fully opening to, and following this deep inner yearning to its source that changed my life, leading me in a direction that was totally unexpected, but yet not completely unknown. Within these pages you will be led through a candid, chronological account of my perceptions, inner healing, experiences and insights that offered me the opportunity to come out of all that I knew of myself, and all that I had suppressed, to eventually awaken into the loving embracement of Heart and Divine consciousness.

A moment of time, and a flicker of Light from deep within during my darkest hour, was all it took to start a chain of events that eventually set me on the path that allowed me to experience God. In its truest sense, this became a Divine journey of acceptance, surrender, opening, and loving remembrance. I felt embraced by so much love and support throughout it that my heart weeps with gratitude, for all of the feelings of emptiness, separation, pain, confusion, and deep spiritual longing that I once held so deep within were lifted away.

I have grown in ways that I could not have imagined. In sharing my experiences, insights, and awakenings, my hope is that you find something that will bring greater clarity, empowerment, love, and acceptance into your own spiritual journeys of remembrance, discovery, and joy.

Believe in yourself, and just perhaps, by walking with me as I lead you through my journey, you may fly more freely on yours.

CONTENTS

Author's Preface		7
Book One:	My Journey Begins	11
Book Two:	Irish Journal	53
Book Three:	Changes . . . and a Symbol	87
Book Four:	The Southwest Beckons	99
Book Five:	Akashic Records	127
Book Six:	Deeper Understandings	169
A Few Closing Words		211

Book One

My Journey Begins

As I set the phone down a massive shiver enveloped my body, and I had no idea just how much my life and all that I believed about life and this reality would eventually change. The newspaper had lain open for two days, and each time I walked by it my eyes were drawn to one particular ad. It was not my eyes alone though that had been drawn, for something much deeper within had been compelling me to look. The universe and my guides must have felt my desperation and this had been their way of communicating, but within this particular moment in time I had no clue about this. In fact I did not have a clue about much at all. I just knew deep within, that something profound was coming.

The roller coaster ride I had put my family through had finally taken its toll, and I had been sitting in a furnished but empty apartment for days. All that had once been so important in my life I had let slide through my fingers and I was tormented by grief.

The realization that something profound was approaching had sparked a glimmer of hope, but it was only a glimmer; every level of my being felt as if it was imploding as all real meaning had now gone. I had torn my family apart, but even watching as it was happening, I could not or somehow would not, stop it. I was not in a good space and I was floundering despairingly. My family had been my anchor in life, though I did not truly understand the full extent of how much until now. I envisioned that I was standing on the edge of a cliff and swaying back and forth imploringly, my heart crying out to the universe for some kind of help.

Awakening to this cry, the token spirit that I still had remaining arose from the depth of my being and surfaced with a surge of indescribable and all-encompassing power. This forgotten part of me had to live, and I was startled by the sheer magnitude of its will to survive. It knew that 'it' still held an unfulfilled purpose. I was so caught up in all that I had become over the years that this aspect felt just as separate from me as it did a part of me. Was it the accumulation of exhaustion, confusion, disjointed love, emptiness, pain, and finally the separation from my family that became the catalyst in my life to heal? Was the culmination of all that had led up to this the only thing that could have really hit home, and shaken me up enough to make this journey to the extent that I have? That surge of power and spirit had engulfed me, and I had never before felt so precisely determined or focused. It was this moment in time where I set my intent to heal all that I carried inside, and it was to be this moment in time, that set the stage for what was to come.

Looking back prior to this, the pure joy I had once felt with my family had led into an increasing darkness as I slowly spiraled into an inner hell.

My life had become a life of constant pain and stress, multiple injuries, and all-encompassing fatigue from working on the factory floor. It had been 18 years or more that I had dealt with this, and I finally reached a point where I could not deal with it anymore. Fibromyalgia had set in and I had become extremely sensitive. I felt as if I was living in the body of an eighty year old man who had had all of his joy and vitality sucked away, and underlying this, I carried an inner tension that amplified and reinforced everything that I was experiencing. I became acutely focused on anger, frustration and resentment, and my pain and lack of vitality were over-riding everything.

In time, I eventually became totally numb and empty. I felt no compassion, no tenderness, no love, no anger, no joy, nothing. I could not feel anything accept the dull throb of pain. I lost the ability to even connect with my own feelings. The protective walls I had built up over the years, as well as my assumption that I had to maintain an image of the strong, quiet and confidant male at all costs were working against me. I had succeeded only in becoming frustratingly adept at closing myself down, so much so that I became numb and devoid of everything. I felt like I was being buried alive.

I was an innately highly sensitive, gentle, emphatic, sentimental and compassionate person, but these qualities at different times over my life had become increasingly fragmented and covered over. On the surface I became harder and more detached. Eventually it had an adverse influence on my family relationships, because it had become a pattern and I could not separate it and carried those characteristics all the time. While my daughters were young I had opened to the joy of play, of laughter, and togetherness, but all too soon the outside world had closed in again. By continually suppressing, even indirectly, all that I felt was good about who I was, I had propelled myself to this place. I understood that if I was to live I had to break that pattern, and I felt that need with every fibre of my being.

To step back a moment of time, prior to my family break up I had sought help through an intuitive Psychotherapist. I had been desperately searching for something within myself to anchor into; my family had been my only real anchor but I had lost the ability to grasp onto them. I was searching for anything that I could lock onto, anything to bring more concrete clarity and stability to my life. I was emotionally bouncing all over the place, and the hardened, detached personas' I had developed over my life were affecting everyone around me. It was during my time with this Psychotherapist that I experienced the first dawning insights into what would follow, for she incorporated energy healing as an integral part of her healing approach. I experienced such a deep resonance with this energy therapy that for the first time in my life I began to feel truly connected with something inside of myself. I felt an inward knowing or recognition that I could not explain, but just experiencing this taste of connection had me hooked.

It was during these sessions that I had five significant visions that I feel pertain to my journey. I would like to share them.

The first vision showed dense layers of cobwebs and dust overlapping a dried out mummy. I had an inner knowing that this carcass of a mummy was me and that I was crying out to be saved. I willed it to happen and the dust and cobwebs began to unravel, slowly at first but then amazingly fast. What surprised me was that it did not stop with this one carcass. The vortex of unraveling energies continued to increase in speed, and one mummified body after another going back in time was being freed. As the vortex became a blur, I knew with certainty that they were all me. I felt that this was an indication of just how many lifetimes I had buried myself; unable to break free of the protective walls I had created. I was left with the feeling that I had not been able to fully express myself in any of them.

I hoped with everything that my heart could spare that I would be able to break free of this cycle, for outside of playing with my daughters when they were young I had always held myself back from truly expressing all of who I was. In one-way or another throughout my life I developed a lack of inner confidence, and I had a deep-seated fear of rejection if I truly opened up. In many ways I felt like an outsider. It was only during the time that my daughters were young that this fear flew aside and I felt that I had been set free. The level of pure joyful abandon that flowed between us had been one of the greatest blessings of my life, and its memory became my primary sustenance in the ensuing years.

In my second vision I was standing in a field watching an incredibly dark storm brew. The wind began whipping in from all directions, and somehow I had a knowing that to survive it I had to project my essence into something else. The awareness flowed in, that no matter how much grass is blown around or pounded down, it will always bounce back. I moved into it. The storm passed and I survived. I wondered; was this vision connected to something that was about to erupt within me?

The third vision was much more vivid; all of my senses were involved. I was in the grasslands of Africa, a long, long time ago. Every fibre of my being was acutely alive, aware, and tuned in. The air smelled vibrantly alive and was so fresh and invigorating that it felt crystalline in its purity. My own scent was a little more pungent. I was walking down a slightly beaten path with the wind gently blowing the tops of the grass. I was keenly alert and listening but walking at a leisurely pace, my head slowly moving side to side. Glancing upwards, I could see the tops of the grass swaying about two feet above my head. Looking down, I watched as my knuckles left slight imprints within the soil. I was walking on all fours and my forearms were heavily muscled and covered in black hair. I was very sure of myself. I felt a deep kinship with this being, and *know* that this was me in another time.

This vision only lasted seconds but its impact on me was huge, and it broadened my view of things immensely. I had vividly experienced my awareness transferring into another being in another time and place, yet the knowing had run deep that it was still me; the abstract concept of reincarnation was no longer abstract, it had become very real. I thought, if I had experienced this, what else was possible? A vague sense that I was only touching the surface of a greater knowing enveloped me.

My next vision felt constricting and made me nauseous and uptight. A large, extremely condensed, black and gnarled energy spike extended from above my head and into my body. It was swirling in a powerful vortex, and held an energy field that was full of acutely strong emotions. I felt this accurately reflected my inner state of being throughout my life. I have had loving times with my family, but having my internal angst reflected back onto me bothered me for days.

The last vision also held some resonance with me, but this time in a much more expanded way. I was a tentacle, or a feeler, in the awareness of a Being capable of being omnipresent at many levels and dimensions of existence. I sensed that it was not alone, and within seconds became aware of two more of its kind. I felt that they were more ancient than much of our known universe. I also sensed that similar tentacles were attached to all life on Earth, so that these Beings would feel and learn from all of this planet's experiences. I later heard that I should read the Seth books by Jane Roberts, as they would offer greater clarity on this vision.

Carolyn, my Psychotherapist, taught a class on energy healing and I was thrilled and honoured when she asked me if I would like to learn it. She combined what she felt to be the best of Metamorphic technique with her own inner guidance to create her own approach. Within moments of this class beginning I realized that energy work was the life path that I had been yearning for. Something had awakened within me that I had not known for a long time, if ever, and my impassioned belief that General Motors was not where I belonged was all too intimately reinforced. I had no doubt that offering, and being involved with energy work would become a significant part of my future. It made me feel alive.

During one class she asked me to assist her in demonstrating how a pendulum could become a tool as a reflection of energy, and then to reinforce our understandings she asked me to think of something sad followed with something that made me feel happy. Holding the pendulum in front of my heart chakra, it had instantly stopped, pointing straight down. This shocked Carolyn with just how fast I could shut this chakra down. It shocked her even more when seconds later the pendulum started swinging fast.

Validating how easily I could control my energy I complimented myself. In my distorted perception over the years I felt that it was this sense of control that had kept me protected from the world. Whenever circumstances caused me to withdraw inwards I would protect myself by throwing walls up, shielding myself from whatever had confronted me. I would keep my innermost being safely hidden. As an adult I became much more adept at this and no longer hid, I developed a persona of solid strength and quiet ability; when people came at me in intimidating or confrontational ways I would just stand quietly relaxed and project a calm, detached look of compressed, unseen power and they would back away.

I began the slow realization after this demonstration that control had nothing to do with it; my misconception of both control and of needing perpetual armor or shields to survive in this world would be turned on its head. As you witness my journey unfold you will see my transformation into the empowered knowing of our, all of our, innate spiritual Light, and my own heart within the Divine. Little by little in the years to come the layers of walls and personas I built up would be healed and fall away, and I would experience a proportionally greater sense of inner peace, wholeness, and spiritual and heart expansiveness. It became amazing to discover just how many layers I uncovered. Yet, it has become an even deeper journey of self-discovery for me, as I know that more layers remain.

It was Carolyn's combination of energy work, along with her intuitive heart centered approach that opened me in the way that I needed to be opened. The person I sought to help me further had to have deep intuition, insight, awareness, compassion, and knowledge. It definitely had to be someone who could view things outside of the established conceptions of society, because I did not fit into or respond to standard ways of thinking. Answering the ad; an ad for a local hypnotherapist, was the next step I needed to take.

The chronicles that follow include detailed accounts taken from my journals. They are a concise reflection of my insights, revelations and experiences. I have chosen to retain their dates as I feel that they reflect my journey in a more coherent way.

I had no idea that when I set my intent to heal it would open me to the extent that it has. I experienced things that may stretch your beliefs or your imaginings, as in truth they sometimes stretched mine. They happened. Much would become revealed, and with each revelation a whole new journey of discovery would blossom before me. I would awaken to the core spiritual Essence that I am, I would awaken to the Divinity within all things and to its full love, support and encompassment, and in time, I would awaken before God.

October 2nd 2003

Today I met with Feir and she seemed deeply intrigued. Most of my life I had kept a huge part of myself under wraps and had felt shut down. I did not think that this society was the way it was meant to be and I seemed to have a hard time fitting in, I always felt on the periphery. Underlying this I felt a deep-seated emptiness. I did not understand it or know why I felt it. I just knew it had always been there. At times I would feel a deep inner yearning for something that I sensed lay unseen, somewhere, but I felt stymied in trying to access it. In many ways as I grew I suppressed integral parts of who I was. I loved my family, but inside, I always felt that I was only living part of my life. The suppressed parts felt confined, unseen, unwanted, and unheard, and though I would have opportunities to bring some of them out, keeping them suppressed had become a pattern. It was for the most part, the suppressed parts of me that reflected much more of who I really was.

I had a constant inner struggle going on. What I saw underlying society as a whole was a poignant superficiality. I saw semblances of people; people struggling for identity and security in life based on an underlying fear, people struggling to conform into a worldview that under the surface, was not in harmony with them. I felt people striving to fill a deep sense of inner emptiness, even those who became adept in the careers or roles they chose, and it did not even occur to me that it might be the same emptiness that I felt. Up close, when I got caught up in the periphery of these people, I would sometimes be fooled by what they were projecting, but when I stood back and looked again it was always the same. People forgetting that they were humans, people becoming automatons, some controlling, some controlled. We all learned to find our places within this structure, but I felt a certainty inside that humanity had fallen away from its heart and soul. I felt a certainty inside that humanity had been taken away from itself, and I did not really like what was left.

In many ways I felt incapable of moving into the hidden aspects of myself. I was strong in some ways, and a deep inner fire of standing in my own power burned in my core, but I was not living from that level beyond moments in time and it would be all too easily swept aside and sabotaged or undermined by insecurities or fear. I was still reliant on others to validate me in too many ways. It felt refreshing to talk with Feir, to talk with someone who was open to understanding, and accepting the whole extent of who I was.

This meeting was my first glimpse of just how important it was to honour whom I was and to not deny my essence. I had shut myself down, so I did not even know what my own Essence was. Brief, tantalizing glimpses over the years, of a Presence inside that I felt instantly drawn to, a Presence that I thought was me in a way that I never understood, but I could not sustain my connection to it. I had been a father, husband, provider, and I had an underlying gentle and caring personality, but what foundational strengths did I really have besides my family; none really, not that I could sustainably latch onto. Ever since my pre-teen years I had sensed that I lived as only a fragmented shell of who I really was. I wanted and needed to know, 'who was I really, who was the whole un-fragmented me?' I wanted to live the whole, gentle and loving me, the whole me that included the stability and calm strength of the Presence I sensed deep inside.

Feir and I talked about our beliefs in the Earth, psychic abilities, extra sensory perception, energy fields, and the supernatural. She recommended that I ask her partner, Anne, who was a psychic channel, to help me concurrently with her therapy. As an aside to her hypnotherapy practice she worked with Anne and another partner, offering energetic clearings. It was only now that my hope truly began to take seed.

October 8th

Today Anne sat in the corner sensing what was happening inside me while I was hypnotized. She told me of the pain she felt in my body and of the multiple spirit attachments I had. She also informed me of two powerful negative entities that were attached to me. I felt sure that one of them must be the gnarled energy spike that I had visualized during Carolyn's session.

Our spiritual essences had met during a guided suggestion and she saw me as a beautiful higher Being. I felt flattered and awed, but it made me even more curious about exactly who I was deep inside, because I had felt that somehow I was much more than I was ever able to bring to the surface. As I was being led through the suggestion, I remembered coming to a beautifully soothing black sandy beach and being guided to snuggle into the sand. I had instantly experienced rhythmic and immensely powerful pulsations with every fibre of my being. I can only describe this experience as being immersed within the heartbeat of all that encompassed the Earth at the same time; all sharing the same powerfully rhythmic beat. I became one with it, and as I did my spirit floated above my body and looked out to sea. It was a powerfully exhilarating experience, and the heartbeat rhythms thundered through me with even deeper impact.

Anne said that she met me as I was enraptured in this and nudged my spirit back into my body. I remember a brief moment of intense pleasure as my heart opened just before reintegrating, had this been when our spirits met? I had not realized that we had until she had mentioned it. I had felt reluctant about going back into my body. I was enraptured within a state of total expansiveness, freedom and connection, and as my spirit re-entered its shell it found it very confined, dense and heavy.

As the session finished Anne asked Feir if she would help me show the spirit attachments to the Light during my next appointment. I felt upbeat and excited, but as time went by I felt increasingly surrounded by spirits. Later as I was finishing my shower, I was sure that when I came out there would be people standing there, and not just spirits. With a lump in my throat I opened the curtain, and did not see anything. It was unnerving. The events of this day brought a lot of things together in my mind. I have been clairsentient, empathic, and have felt inner knowing's all of my life, but now it felt as if these abilities had really begun to awaken.

October 9th

I decided to practice bringing myself in and out of hypnosis; I wanted to be able to enter the altered state at will. I had an innate knowing that until I truly realized all of who I was and then anchored into it I could never be there for anyone in the deepest sense. I also knew that I might lose everyone before I found clarity, but I realized that there was no other choice. In the last few years I had been emotionally erratic in quietly disruptive ways and I could not continue to impose that on anyone.

October 11th

Last night I was jolted out of a deep sleep as if something inside had suddenly exploded. I was terrified, thinking that I had never been this terrified about anything. I stayed awake, quivering, and it was not until the light of dawn that I had the courage to open myself to whatever it might have been.

As I opened my eyes I could see in every detail, the spirits that were surrounding me. I visualized some of them slowly walking towards a row of doors, turning to look back at me, then opening the doors and stepping through. I told them that I would help show them the way as best I could. The other spirits seemed curious but began to fade from view, though I still felt them moving around my apartment.

Within a minute of my telling the spirits that I would help them, something that held awareness knotted itself through my abdomen and stayed there for about a minute, then stretched itself out pulsing through my system before subsiding. That was definitely not a nice feeling. As I walked into the bedroom later my spine and skin still crawled.

In the evening I became aware of a more concentrated Presence observing me. I felt that it was very old, knowing and calming, and that it seemed equally male and female. I had sensed this Presence before, at different times in my life and I have always been comfortable with it. Having it with me now gave me a sense of completion and wholeness. It surrounded me and gazed through my eyes, and as I experienced this a great deal of love flowed from it. My own heart opened in response and I felt overwhelming warmth and gratitude for its presence.

Something about being immersed in its energy triggered an image of waking up abruptly in the womb, fully alert and aware, and sensing that something was infiltrating my cells. If this had been the awareness that had pulsed through my system this morning, or one of the entities Anne had mentioned, that would explain a lot about my life.

October 13th

I could only partially relax. A current of tension started from my abdomen and flowed along my spine, concentrated in all of my joints and then continued circling inside my rib cage. Consistently the tension in my body and mind was more apparent. I felt that the visualized protective shield that I had learned to use should be aimed more at what was coming from within me, rather than from what might have been coming from the outside.

October 15th

I sensed an ominous Presence expanding inside. It felt different than what had pulsed through my system earlier. This one felt like a heavy, dark, and constricting shadow. I would not allow it to grow or intimidate me, and told it that its days were getting short because I was close to taking my life back. I was relaxed and calm, and started to taunt it because I could feel myself getting stronger. I had no doubt that Anne would soon look after it so I kept repeating *"Peace, Love, Harmony with all things, and Happiness"* until it subsided. I felt pleased with myself because I could now feel, without a doubt, that I was taking my life back.

October 16th

Today Feir had me imagine looking into a magical mirror, one that would allow me to see both my physical and spiritual selves.

Looking into this mirror under hypnosis intrigued me; I felt that this was what I truly looked like when my conscious perception was by-passed. A dimly lit, shadowy, and semi-solid human form, encased within a slightly translucent, narrow band of pale light was what I saw. That however, will change.

She asked me to surround any sections of my body that were shadowy with Divine Light and lift them away. Almost my entire body had seemed to be in shadow. She then guided me to mentally map my body to show where the spirits had attached themselves. Again it was most of my body. As I focused on my neck, the first image I had was of a young boy and two women.

The boy I could see with perfect clarity, the women only somewhat, they appeared almost transparent. It felt as if the women were the boy's guardians. They were in a gloomy forest and the excessively gnarled trees looked as if they oozed slime. They all felt lost and apprehensive. Becoming aware that I was observing them they cried out to be helped, so Feir asked me if I could show them to the Light. Many people know this reference to the Light, as the portal leading into what they feel is heaven. I focused all thought on bringing it forth and it appeared, but as soon as it did an unseen sense of disruption erupted from all around.

The boy and I had felt an instant familiarity and warmth towards each other. I do not know how we knew each other, or even if in some sense he was a younger aspect of me, but it felt good to meet again. There seemed to be a bubble of calm light around all of us, for the disquieting feeling of rot permeating from the trees and the ever increasing turbulence of the disruption were kept at bay. The boy wanted to stay with me but I knew that the women were yearning to go into the Light, so thanking them for all that they had done to keep the boy safe I opened my heart to them. Feeling free to leave the women struggled with every ounce of strength they had remaining towards the Light, and as they made it their immense relief, joy and gratitude flowed out. It was interesting what happened next, for as soon as they entered the Light and their joy and gratitude flowed out, whatever had been causing the disruption lost its power and the disruption disappeared.

Feir had me shift my focus to my throat next, and I visualized I was standing in a field with two almost totally transparent spirits. They were trying to solidify their images but were experiencing a lot of difficulty. I asked them to identify themselves but they could not remember who they were. Without thinking, or understanding how, I projected myself into their awareness and looked through their eyes. They were looking at their hands and having a hard time comprehending everything; they only had a slight memory that these had actually been their hands. Feir wanted to know why they were there. They could not answer but I picked up a vague memory of a fire, so she asked if they died in this fire.

With an anguished "*Yes!*" it became a traumatic moment for them as they shared a sudden realization that they really were dead. She asked them if they wanted to be shown to the Light and set free.

Still reeling from their realization they voiced a subdued *"Yes."* As they said this many other waiflike spirits began appearing, also wanting to go into the Light. I found it much easier to call forth this time, but as the Light appeared everything sank into a deep fog enshrouded and murky gloom. I could feel the dark Presence that I experienced yesterday and he was casting his shadow over everything. He definitely did not want these spirits to feel that they had any capacity to leave and I sensed something indistinguishable holding them back. Feir called in Archangel Michael for help and all of my previous skepticism about the religious concept of Angels vanished.

He came in the form of a dark haired man in his early 30's, focused his thought, and the tentacles that had been holding the spirits were instantly pushed away. After watching them recede he turned towards me and looked into my eyes, smiled, and then disappeared. It was a profound moment and I was stunned. I did not know it yet, not fully anyway, but he was demonstrating the power of pure focused intent through his inner state of calm knowing.

When Michael left the dark Presence found other ways to interfere, so Feir called in the Beings of Light to assist. The spirits trusted me so I was determined to see them safely into the Light, but I became extremely agitated when I sensed deceit from many of these particular light beings, and yelled out *"Pretend! Not Real, Pretend!"* They were evil in disguise. Feir commanded them to leave and called in more Beings of the Light; some were real some were pretending to be. She put pressure on the spirits who wanted to go, to leave, but the spirits were uncertain and scared, as the Light did not seem pure. The false light beings had pulled back but were not gone.

She was positive that we were being deceived about the Light, so some of the spirits put their trust totally in my hands and I took them into it. They immediately erupted into joyous gratitude. The other spirits could feel it and now they all wanted to leave, but as they moved forward a second portal of light appeared and a mass of evil beings sprang from it. I had the distinct impression, seeing their long and distorted clawed fingers, that they were the devil's minions.

Fear and confusion erupted and Feir and I became increasingly frustrated. Everything that could be seen had dissolved into chaos, and as the emotions escalated to fever pitch my body became taut as a bow. My spirit no longer recognized which Light was true, and my impression that there were now more false light beings than true ones was over-riding. I had absolutely no doubt that the false ones wanted to take these spirits to a much darker place.

Feir yelled to flood the field with Light and I did instantly without knowing how I did it. I saw a blinding flash of Light, felt a whoosh, and heard myself saying 'Gone'. When my eyes refocused, the field where this all took place was completely empty and the air and sky were clear. I wondered if instead of the spirits finding salvation, I had just blown them and the minions out of my psyche. I hoped not. I had really wanted to help these spirits and did not like it that I might have just betrayed their trust instead.

From the time of Michael's disappearance to the flash of Light, my right hand had been resonating rhythmically to energy surges that were pulsating throughout my body. The greater and more acute the stress, confusion and emotions, the more intensely rhythmic my hand jerked. My muscles were still quivering for about twenty minutes after this session had finished, as it had been very intense.

October 17th

I decided to use my pendulum to contact my grandfather tonight, hoping that he would help me defeat the darkness.

He answered, *"Yes, I can help you."*

The pendulum only answers 'Yes' or 'No' so my communications with him were enhanced through a telepathic connection. This, in thinking back, had been how all of my communications with the spirits had been carried out. I was tired, so I asked him if he would tell my spirit anything that I needed to know as I slept.

"Yes," and he surrounded me with his love.

October 18th

When I contacted my grandfather tonight other spirits kept butting in. His presence was not as identifiable as last night and the answers were inconsistent. I told the other spirits to leave and that only Ernest was allowed to answer. He came in more focused after that, but at the same time a pulsating sapphire blue and white light encircled the pendulum. I thought it was his way of showing his presence and it was beautifully fascinating to watch.

This pulsating light had first encircled the pendulum, but transformed itself to spread out along one side. As my questions went on, it slowly started working its way up the string exactly like an inchworm. It had only been an inch long at the bottom of the string but by the time it reached the top it had grown to four inches. Here, it arched one more time like a snake about to strike, then leaped forward and disappeared into the palm of my hand. I felt a sudden whoosh of electric current penetrate my skin, and could feel it continuing to pulsate as it moved through my wrist and forearm. I was so energetically and emotionally drained that I only felt mild surprise and took it in stride. I know that it was Ernest I was talking to, but now I was not quite so sure that he was the vibrant light that I had been fascinated by.

According to Ernest this darkness had been coming through his family lineage for generations. I counted back the centuries, wanting to find out how long and the pendulum never stopped moving. As I thought of my family, I wondered if he had lost his concept of time.

He told my spirit what I needed to do. The dark Presence needed to become concentrated into one spot, prevented from being allowed to escape with walls of Light, immersed totally in white Light, and then sent into the Light. I felt the truth of this. I once again confirmed that he would help me clear this darkness, and then I had asked him if Feir was in danger if she tried to help me alone. His answer caught my attention.

"Yes, it is important that Anne be there." It had been Feir's intent to deal with this entity during our next session, but I was going to tell her to put it on hold until Anne could be present.

October 22nd

Tonight, as I arrived at Feir's I could not help but notice that things were becoming more surreal. Anne was there unexpectedly, but so too was Sheri, their other partner. They had been surprised as well, but their spirit helpers had told them that they would be needed tonight, and that they would learn something from me. Now we were all curious.

I told them what Ernest had said and of my experience with the vibrant light. They warned me to be extremely careful contacting spirits, and to be specific about which spirit I wanted to contact and what questions I asked. They told me that there were a lot of manipulative spirits who did not really care about our wellbeing, but instead had their own agendas. We went into the session room curiously exchanging looks, eagerly anticipating what may happen tonight. All of us were caught off guard.

As Anne began going deeper into hypnosis for channeling I felt the dark Presence fly out of my body and into hers, attacking her. She kept gasping. Feir told Sheri to grab Anne's hands to lend her strength and to throw a wall of Light up. The dark Presence was controlling Anne and was shaking her off but she regained herself long enough to grasp Sheri's hands and became strengthened. This had been totally unexpected, but just like a Hollywood movie this 'Presence' possessed Anne. Her mannerisms changed and the spirit demanded to know what we wanted and why we were interfering. Feir told him that I no longer wanted him interfering in my life and that I wanted him to leave. She asked me if this was right and I said "*Yes*".

He sneered, "*There is no 'conviction' in his voice*" and he really emphasized 'conviction'.

I said, "*There does not need to be, my mind believes.*"

He looked suddenly doubtful. I was just as doubtful, though I tried to cover it up. All that I could think of in the spur of the moment was to try as best I could to convincingly bluff him. I was still shocked about everything that had just happened and that I was actually talking to an entity. I felt that he was exerting some influence over my voice because I had sounded pretty unsure of myself.

His voice oozing with contempt, he replied, "*Others have tried to get me out but they all failed, what made us think that we could succeed?*"

Feir answered, "*Because we have the Light on our side.*"

At this he tried to jump out of Anne and into her, but hit the wall of Light that Sheri had put up. He could not believe it and looked stunned, as nothing had ever stopped him before. I felt that he would have tried to punish her before jumping back into me, but he was trapped. Feir gave him a choice of either voluntarily going into the Light or going further into the pit.

He said, "*I am the pit.*"

She replied "*Oh no, the pit goes much, much deeper. Do you really want to go there and be eternally frozen in time and space?*"

He wavered with indecision, as he was just as afraid of the Light as he was of going deeper into the pit. With growing impatience, Feir finally had enough and called in Michael to surround it in Light and take it where it needed to go. He came instantly with an escort of Light Beings, and I watched as they swiftly glided away with this entity safely inside a radiantly pulsating cage of Light.

Anne was brought out of her semi hypnosis and slumped exhaustively. She thanked Sheri for holding her hands and found it amusing that she had tried to push her away. She looked at me and said "*That spirit was Big.*" Thanking Feir, she ran out to the yard to stand barefoot in the grass. She returned minutes later and Feir hypnotized us, and we continued the session.

Anne and Sheri had their hands on me and were tuning into all of the entities henchmen spirits, estimating them to be in the hundreds. These were the same spirits that I had thought to be the devil's minions in our last session. This time though I had the impression that they were like slave overseers to all of the good spirits who had been drawn to me.

After we corralled all the henchmen Feir told me to visualize the top of my head opening, and then she also put her hands on me. They sent a great surge of white Light through my body pushing all of these spirits out with it, and I watched as they dissolved into the Light. This experience was powerful, and I felt totally invigorated and purified by that surge of energy. They smiled and asked how I was doing, so I told them that I could sense Michael, and that he was not sure of something.

They said *"Oh no, Michael is always sure."*

I replied *"No"* and that Michael was not alone.

Feir asked Sheri's guide, Kamut, to check it out and he sensed a power, a vastly powerful Being standing with Michael and looking down at the dark Presence. This Being's essence radiated distinct disapproval, while Michael stood in calm neutrality waiting for a decision. Feir asked if this was God and Kamut said no, but this Being was much more powerful than Michael. Anne's guide, Anya, then put her hands on me to see what was happening and as she did I could see everything with clarity. We were in some kind of chamber and the dark Presence was cowering inside his cage of Light, curled up in fear close to the far side of the cage. He was trying to move away from the intense look the powerful Being was focusing on it, but it seemed he was also doing his best not to touch the bars of Light that comprised the sides and top of his cage. Elsewhere in the chamber, behind a raised platform, were three older Beings looking on impassably.

This vision only lasted seconds but it was pretty profound to all of us. We had observed something that had been directly related to us, and that was now happening way up on the spiritual ladder. None of us had experienced this chamber before, but the ladies felt that this was quite possibly the chamber of Elders or of Judgment referred to in Theology. Feir brought me out of hypnosis and I saw them looking at me in wonder. Seeing their expressions, I also began to wonder about this chamber. How had I opened the door that had allowed us to be taken there? Inexplicably, the segment involving this chamber never transcribed onto the tape. I have since heard that 'omissions' of this type sometimes happen when it involves higher spiritual interventions.

Anne told us that the 'Big Boss' entity had entered her home and pushed her against the wall a few days earlier. She had not known what it was, or recognized it as the same energy until tonight. I wondered if it was related to my taunting; of what I assumed was this entity last week.

I mentioned that when Anne was going through her experience with the entity I felt compelled to reach out and comfort her, but something was holding me back. They rolled their eyes and said thank God I had not touched her, because that spirit would have been able to transfer back into me. They feared that they would have had a lot of difficulty drawing it out of me again.

These entities are not constrained by the same perceived reality as us. They are not only able to bounce easily between people, but if they are energetically powerful enough, they can separate themselves to latch onto multiple people. They are also able to flow through doors into other realities, other times, and other dimensions. Some stay with us for multiple lifetimes. Others pass themselves down generationally to different members of a family. Yet others test us to see how anchored we are within our own Light, our own spiritual power. If they can influence us and experience more of their own accustomed realities through us, they will.

If, in your own experience, you recognize an attachment, you do not need to fear it. Remember the first time I met Michael and what he tried to teach me then? He was showing me that through pure loving focused intent, we possess the same power. We do. As you progress through this book you will witness this understanding unfolding within me.

As I was leaving the lady's said that I should start feeling better from now on. I smiled. I was already feeling totally alive and super-charged with energy, and I felt that I had great things to look forward to.

On my way back into Peterborough I saw people gathered around a deer lying by the road. Its essence was all around me, so I closed my eyes and instantly became my higher self. I experienced the same deep resonance of the Earth's rhythms that I had felt previously. I was in another dimension and felt total exhilaration. I sent a powerful wave of love and healing towards the deer and a minute later I did it again. I never did find out if it had any effect but I hoped it had. During the night, the internal workings of my brain felt that they were flipping erratically all over the place, so I could not sleep.

October 23rd

I had been practicing my protective shield and filling my body with Light. I had also been telling all negative cell memories to leave. Light surged through me in response causing whole body goose bumps with each surge. Eventually my face took on the life of the departed 'Boss' spirit. It felt as if I had the same expressions and way of moving as Anne had displayed during her possession. This lasted for about a minute and then I was free. Its memory had now left my cells.

I started talking with what I was assuming was my guardian, the Presence that Anne and Sheri had witnessed standing behind me observing as I was being cleared. I asked him if he was my protector for more potent entities.

"*Yes,*" he sneered, "*dark human presence was only a fly to be stepped on, a fly in the dirt.*"

At this point in time I was still being introduced to the existence of spirit guides, so I did not yet know the difference in their integrity. I thought that any spirit guide must be good.

I asked him if I was going to be coming into contact with these more potent entities.

He answered, *"Yes."*

As a child I had imagined myself as one of the saviors of humanity and the Earth, but at the same time, I had also unerringly sensed that I would die in my mid-forties. I believe that instead of dying I was being transformed. Perhaps this was why I had pushed back everything that was once so important to me, so that I could set the stage in preparation.

One of my daydreams as a teenager had been that something significant was about to happen towards the Earth and mankind. As I had aged and more time went on doubt crept in and I wondered if it might have been just my imagination all along. After hearing this I believed it again, so I asked this guardian to teach me everything that I needed to know.

This Presence ordered me, and all my protective spirits to, *"Buck up and focus on everything being taught"* and kept reinforcing how vitally important it was. *"Learn until every fibre in your being knows without hesitation or doubt what to do with each kind of entity. Learn until teacher becomes student and never stop learning. Learn each strength and weakness, manipulation and deceit. Learn. Learn. Learn. Know yourself. Know your enemies. Know them better than they know themselves."* With surprise, I realized that I had known this litany since I was a boy, except I had always believed that it was in reference to an enemy. I did not realize that it also implied another type of entity.

Thinking back on my conversation with the 'Boss' spirit last night, there was something about the way he said, *"There is no conviction in his voice"* which made me believe that he exerted some influence over my voice or thinking. In past attempts to remove him he, or his helpers, may have reinforced self-doubt in the person. If the person could not sound confident, then the person would begin to doubt and the spirit would triumph, and retain its hold and influence. I know in some ways, that I had felt a longing for its return. I believe that past generations did not know the importance of surrounding this type of spirit with Light in order to permanently release them. I think that my answer, 'It does not need to be, my mind believes' was right because of the sudden look of doubt on his face as I said it.

It was fortunate that Sheri was present and had put up the wall of Light. There would have been nothing to stop him from jumping into Feir if it had not been there. I felt that he had known my thoughts. I had believed that both Feir and Anne would be needed to clear him, so he had made his plans accordingly. That is why he immediately jumped into Anne as she was going into hypnosis, and in her most vulnerable state. He was intending to terrify, hurt, and unbalance them. However, he was caught totally off guard because I had not known that Sheri would be there. She had lent Anne the needed strength and had held him within the Light.

I owe Earnest a great deal of love and gratitude for assisting me to understand. This had become an enormous eye opener about how easy it was for these types of spirits to jump from one person to another. No matter how unnerving this is to have a lower energy attach itself to you, I now know that I need not fear it. I just needed to hold myself in the Light and call in the Light, Angels and Light Beings to surround and take it away.

Later, I sensed something awakening and wondering why all was quiet. I sensed a lot of pent up aggression, power and purpose. I had a sensation of a serpent slowly uncoiling from around every inch of my ribs, spine, tailbone, and skull. It took almost an hour to finish uncoiling, and then I felt the power of its focus. It was looking through my eyes, turning my head, and appraising my surroundings. Could this be the same awareness that I felt circling around my rib cage a few days earlier?

I suddenly slipped into a semi-altered state and vividly sensed this serpent and its intent, then watched as it flew towards Anne and flung her against the wall. Another spirit shot out of me. I watched as it grappled with the serpent, forcing it back towards me. I instantly went into a trance, calling on the Guardian, Michael, Feir, Sheri, Anne and all of our spirit helpers to help contain it until we were ready. I then psychically yanked it back inside, sealed it in a shell and smothered it in Light. I told Michael to take it away. This vision had not lasted more than a few seconds but I was extremely tense, agitated, protective of Anne, and furious that he threatened somebody I felt close to.

I was still in the trance when, what I could only describe as an incomprehensibly alien awareness possessed me and my awareness was transported into a totally foreign reality. All that I could see was continual waves of energy flowing like ripples through a gray and empty void, a void that seemed to stretch into infinity. I felt immersed by a slight hum but I did not sense any other presence. This awareness began slowly turning my head in an extreme range of motion. I was aware of everything, but I was not the one moving my head. It was scanning for something but I did not know what it was. All I felt was the emptiness of this space. My breathing during this time was slow and deep.

A voice came that sounded like my guardian asking whoever was probing, *"Who are you?"* The voice kept asking but there was no answer.

Now a different voice said, *"We want John back."*

Someone counted to five and I came out, but then slipped right back in and continued to probe. I was still looking through my third eye, turning my head side to side, and breathing slow and deep. After another couple of minutes my head finally went straight up and down and I came out.

The period I was being used to scan seemed to last minutes. I had been taken somewhere that I had never before or since experienced. It was vaguely similar to, but was vastly emptier then the experiences I had felt becoming my higher self. There was not even a trace of the exhilaration. I felt that I had been used as a mechanical probe. I had no idea what "I" was probing for, but I could feel the expansiveness around me. I did not think it had anything to do with this universe, as we know it.

October 24th

I found that my guardians name was Akorbak. I asked him if he would help clear others as I was cleared.

He replied, *"If it is worthy of my attention."*

Hearing this, I decided to just go back to learning.

I had been stretching both arms up to a 45-degree angle for the last couple of days. I had not done this before. I was also stretching and breathing in deeply as if enjoying the sensations of this body. It was not until later that I realized that this was not me who was relishing in these sensations. I had opened myself for something else to share my body.

Another presence re-appeared as well, a presence I had not felt for a long time. I remembered scary episodes since early childhood, where a word would come out of nowhere and flash through my mind. It was a simple word actually, but the way it was said and repeated terrified me.

"*Faster.*" Yes a simple word, but I learned to instantly totally shut myself down and become very still. The more "*Faster*" was repeated the faster and more agitated the cadence became. Before I learned to become totally still, I felt increasingly agitated and unbalanced. However briefly and intermittently these episodes lasted, I always feared that one day the words would never stop, and my ability to hold my stillness would be pushed away, never to return.

Many times in the last little while I had also been merging with the awareness of my pre-human self as I walked through the grasslands. I wondered if I was starting to slip through time.

I had not sensed the serpent all day, though I had started to second-guess myself about whether or not the vision of it actually happened. The trance and possession had definitely happened though. My neck was still really stiff. I wondered if the serpent was the second 'Big guy' Anne had sensed, and was playing games with me.

October 26th

Exhaustion was definitely settling in due to my lack of sleep in the last few days and it was getting hard to focus. I could not deal with pressure, even subtle pressure. I was feeling helpless. I could not think. I felt as if I was possessed, but I was so tired that all I wanted to do was sleep. I could not, and I sat in a state of confused turmoil all day.

October 28th

I was feeling more at peace today. I still had many good spirits inside so I asked Michael if he would show those who wished to leave into the

Light. In my inner vision, I saw a ball of Light instantaneously encompass the interior of my torso, and as the spirits flowed towards it my sense of peace deepened. I saw myself standing at the entrance wishing them all well as they went by. Michael came and stood beside me. After a little bit he turned to me, looked at me with warmth, and smiled. I felt blessed and full of gratitude. There seemed to be a close, respectful, almost brotherly friendship between us. He left, but within seconds a consciousness popped into my head that did not like what was happening, and it felt like the serpent. I became suddenly agitated, knowing that it was still with me. Anger rushed to the surface, but so to, did an overwhelming deep fatigue. I held my ground until the serpent receded again.

I had been feeling a couple of pounds lighter overall though as a fair amount of inner tension was now gone. However this had turned out to be a mixed blessing, as now I ached more.

October 29th

I had another session today. I told Anne about my vision of the serpent attacking her and she told me that she never experienced anything. This left me confused. I also told them about my growing apprehension about being possessed and used as a probe. They had no answer for this one. When I told them about Akarbak and of his general distain they were upset. They told me that any spiritual helper that does not radiate heart energy was not a good one to have, no matter how much they appeared to be helping you.

During this session we found out the truth about Akarbak, the serpent, and the Faster Faster Faster entity. I also learned another valuable lesson about having greater discernment towards any spiritual energy that I let close.

Spirit helpers that are truly aligned with our highest good will not impose in a way that takes our power away, or the power of another. I had sensed truth in what Akarbak had been teaching me, but I had been taking his words and arrogance in stride, without thinking or questioning, and that was not good.

This session turned out to be another interesting one, but only half of it was recorded. Things had become quite intense as the first side of the tape was ending so it was totally forgotten about. I will share with you exactly what was recorded. I later sent a copy of this tape to the director of the Planetary Society in Pasadena, California, more widely known as S.E.T.I., but I received no response.

The first thing Feir asked Anne to do was to verify that all of our auras were secure and protected by Light. She was not going to take any chances today. Once done, Anne began channeling a Being. This was my first experience with an intentional channeling so I was a little bit in awe. The energy radiating from this Being felt good.

His first words were *"You come to seek guidance, hmm?"*

It identified itself as the Teacher, then looked at me and said, *"John is asking for guidance, hmm?"* We said yes.

Feir asked, *"Can John first have higher spiritual help brought in to guide and protect him?"*

The Teacher searched within and said *"Yes, there are two Beings available that can assist you at this time. You may call one James if you choose and the other Otto. These Beings will walk by your side. You can connect to them through your vibrational frequency. You will learn to access knowledge available to you through their consciousness. As you progress with your vibrational frequencies, more will become available. If you choose to enter these areas, protection will be automatic and you will be safe. Your vibrational states may vary and it may be at times disconcerting, but these Beings will assist you in maintaining your vibrational state. You have at your disposal many levels of activity, and as you progress in frequency more will become available."*

Feir asked, *"Is Akarbak really John's guardian?"*

He reflected and replied, *"This is of low magnification and is of a different nature; it is not discarnate. This is a projection from another place within your galaxy."*

Intrigued, she asks, *"Is this an Extra Terrestrial?"*

He replied, *"From your understandings this is how it would be perceived. This is part of an experiment to study the emotional manifestations of the human form. If John does not wish to be studied, he can make it clear and understandable to this being that this is against his will, and this being will have no choice but to withdraw. This experimenter is not very qualified."*

I smiled at the way he said this last part, I 'would' have to get somebody who did not really know what they were doing. She asked about the serpent next, and we found out that this was also a manifestation of this experiment. As I heard this, my initial amused curiosity quickly faded and I became more annoyed. Anger set in as I started reflecting back on my life. How dare these Extra Terrestrials disrupt any real chances for me to experience deep and prolonged joy, and why would they? There had been times when my emotions would instantly flash into extremes, and other times when I would, seemingly out of the blue, do something that would hurt the feelings of others. I would not have had a clue why I had just done that. There had been many times during these episodes where the acuteness, and suddenness of my reaction confused me just as much as it had other people.

The Teacher shared some wisdom about dealing with this being, or any other spiritual Presence. He told us that, *"Focus is in our intent. All comes from intent. If you need more surety that you are doing it right, voice 'out loud' exactly what you want and it will be respected. All else will not be allowed in."* He advised me to attune myself to the higher frequencies in both my conscious and unconscious states, and that Otto and James could assist me in this. I asked if I already know how to do this.

He replied, *"Your time is an odd thing. You have known how to do this in what you refer to as the past but have now forgotten. Your energetic structure has been altered in this incarnation and must be re-aligned with the energies of Home."*

Feir asked about my fibromyalgia and he said that if I focused 'My Light' into my body then my body would heal. He said that my muscular structure could be compared to a tight elastic band, and that deep tissue massage, attention to diet and a release of stored toxins would be beneficial.

She now asked about my experiences with the Faster, Faster, Faster entity. He allowed Anne's guide Anya to answer and I quickly warmed up to her.

Anya told me, *"If something comes into your mind or your body that you know is not yours, you have the power to release it so that it can no longer influence you. You have control of your body. You have to believe, feel and know that you have this power, and then you just have to tell it to go away."* I had never felt this empowered control over my life before. She kept reinforcing my understandings until this knowing sank in. I slowly began to feel this truth.

She said, *"Just tell this experimenter to shoo shoo go away, do you not think that he just keeps poking and poking until a reaction is forced, and then his experiment just continues? Do you not know it affects everything about you, your body, your mind and your emotions when he does this? You are in control of your body. Do you want this experiment to continue or do you want this to stop?"* I chose to stop it. Anya laughingly said, *"Now that you have had your pep up talk do you feel better and can I go now? You do not need me anymore. You can do the rest by yourself now."* Feir and I laughed and I told her that I liked her. I was then hypnotized but my body resisted. The awareness of this experimenter, coming through the serpent, was blocking my attempts to go into a deep trance.

Feir asked where the experimenter was attached. As I scanned my body, I sensed that he had attached everywhere. She told me that my conscious and altered states were one and the same for me and asked if I could see anything approaching. Yes I could. It was a Light Being that I instantly recognized as me, and I felt a mixture of awe and wonder as my two selves merged together.

Anya returned and asked if the awareness was receding yet. It was not. She told me to strengthen my focus by bringing the Light from the Earth up through my feet and into a focused intent to recede it. It still did not recede, but I established a connection with the experimenter. He was humanoid, and was surprised and uncomfortable that I had tuned into him.

Feir told him, *"You are disobeying the Prime Directive concerning humans; you must stop interfering in John's life."*

He sneered and said, *"I do not believe in it. What do you want?"*

She asked him, *"Are you John's guardian?"*

He snorted and laughingly said *"No."* She then asked him how long he had been with me and he said *"A long time."*

She demanded to know what he wanted and he was taken aback by her tone. He replied meekly *"To observe, to study."*

Once again she told him that he was interfering and he snarled, *"Humans are like mice in a cage and are a lower life form. I am not done with my experiment."*

Anya returned and told him to leave but he became amused when she mentioned the extent of spiritual help that had gathered.

He laughed and said, *"I think we are stronger than you."*

Anya said, *"You do not really think that do you?"*

Contemptuously, he snarled *"Oh yeah, I think that."* He was not going anywhere and was calling in reinforcements.

Feir angrily jumped in and said, *"I want to talk to your boss."* This was where the tape stopped recording, but this was what I remembered.

The commander and half a dozen others arrived, all excited that humans had tuned into them and were demanding freedom. As Feir began explaining the Prime Directive, the commander quickly angered. She dug in. He was not impressed and would not back down, so she called Michael to break their attachment. He did, once again through intent alone.

I still maintained communication, so she told the commander to look deep into his heart to find the Light, and for some reason he had no choice but to obey. This was her gift, as she knows intuitively exactly what to say in the right moment.

Looking within, it shocked him to find that he actually had a little spark of Light, and was surprised at the feelings being generated in him. All of his previous anger washed away and he stood in humbled curiosity.

Feir asked him, *"What do they really want by studying humans?"*

He replied, *"Humans are only a curiosity and an amusement. We are searching for a planet to settle on."*

She introduced Michael saying that if he could find them a suitable planet, other than Earth, would they stop interfering with humans? He was skeptical that Michael could have this much ability but agreed. Within seconds Michael returned saying that he had found a suitable planet and the commander's awareness shifted, and he left with Michael to view it. He came back happy and relieved, saying he would take his people there. Communication was now broken and Feir thanked Michael and he left. Anya then asked me to scan my body to see if anything else was still lingering. Tuning in, it felt really quiet and empty inside. The vision I had of the inside of my head though, looked like a devastated urban area, as all I could see was debris.

I had been slipping in and out of hypnosis since being put under without leaving the altered state, so I was 'awake' again when Anya and the teacher withdrew. As Anne was brought out Feir mentioned that she wished that she had our gifts. I replied that she had a special gift of her own with her amazingly timed intuition and knowledge. I thought it would be nice to have her gift. We all complimented each other and it seemed that it was just the right combination of people and higher help that was needed for these clearings. I was feeling blessed and thankful at the spiritual orchestration and synchronicity involved, but I could not help thinking though, about how we humans are really no different than these Extra Terrestrial's. Do we really think that apes, dolphins, frogs, mice, and all the rest do not warrant more? We look at them as lower life forms just as much when we experiment with them.

Days later I was looking at the stars when I felt the same Extra Terrestrials trying to latch back in. I would not allow it and they backed off, it was that easy. By this time my feeling of empowerment had grown so their attempt did not faze me. I was calm and felt at peace. I now *knew* that I had the power over my life. My awareness was expanding, and I was now able to recognize energies with greater ease. I felt that they were just curious about me now and wanted to hook back in for more precise experimentation.

I tuned into the Teacher and asked him if he was also an Extra Terrestrial. He withdrew a little, unsure how to answer. I told him that it did not matter whether he was or not, I had a lot of respect for him. With this, he immediately came around me again with warmth and happiness. I felt content, peaceful and happy inside, as I was already starting to notice significant changes in my life. I had developed though, tunnel vision into almost exclusively focusing on finding my own niche. I needed to find out, and be fully accepted for who I was becoming.

In my innermost yearnings since I was young, I had yearned to go to a place where I could truly be the free expression and wholeness of all of who I was, a place where I could truly feel connected to everything, and everyone around me; a place of all-consuming love and friendship. Deeper even than this though, when I would feel that inner something, that something that would come out of nowhere and instantly envelope me from the inside out, with its depth of calm empowered knowing and purpose, I would feel that I was connecting and merging with me, but a me that was completely beyond anything that I knew. I would feel the deepest sense of peace and embracing comfort, and I would feel a remembrance to something that went beyond this world. My heart would fly open as if it could not get enough, and the sense of familiar expansiveness and connection that I felt made my soul yearn to permanently stay immersed by it. At this point in time I had lost all meaning to my life, any meaning to it had imploded as my family imploded and I was grasping to know who I truly was, I was grasping for a place to fit in, and I was grasping to find what had touched my soul.

November 11th

Today was my last session with Feir and we did a past life regression to heal issues that I had carried forward. I found it appropriate that it was Remembrance Day. I was to walk away though, uncertain of exactly who received the healings.

My grandfather, Earnest, had been so much in my awareness that I was unclear if I was experiencing his life, or truly experiencing my own past life. The scenarios were remarkably similar. A form of claustrophobia, where we would panic if we were constrained in any way that affected our movement or ability to breathe, had definitely been part of both of our lives. Earnest had been buried alive for what seemed eternity as a result of a shell landing on his position during the First World War.

We felt that we should have died in the war because of who we became after. We went from good, gentle young men, to hurting anyone we got close to. We wanted to love, and needed love but felt that we were no longer in control. We felt as if we had something else that had taken hold of us and was looking through our eyes. An acute belief that we were evil haunted us and we were angry with God and the world for not killing us in the war. We blamed ourselves for drawing our families into our own inner hells, because we knew they still suffered because of it.

It was much easier to trace the shell back to its source, look into the eyes and heart of the man who had fired it, and then set him free than it was for us to forgive ourselves. That man shared the same terror, sadness and disillusionment that we did of a war that he felt trapped in. I had an inner knowing that this man never survived the war, but at least now I was not holding onto him in blame.

We could not stop berating ourselves for not walking out of the war. We did not believe in it, it was all a lie, and we were instrumental in killing and maiming others. We believed that because we did not walk away, our own lives and all that had been good within us had also been taken away. We were not worthy enough to live.

This belief might be the underlying reason why I had drawn so much pain and suffering into this life, and, the reason that no matter how much good and happiness I could have shared with my family, I still found a way to undermine it. This gave me my first solid hint at how this possibility could affect our lives now.

My previous self was struggling. He needed to find validation that that lifetime had some good to show for the fact that he had not died in the war. Feir had me go to the other side of the veil to find out what the purpose of that life was. Surprisingly, the first thing that popped out of my mouth was, "*It was so that I would be born.*" I sat there stunned. She counted to three and said that I was now in a room of older Beings that could elaborate further. I was told that it was important that I not die in the war. There was a reason that my family line had to continue. A descendant was going to play an important role in the future.

Feir said, "*You see, the purpose that you entered that lifetime was successful. It does not take away what happened in it, but you fulfilled your purpose.*" She asked me to ask them what the purpose of this lifetime was.

The elder Beings responded, "*Prepare your children for the future as they will be the ones. You can only prepare them if you truly know who you are, and if your children know who it is that you really are. Attach yourself to the Light within, not the Light outside of yourself. Follow it to discover yourself as a pure soul, and open to the healing energies, releasing all attachments that do not serve, as they are superficial to your true self.*"

I had become aware that we could be psychically open in many ways, even inadvertently. My energy field had been wide open and full of holes for years, which was a contradiction when you think of all the walls that I had put up to protect myself. Consciously I had been closing myself in through intentionally suppressing things. I had thought that whenever I would close my energy tightly around me I was protecting myself from the world. I was now gaining greater clarity, and understanding that there was a much broader picture.

My sessions had finished, but my mind could still not stay focused and it would drift into nothingness or abstract thoughts. It had been re-enforced how important it was to really find out and start living all that I am, and heal all that I am.

A couple of weeks later I relinquished my once prided self-control into the hands of Otto, James, the Teacher, Nature and all beneficial Beings. I surrendered all of who I was and opened my soul to Divine guidance. I had been floundering along in too many ways in my search for peace and clarity. I began to feel a real sense of what being humble was about. I was now choosing to go with the full flow of the spiritual support that I was beginning to truly understand was around me.

Loving waves of energy immediately surged through my body. I was being honoured with joy and welcomed, and this was to humble me even more. I felt so much love and appreciation for their unconditional acceptance and support that it would truly become the moment where the spiritual Essence that I am awoke into my experience.

I soon began to learn Reiki and another path would open for me, a path that was more deeply spiritual in some ways. This new energy began to make a greater overall difference in my life. I came into greater mental and emotional balance, and my innate gift for working with and channeling energy became more refined. After receiving the 2nd level attunement though I had been feeling an increasing urgency to open myself to the Spiritual one. This attunement was to have a profound effect on me. In receiving it I went into an altered state for minutes, and I was fully aware as it began integrating my spiritual Essence more integrally into my body. Everything in the room felt alive and I could sense all of the varied energies out on the street.

As time passed it enhanced a greater conscious connection with my core Essence and the higher Spiritual realm. It also significantly increased my perceptions and experiences when I channeled. I would feel vibrantly alive as the energy flowed through me. It would fill the room with its swirling as if I was in another dimension all together. I thrived on this.

It would be many months later before I was to feel that the energies opened through the attunement had completed their transformation. It was not until this time that I felt that I was beginning my journey into truly being a Master. To me, until I was fully healed within my own being I would not be a Master in the truest sense. This was the only sense that held any importance to me.

During this time period, I attended all self-healing related workshops that I could. I had become addicted to learning, going deeper within to heal and expanding further into the energy. I was meeting an increasing number of like-minded people.

Work, however, was becoming increasingly difficult to be at. The more I was exposed and opened to increasing frequencies of energy, the more conscious I became of just how sensitive I was to everything around me. At General Motors I worked in the Body shop, and the irritants, electromagnetic fields and underlying unhappiness was amplifying my own spiraling experience.

I was introduced to a woman who worked with the Light Beings next. Nadine's work was to enhance deeper energetic clearings and healings. With all of my exposure to energy and the healing work I had been doing my brain still felt sluggish and foggy, I had chronic pain, and I was waking up with my hands, arms and shoulders constantly half or totally numb. I felt that there was a lot that she and the Light Beings could help me with. All of our sessions were done over the phone with her guiding me as I tuned into my body in a semi-altered state. Once again, I was being introduced to new broader ways of assisting people that were more heart and spiritually based. Once again, it enhanced a greater and more fulfilling response from me.

I became much more comfortable working with the Light Beings during these sessions and was able to do some deeper healing. At the same time, I found out that I still was not aware of some forms of energy, as I had inadvertently opened myself to more energetic attachments. I also found that I was dealing with powerful fear based beliefs that had genetically come down the family line. These beliefs were exerting an underlying influence in my inability to move forward. I know all too well, that I added my own share to this mix.

I was reminded to fully open to my inner essence, my awareness, dreams, the Light Beings, and to express gratitude! I had not always remembered to do this. I was still concentrating more on my aches, pains and general listlessness then on the inner healings that were happening. I was learning a deeper lesson about where I let my focus rest, and returning it to a more positive focus when I did catch myself slipping. I also realized how entrenched my pattern of dwelling on negative thoughts was. It became a hard habit to break, but gradually it began to shift.

When I tuned into my body during a session my ankles unabashedly shouted out *"Do not ignore me! Your feet are your connection to Earth energy, honour and look after them. The more harmonious the energy flows within your feet, the greater you maintain your connection to the Earth."* This was another wake-up call as outside of their usual discomfort I generally have ignored them.

There was one vision that I had concerning my body during this session that I will share, as I feel it is an indication of our innate power. I will also share the attachments I had just to let you know that you do have power to keep them out of your existence.

My wrists, hands and forearms were blackened and shriveled from being severely burned, and I was experiencing it with all of the emotions and sensations as if it had just happened. Through Nadine's guidance I visualized, as though I was looking at time-lapsed photography, my arms and hands completely heal. To me, this proved the power of focused thought for healing when you open yourself to Divine assistance. Be in the calm, loving, and detached anticipation and knowing that it will happen, and it will happen.

I found out that I had other Extra Terrestrial attachments and déjà vu comes to mind. I was still inadvertently advertising myself to the universe. I visualized myself as being an old-fashioned pincushion going ouch, ouch, ouch, ouch, ouch, until I finally learned to come into the empowered wholeness of who I am.

One was attached to my lower spine and I saw it as a big grey lump whose ligaments spanned my body, and, attached to my right shoulder and wrapping itself around my throat was a serpentine energy stretching into another dimension. We called Michael in to sever its connection, but it tried to come back so he posted a Light Being to block its attempts and it could not return.

Between this session and the next I developed swimmers ear and was more lethargic, depressed, fearful, anxious, and my right knee flared back up. The numbness that I had been experiencing though had diminished a fair bit. These symptoms were all manifestations of my body processing and releasing all that had been stirred up in the last session, so I was actually thankful for it in the end.

Entities were found in my next session that Nadine called Hydra's. There was a big one at the base of my skull, little ones on my ribs, and miniscule ones in my brain. I could feel the release happening in my head, eyes and throat as they were removed. The whole existence of these entities revolves around one particular frequency, fear. They will hone into this frequency wherever it is being generated, so I am not surprised that they became latched onto me. According to Nadine, not only do these entities latch on to sustain themselves but that once fear is triggered they can amplify your experience of it many times over. They do this so that they can feel more invigorated themselves. We all thrive on something, and they are just another part of creation.

Up until now, whenever I would become aware of a lower energy presence my first reaction would be an instinctual fear that it might somehow latch onto me, and I would start pushing it away or throw walls of Light up. Anya had taught me that I had control over my body, but I would still feel afraid, so, this teaching had not yet fully anchored in.

My perception and awareness has since deepened; whenever I become aware of a lower energy presence now, I just choose not to allow it to attach, or remain attached. I have realized that by putting walls of Light up we are coming from a place of fear, even if only subconsciously. I am choosing to come instead from a place of inner knowing, empowerment, and the acceptance that they are what they are and I am what I am. Neither has power over the other. I have learned to understand the Light of my Essence. From the most miniscule speck of Divine Light, deep within my heart, I feel it radiating outwards. I am this Light. We are all, this Light. Knowing it, we are automatically safe and protected. I just know that this Light, my Light, surrounds me, and I can expand it at will. It is in our perceptions, and our fear, that we allow this balance to shift. I see these energies as flowing through me and I do not become attached to them. I anchor in the knowing of my own Divine power. I recognize fear as the separation from truth that it is. I know that it has no power over us unless we give it that power. I remain centered and fully present in the moment, intending the highest good for all. I surround whatever I am focusing upon with Light. I come from a loving heart, and I intend that the Light go to all times, places or dimensions that we may exist in. It is then that I call in Michael and the Light Beings if I feel the need.

In time, after finishing a psychic development course, two friends and I started a group of our own. I would like to share an experience that I had during our start up, as I feel it is a cautionary lesson on being discerning on what energies you let in. I can only relate this from my own perceptions and experience, so I must leave you to find its truth.

Some people eagerly embrace messages from any spiritual source or presence, automatically assuming that if they are in spirit form they are all knowledgeable and their intents are pure. This is not always true. There are many spirits and other entities that still retain their egos and lower thoughts and emotions. These particular entities will feed you, or others, tidbits of truth and they will feed your ego. They have their own agendas, and will sooner or later have more prominence in your daily life than you do. If you are holding thoughts that are in harmony with these lower vibrational spirits or entities, they will feed off these traits. This widens their doorway into your energy field and this level of existence. They will then amplify these traits, especially if you focus with an intense emotion.

This was my experience. Our course teacher, a Spiritualist reverend was invited to join us. However, when he was denied a controlling influence in our group he glared into my eyes, but the thing was, it was only partially him; he had allowed himself to become a conduit that offered focused intent to these lower energies because of his own thoughts in that moment. When he channeled them I was hit hard, so hard that I had to leave and head home. I was energetically, physically and psychically depleted and it took me three days to bounce back. I was furious. We had wanted the highest good for everyone. It was to be a group where everyone could be empowered and grow in all ways, with no one on a pedestal. There was no way I was going to allow him to come back after that.

Half the people who started with us dropped out because they looked up to him and thought it was my ego that was the problem. Outward appearances, especially when people are charming and have established reputations in the community can be deceiving. Look deeper and trust your instincts, no matter what outside influences or appearances may say otherwise. Discernment is perhaps one of the most valuable attributes that you can develop if you wish to go on this journey. You will find though, that there will be many increasingly empowering layers to it.

What is true for you? To find this you must be really honest in acknowledging, understanding and honouring your perceptions, intuition and instincts. Our learned or programmed reactions are just that, learned or programmed. What is true for each one of us? We can only really find that once we learn to tune in, really tune in to ourselves and trust our innate, first response feelings or instincts, before our brains have formed a thought response. Honouring our own discernment, not someone else's, can become one of the most valuable tools to us in life, as we all live with different variations of how we interpret our perceptions. This is also true in how we interpret our world and our experiences within it.

Become aware of whether you are viewing and forming a reaction to something or someone based on your true discernment or pre-programmed judgment. This is not always easy to differentiate, as sometimes it can be only a subtle difference. This is a re-learning on how you view and react to life, and with practice and self-honesty this can become very empowering.

What is harmonious, what is disharmonious to you? What is the first reaction in your heart? What is the first reaction in your body? Did you pull back, ever so slightly, or did your body and heart become drawn towards it, if only ever so slightly? In our human experience this can be our first guide. There is an old saying, "If it feels good in your gut go for it!" and if it does not, run, no matter what the appearance of it. Trust even slight hesitations if they are truly the first response. This is one of the main ways in which your body and heart can consciously communicate with you, for they are tapped into the underlying energy of the person or situation whereas your brain is not. Your heart and body hold more innate intelligence and awareness than your brain, and both, are centered on your highest good. Your brain cannot always differentiate what is in your highest good.

Until you become adept at bringing awareness to your body and hearts split second initial response, it helps to give yourself permission to mentally, or even physically, step back for a few seconds and become the witness to yourself. Ask, how does this feel in my heart and body? Bring your focus and awareness to it, and allow yourself to journey inwards. Am I reacting or discerning from an unbalanced state of being, or am I fully present and grounded in the now of the present moment and fully aware of the subtle nuances in my surroundings? Is this something that I wish to add my power to? Is this something that I want to bring into my experience? Am I being caught up in the emotions and reactions of others, or the insinuations of the media, or is this truly my own perception and response? This takes practice and a conscious willingness to take the time, but through time and practice it will become instinctual. Trust yourself, trust yourself, trust yourself. Sometimes our inner guidance only makes sense at a much later date, even if there has been no logical reason to back it up.

There is another unrelated experience that I am going to share, an experience that terrorized another man and I, filling us with an abject dread that lingered for days. I am sharing it because there may become moments when a similar thing may happen to you. This is not something to fear though, now that I understand, but it can still be very disconcerting to go through. I had no idea about this part of it though until weeks later.

We were sitting at the end of a train bridge and talking about spiritual things, when we felt something ominous approaching and knew we had to get out of there. Coming towards us over the bridge was a dark and powerful presence that we could not see, but every fibre of our beings knew it was coming and honing in on us. When it felt like it was about to overtake us I spun around calling in Michael and Gabriel. It had felt like pure evil before, but when I spun around it became amplified many times over and I found it hard to breathe. I could see it in shadow form and it was huge, many feet wide and stood two thirds of the way up the lamp post. The waves of dark energy that flowed from it seemed to permeate our souls, and the fear it generated felt like it would shut our systems down. As we stopped and faced it, it also stopped. I was given the impression that by turning and facing it something changed, because it did not continue after us. Was it us that stopped it? Was it Michael and Gabriel that stopped it? Or was it the combination of all of our energies? We did not know, but whatever the reason was for its' stopping, we were only too grateful that it did. We turned and left, and I knew that it did not follow, but its radiating waves of energy kept after us, choking us. The people walking by did not even subtly seem to notice anything amiss. It had focused specifically on us, and it really shook us to our core.

I was told that this was a Test in Motion. Sometimes in order to see if we are really ready to move on to the next spiritual level, the universe will throw something in our face that is of equal but opposite power to ourselves. This may occur during specific stages of our evolving spiritual journey. There was a part of me; the primal part of me that the fear had triggered that had felt like running in pure panic. I think most of those triggers were from barbs this Being was projecting at us, because there was also a huge part of me that seemed not to have any fear and had just been appraising this Being. I think that must have been the Spiritual essence part of me. My body felt seized with apprehension for the next few days and always on the verge of throwing up. The primal fear had not left.

When we are anchored in the knowing of our own Light and have grounded it through our bodies and into the earth, and fully re-integrated into oneness with our own hearts and the Divine, there is nothing that can unbalance us unless we give it the power to do so. Until we heal and release all patterns of fear that we hold inside though, this giving of our power away can be a subconscious knee jerk reaction. Coming into our full spiritual Divine power, and our full authority as Divine Beings takes time, but it is worth it.

Later, I was to be guided yet again to two people who would become influences in my life. Peter and Raven. They were stewards of one of the purest water sources on the planet, and their springs held distinct awareness of old Earth knowledge.

They told me that people could be led astray here if they were not aware or coming from their hearts, and they gave me an example of their own experience. While walking on paths that they knew well they realized that they did not recognize where they were. They were on the same path, but the woods and the path before and behind them had changed. This had caught them by surprise, and it took a few hours before they got re-oriented. The Earth and the elementals were showing them that they could protect what needed to be, through opening doors into alternate realities and misdirecting you. Peter told me that the water had let him know that it will recede if its essence is compromised. My awareness increased as I was reminded of just how much water, or anything else can be a conscious and self-determining entity within its own rights.

There was one more intriguing thing that Peter told me. At one time there was an indigenous community living in this area who called themselves the Children of Light. I now, became even more keenly interested. I left Peter and Raven with a great deal of gratitude, feeling that I had moved into, and was being accepted into, broadening circles of people that were in greater resonance with who I innately am.

A little while later, I sensed the curiosity of well-intentioned Beings. Two were somewhat humanoid and the third seemed similar to a jellyfish. I felt comfortable and told them they were welcome to check me out, but it astonished me at the speed at which they instantly began going through my memories. Surprisingly, I realized that they were also going through my memories from previous lives. We kept a shared awareness going into the next day, and I felt that they were learning from my senses and perceptions as well.

The following night I had a dream that I was being energized within a fluidly moving, semi-transparent essence. I felt aware and alive, and completely safe and honoured, but I was not sure if I was actually being scanned or re-configured by these Beings. I was grateful for this experience though. I was grateful for the knowing that I am becoming more in tune to vaster understandings of what lies beyond our concepts of the universe. Shortly after, I was to have a vision of myself in a bubble. I felt that the entirety of my essence, all that I was within the Divine seemed as if it was manifested into this vision. I was in the form of a baby, fully aware and focused. It reminded me of the scene at the end of the movie 2001: A Space Odyssey, where the baby is hovering and all knowing.

Months later, in the hope of being able to communicate more effectively with my guides, I enrolled in a workshop on developing intuition and channeling your higher self. Gratefully both occurred. I would like to share information received from my guides because it can be pertinent in many people's lives, and I will share what I channeled for another person for the same reason. I will start with this channel.

"You see yourself as very small but you are one with all things. Your Essence is Light and beauty. You have allowed others to surround you with their thoughts and limitations. Know that your Essence is just as powerful. You are one with all things. Walk in your own Light. You have a beautiful Light, though it seems hard for you to believe. Your spirit is enormous. Walk on both feet. Surround yourself with people who think the same way who will help you grow and shine. No need to hold back anymore."

I had many guides, all of whom were assisting in different areas of my life, and I was happy and thankful to know that they were helping. I was even more happy and intrigued to find that I had known them in other lives.

Lazarus and I were Romans together and had a loyal and strong bond, always watching out for each other. Celina was my wife and was helping to open my heart. Faith was helping me to believe. Cassandra was helping me remember how to flow. Rolph was reminding me to see with clear eyes, and there were more. They told me that I had many guides who came and went as I needed their specific assistance, and that many of them are and will be my teachers. I came into this lifetime to feel whole, and that the best way to access them was to play, create, believe, and to just have fun. They stressed that, "*The more open, relaxed and joyful you feel, the easier they are to connect with. There is no need to fear, trust your-self!*"

When I asked Ramsey why he was with me, he said that he was my connection to Home and that we were like brothers. He reminded me that I resonated with the high frequencies and was more than I thought I was. He also reminded me to remain an open and clear channel for wisdom and healing. Hmm, the greatest wisdom I think that I could ever give to anyone is to allow yourself to find, and then live your own truth and joy.

Everything else will fall into place if you just flow with it. Love yourself enough to take responsibility and accountability for your life, then, joyfully grow into your fullest empowered and creative potential.

Ramsey's remaining message was, *"You have a vast storehouse of knowledge, and there is more available to you. You understand that you are one with all things. All that you have to do is to think and you establish a connection. You are a Being of Love. In your world that is sometimes easy to forget. Know that all life is beautiful and that you are on the right path. Help others to see their Light."*

Breaking off into groups we took turns seeing what elemental, intergalactic or animal guide would come to us. We were then to imitate whatever it was with the intent of establishing a deeper connection. As my turn came, a progression of animals, one after another appeared, but I sensed that they were only showing themselves before the main one. I could feel the absolute power of it before I became aware of what it was, and I was not sure if I had ever experienced this kind of earthly power before.

It was an earthworm. We asked if it had a name but it said that it needed no name; it just was. It held a power that was majestic, grounded and sure. Its' role was to enhance my understandings of stability, and show me that nothing could knock me around when I was in my power and fully present. It was here to remind me that I always know that I know my purpose.

Asked if it had a message for me, the earthworm said, *"You know your message. You know what you need to do. In time another guide will come."*

All that I could think of was to keep following where my path was leading me, but I did not have a great deal of conscious clarity about it. In fact, part of the reason that I signed up for this workshop was to get greater clarity about my life.

The earthworm's message for the group was, *"You are all bright lights. Believe in your own Essence. Do not let the outside world distort the Essence of who you are. Believe in yourselves, everything will flow when you relax and enjoy. Stick to your own truth and feel joy. Your Essence is joy; remember that. You cannot fulfill what you came here to do if you are not relaxed. You all have great inner wisdom, trust it. No need to worry."*

I asked my guides how to access them again and they answered, *"It is all intent, just think specifically who it was that you want. If you do not know, then intend that the best one for whatever your concern is be the one that comes."*

I was reminded how similar this message was to what I had learned during my sessions with Feir and Nadine. It was all intent and a clear focused knowing of what you want.

It was around this time that I met Tim. He agreed to teach me how to make a native drum as close to the traditional way as possible. I felt, with a deep hearts knowing that it had to be only my energy going into it. It had to resonate completely with my Essence, the heartbeat of the Earth, and the heartbeat and unconditional Love of the universe. My intent was that as it was being drummed, the combination of these energies would ripple out to affect heart-centered change to all that the vibration touched. It was to be one of my ways to assist in the co-creation of a new Earth, enhancing healings for all.

I learned Therapeutic Touch and became an Integrated Energy Therapy master as well during this time, but my priority was still healing what remained within me. I understood that I had to be anchored and clear in my own foundation first, before I could shift my focus more exclusively to others.

My countdown for leaving General Motors had now begun in earnest. I had become acutely sensitive to my working environment. I was increasingly tired and depressed, and my overall constant stress and agitation became exceedingly frayed. My nerves had become so on edge that I instigated two altercations that got me time off. This was not my way, as prior to this I was always the one to calm people down. I was desperate and could not change my plans. I could not turn back, and even the thought of remaining at work virtually had me on the edge of a breakdown.

The day before I was to finish at General Motors I woke to a significant dream. It was my second appearance before this young native man. He had a welcoming, good-natured smile but did not talk much. Inviting me into his room he motioned for me to kneel on a mat; then knelt facing me on his. He then put himself into a trance, probing with his awareness.

He flapped his arms in imitation of a bird and I sensed a reality shift happening. As his arms moved faster my altered state deepened until I was in another place and the room at the same time. He transformed himself into what appeared to be a thunderbird, and I fell onto my back because of the intensity of the swirling energies. He crawled over to my right side, back in human form again, while a woman crawled to my other side. They told me to breathe in and out deeply in order to clear my system and I started coughing; I had a lot of blockages in my throat and lungs. They looked at each other and said that I was the Light of the tunnel, and then acknowledged me with happiness and welcomed me. They then made me more aware of my purpose, gifts and energy.

Moments later I could still feel them around me but not in physical form. My perceptual range had altered and increased. I was told to continue focusing on my vision and to continue clearing the blockages and toxins from my system. Around me were many guides; ancestors, nature, the Earth, Celestial Beings and Jesus. I felt without a doubt that I was not just leaving work and my old life on a whim, or because of anything else that I had thought or experienced until now. I sensed that I was being guided into what seemed to me, another higher purpose.

The next day, my last day of work, I found out that my union representative never bothered informing Management of my desire to leave. Any chance of a buy-out was now gone, but I controlled my anger because in a few hours I was going to be free of General Motors and the union forever.

I left work with only my holiday pay and lots of uncertainty and hope for the future. Even though I did not have concrete confidence in my outer self, I had implicit trust in my inner Essence and Divine guidance.

Leading into the last weeks though, I had pre-paid my airfare to Ireland as a gift for surviving General Motors as long as I had, and I was lucky enough to combine it with a tour of its spiritual sites with Caroline Myss. As I excitedly anticipated this trip, part of me felt as if I was in seventh Heaven, and I focused on recouping my energy as much as possible. However, in the days leading to flying out I think my trust in the universe was sorely tested, because two days before leaving I had only four dollars left to my name. I thought that I was about to become a transient outside of my time on the tour and figured that I would probably starve a lot. I did not know how far that I would be able to travel, and I did not really care what happened to me after I returned to Canada. I just wanted the best possible experience that I could have while I was there.

My guides and the universe were about to pull the proverbial rabbit out of the hat though. The day before flying out a notice came from a credit card company stating that if I did not activate their card within 48 hours I would have to re-apply. I did not know that I had sent away for this card, and I definitely had not realized that it might be lying around aimlessly somewhere in one of my drawers!

Book Two

Irish Journal

Without hesitation, I feel that if I had not previously set my intent to heal 'all' that I held inside, I would not have experienced the beauty and freedom of spirit that I was about to. It was this intention, along with immersing my-self into energy healing that began my transformation, setting me free enough to experience what I did, and had to, in Ireland. If I had not experienced what I did with such heart expanding depth, I sincerely do not know if I would have turned my life around to such a depth. I needed these experiences of connection. I have grown since this journal was written, but I felt that it was in Ireland that I was given the first true glimpse of my soul. The spirit of this land will forever be in my blood, and for that I have become eternally grateful.

August 17th 2006

I flew into Dublin, having rested but not slept. When the airport bus passed by an Internet café and accommodations, I joined the flock of people leaving at the next stop. I was hoping I was close to downtown and the bus or train stations but I really had no idea where I was.

I sent word to loved ones that I had arrived safe, found a room, and went searching for an old bookstore. I had a week before I was to hook up with Caroline's tour so I figured that if anyone had knowledge of interesting mystical or energy places, it would be found in such a shop. Although the proprietors happily shared standard tourist destinations, my spirit was pulling me towards something else.

I found that Dublin, regardless of its history did not resonate with me. The land was calling and I did not want to waste any more time in the city looking for other bookstores. Which direction will I go? I did not really have much of a clue. Eventually I would head north to visit relatives but for now, it was quite possible that it would be the next train or bus leaving the station.

It was slowly sinking in that I was here, and I could feel as my spirit gently moved around me, opening to whatever was meant to happen. Part of the reason I was here was to re-connect with the Divine, the Earth's energies, and myself. I had been on the healing journey for some time now. It was time to bring it to completion. It was time to heal. Time to glow in the joy and love I held inside, and, it was time to be free.

August 18th

As I left the hotel a flyer caught my eye; the Hill of Tara, an ancient royal site of the Irish High Kings. What better place to start!

Hauling my backpack I searched for the Busaras station, then hopped on the bus. The driver gave me an eye as he called out Tara cross, but as I looked around I did not see any sign of a hill, so I did not clue in. I ended up making an hour and a half extra bus ride to Cavan, where the return driver obligingly offered me a free ride back. This area was just like the Cavan area, back home, so as I watched the rolling hills flow by I did not end up minding the extra trip.

It was a twenty-minute walk from Tara cross to the hill and it was beautiful countryside, but I was surprised at how unassuming the hill was; I had expected with its significance that it would be a more prominent part of the landscape. There was a good 360 degree view of the surroundings though, and as I thought about it I was glad that it flowed so smoothly with the land.

Admiring the countryside, I caught up on my notes. It felt good sitting here, the fresh country air, the breeze, watching the sheep grazing, and just absorbing the energy. Rain was falling nearby, but there were still many people freely wandering the pastures. I was feeling a deep sense of serene contentment, but as I felt something crawling on me I looked down and found myself covered in red ants. Brushing them off, I moved away from their nest and returned to soaking everything in.

I lingered for a long time and then set off to see the rest, and I was so glad I lingered. At dusk a group of people arrived who were on the last stage of their pilgrimage. They were led by the reverend Brenda McLellen and two Irish guides. Kevin O'Kelly and Una Coghlan were guides that I would love to walk the backcountry with some day. Kevin shared the same spiritual Light as Brenda, and highlighted on his map some high vibrational spiritual places that he was aware of. He said that he would have marked more but most of the sites were located in the backcountry. Offering me his map he said that my energy felt at home on the hill, then welcomed me back saying I had been gone for a long time.

I shared an unorthodox Eucharist, a mixture of pagan and Christian with them. Terri, a beautiful spirit from the group, gifted me with a Chinese necklace, one side showing a dragon, the other a Gratitude symbol. She also offered me Gratitude tassels to leave where I had the most profound experiences, so I gave her a huge hug and then gave hugs all around. All of us felt that we had been together before and I thanked the universe for influencing this day.

According to Kevin, not only were High Kings crowned on this hill but Saints and honoured guests were brought here. The Druids considered this a sacred place.

I was drawn to sleep beside the Destiny Stone, feeling that it was somehow significant that I would be starting my first night on the land here. Soon though, a thunderhead rolled in and it started thundering and raining. A tent would have been nice. I knew that if the rain kept up it would be only a matter of time before my sleeping bag was soaked, so I got out, put my rain-suit on to retain body heat, and got back in. I asked the hill to keep me warm and it was a good thing, for it rained steadily all night.

I never slept. I spent the night holding my bag away from my face so that I could breathe. During the night though, I was visited by one of the High Kings of old. His presence was strong, confident, and aware. Aside from his visit, the baaing of sheep, and the sound of the rain, it was a quiet night. I found it fascinating that the hill seemed to have heard, and responded to my request. The energies seeping in from it had kept my back warm.

August 19th

I dropped my wet gear off at a laundry in Navan to be dried. The rain had added about twenty pounds to my load earlier, but now that it was dry I felt invigorated and alive. I decided to walk to Newgrange and found a scenic backcountry road. I needed quiet, and I wanted to absorb and connect with the land as much as possible. It was a quiet, contemplative, peaceful, and enjoyable walk, but after about fifteen kilometers the strain was wearing me down. When a couple pulled up asking if I was walking to Newgrange, I eagerly accepted a ride.

There were three significant Neolithic mounds in this area; Newgrange, Knowth, and Dowth. Newgrange and Knowth were the only sites offering guided tours, but when I arrived I found that both were sold out so I walked to Dowth, the most run-down of the three mounds in this area. I felt that if they were not offering guided tours of it, it would not be patrolled at night. I planned on sleeping there.

I arrived at the earth-covered mound at dusk, and found that only a faint semblance of its former self remained. A gated entrance leading into the mounds interior was the only way inside, so I would have to sleep outside again. I looked to the sky and prayed for a rain free night. All the rocks nearest to this mound, especially one, held amazing energy. I sat on it for a long time, resonating with the energies that surged through me. It was a fantastic experience of connection. I later fell into a relaxing sleep under a tree, all the while listening to the cows and sheep serenading each other in the background. Thankfully it did not rain overnight.

August 20th

I toured Knowth first. This was a significant, high-energy site. It had once held the largest collection of Neolithic art found in Western Europe, and the craftsmanship of many of the artifacts had only been able to be duplicated by using laser technology. Most of the rocks forming the outer wall of the mound had been etched with symbols.

There was much more, but as I sat waiting at another bus station hours later, with my journal open in my hands, I was trying to go by memory. I was tired and my rough copy notes were rain damaged. It was no use. I could not focus enough to offer this site, or Newgrange, enough justice. There was too much information to absorb. The only way the general public had access was through hour long guided tours, and for me that was not nearly enough.

At Newgrange, I did not explore the whole sight. As I arrived, I had been drawn to a triangular shaped stone located down the slope from the entrance. It stood over six feet, and etched on its upper left side I found a barely recognizable spiral. As I placed my palm on the spiral an intense energy rush enveloped me. This must have been why I had been drawn to it; there was something within this rush of energy that I was meant to connect with. My eyes lost their focus and I fell into an altered state. I felt only half within this world. I was looking around and into the rock, totally connected, and I stood like this until the guides called us to go inside. It took me a minute to fully come back.

The guides gave us a demonstration of what the experience of solstice would be like inside the main chamber, and what an experience that was. I could easily see why people would have thought that the light cascading in would lift the spirits of the dead into the heavens. It was electrifying and I could feel the magic of it!

Hours later I was in Drogheda looking at a five hour wait for the next bus to Newcastle, so I spent time catching up on my notes. Slieve Donard, the mountain that overlooked the town of Newcastle, had not left my mind since I found it on the map. Something that lay buried deep within my essence was compelling me forward.

August 21st

I spent the night at a youth hostel in Newcastle. It was clean and quiet, but it took me a long time to fall into a disturbed sleep. It had rained with gusts of high winds overnight, but I was not sure if that was the reason I felt so restless. I did not feel rested. I felt sluggish actually, so I stopped into a restaurant for two servings of breakfast and it gave me more of a spring in my step. Outside of my time on the tour I planned on avoiding restaurants as much as possible, so this had been a treat. I was living on the most dense, uncut loaf of bread that I could find, bananas, and as much water as I could carry. Breakfast had provided me with more vitality, but I was still in no shape to climb the mountain. I did not know if it was the mountain itself that was calling me, or something around it. Whatever it was, I now realized that I would have to come back to find out.

Curious about other possible significant sites in the area I looked through the tourism office and the Ballynoe stone circle literally jumped out at me. It was a bus ride away, so I hopped onto the next bus to Downpatrick. I had to wait again for the next connection to Ballynoe. All of this waiting was tiring me out more than anything, as I felt alive when I was on the land.

A car would have been convenient, but since arriving in Ireland I had been glad that I was not driving. There was just so much of the natural world, in all its facets, that you could miss experiencing through being separated from the land inside a car. One of the main things that I had observed within people was a deeply buried inner sense of emptiness, or disconnection. Our modern society seemed to promote that basic feeling, regardless of how much it was covered over. I had felt it most of my life, and I was tired of it. I had a knowing, and a yearning inside to re-find that connection. I sensed that my journey was expanding, and I had begun to realize that there were many layers to it. I felt it necessary to be outside of a vehicle as much as possible on this trip. I needed to directly connect to the energies of this land; something within was expressing a sense of desperation for it.

Ah, the Ballynoe stone circle! I could feel the surge of its energy envelop me as soon as I saw it. Nice! The first real patch of blue sky that I had seen since I arrived in Ireland had just opened up above me, so without hesitation I stripped down, walked around, and entered the circle naked. I lay on top of the mound soaking it all in, and it felt great.

There were many friendly and curious spirits still here. After sitting with them awhile, I asked if any were ready to enter the Light. I sensed from those who had chosen to leave that it was important that I sing, honouring them and their journey as they prepared. I sang until my throat went dry, and then called in Michael and the Light Beings. Many left, but there were a couple who stayed behind who felt that I had been trying to usurp their power, as many of the spirits who had been with them had left. When all was said and done though, they backed off.

The local priest showed up later and told me that there used to be seven rings of stone here. Hearing this, my fascination for this site increased. It would not be long before the last bus passed by my stop. Do I stay indoors somewhere warm and dry, or do I sleep on the mound within the seven circles of stone? I smiled and dug out some warmer clothes. I felt the moment that I saw this circle that I would be spending the night here. To me, it was immaterial whether the seven circles still existed in form. It did not matter where the stones now rested, their energetic imprints, and the original intent behind the circles remained.

Well into dusk I had to laugh; a couple of farmers were dropping off a load of cows to graze. I would have company tonight. The cows walked around the circle of stones, stopping occasionally to check out my gear, but they had not entered the circle. I had not brought my gear into the ring yet. As I had first neared the circle, I had had a feeling that I was meant to only bring the truth of who I was into the ring. To me, that meant that I could not hide or distract from my essence in any way. Later, as I prepared to bring my gear into the circle, I leaned it on one of the entrance stones and was swept by a rush of energy that held definite masculine vibrations of discontent. Stunned, I apologized, then asked permission from a stone on the inner circle to set my bag there and was warmly accepted. I connected with the strong, gentle, regal and feminine spirit within this rock. Her name was Gwyneth.

As I sat absorbing all that was around me, I realized that all of the stones in the inner circle had feminine energies. I felt peaceful, relaxed, happy and serene. A family of rabbits was playing outside the stones.

One of the farmers returned with more cows and was eyeing me curiously, so I approached him to see if this was his land. He was only renting the land but said that if I was not here to bother the spirits I was more than welcome to spend the night. He was a pleasant, down to earth young farmer and we talked about our travels.

After he left I pulled out one of the Gratitude tassels that Terri had given me, honoured and thanked the circle with it, and then said that I was offering it to Gwyneth. This made her happy and her spirit turned playful. I liked her, and chose to sleep beside her tonight instead of on the mound.

I lay a long time just staring at the stars, though it did not seem to get really dark at night here. There was a soft luminescence permeating everything, even though there was no sign of the moon.

I woke up with a start! There was a loud snorting of breath and I could not for the life of me figure out what on Earth it was. It sounded unerringly close to the raptors on the movie Jurassic Park and my heart about stopped. I sat bolt upright and there sticking its head over top of Gwyneth and looking down on me from not more than a foot away was one of John's cows! I shook my head smiling unbelievably and laid back down laughing.

As I slept there had been many spirits on the edge of my awareness still enacting life as it was for them, even Gwyneth. At one point I felt the earth shake, and watched as a large group of medieval horsemen galloped in my direction. The leader was coming for Gwyneth and ended up carrying her away. I felt a growing sadness, for as time had gone by we had been getting close, and I missed her.

A couple of times in the early morning hours I heard what I could well believe the people in bygone days feared as the banshee. The sound carried a definite haunting, wind-blown, lingering resonance to it. It was however, only a litter of young pups howling away.

August 22nd

In the pre-dawn hour I sat quietly beside the stone to Gwyneth's right. Gwyneth was gone and her stone felt lifeless. The spirit essence within this stone was Moldred. She felt friendly, quiet and down to earth. I welcomed her to the new day.

At dawn I watched a jet crisscrossing the sky trailing a stream of particles. I watched it curiously. I had never paid attention to this before, but seeing it in practice had triggered my memory. It was on the Internet that when governments had been asked about the particles, or who owned the jets, there was not one that seemed to know anything about it, or was willing to take responsibility. Whatever these jets were doing had been witnessed throughout the world. Within minutes it clouded over and the clouds seemed to appear from nowhere.

I should have left on the first, then the second bus from here, but I could not leave this place yet. A stone on the outer circle had been gently drawing me since I had arrived, and as I answered its call it became a profoundly powerful and deeply personal experience. It stood over six feet tall and was about five feet across. Stretching my arms sideways as far as I could, I found finger holds that seemed meant for me. I embraced it with a full body hug for a long time, much like a small child clinging to a nurturing parent. My inner child had come fully to the surface. In these untold minutes this stone, my inner child, and my adult self really connected. The energy within this stone was not male or female, and it was not overly amplified. It just was. It worked on a deep subtle level.

As I finally released this stone, it was like leaving a long gentle embrace from a close friend. I slowly stepped back and brought my hands together in a prayer of thanks. My inner sight was instantly sent journeying through passageways and other places that passed by so fast that I could not recognize them; yet my inner knowing understood that they held importance. Warding off a chill I brought my hands over my third eye, tensing my back and shoulders. My vision shifted and I was passing rapidly through the stars. I almost lost my balance and had to take a step forward. The Earth immediately thrust her energies upwards, re-grounding me, and I felt so profoundly moved that I went into a deep and quiet place inside. Moments later, still in this place, I retrieved the second Gratitude tassel from my bag and raising it to the circle, I turned slowly so that all could see and I called out that I was honouring this stone for nurturing and affecting me in such a way. I set the tassel in front of it. The inscribed writing on this tassel said 'Joy of Discovery'. I had been softly crying ever since, and my tears had dropped onto the pages as I had been writing.

I noticed other interesting things about this site. The elongated mound was not perfectly aligned with the sunrise, and anywhere that I had traveled the crow seemed to be the predominant bird; here it was the dove. Surprisingly, this site was not one of the sites highlighted on Kevin's map. To me, it now held immense meaning.

I did not want to leave but my time was running out for visiting my relatives and my Dad's homestead. I took one last look around, told the stones we would meet again, looked over at Slieve Donard, again with its peak swirling in clouds, turned and left.

On my way out to the road I came across a beautiful flower, one that I had never seen before. Shades of blue, with the sweetest of fragrance, but it was not this alone that held me; where it was situated felt magical in it-self. Nature had formed a tunnel of branches that gave you a sense that you were walking through a portal into another time or place; thinking back, that was exactly what I did.

John drove by and offered me a lift into Downpatrick where I caught the next bus into Belfast. Of all the places that I had been the energy in Belfast was the heaviest, almost oppressive. The whole city appeared more unkempt, the people more wary. I did not have to wait for my next bus transfer and I was relieved. I found it hard to breathe.

The bus passed through Moira and I thought that one day I would like to walk through this town. Portadown also seemed like a friendlier and nicer town. By evening it had started to rain so I decided to stay here instead of continuing on. My guidebook did not have this city listed so I found the heavily protected police station and asked for a referral. The amount of protection around the station was unexpected but the officers were friendly. They directed me to a place where the owners were friendly and the food good. My room however, had no window and after being outside so much I found it very closed in.

August 23rd

I had a terrible sleep last night. The re-occurring dream lasted for hours and it concerned three pedophiles. I was in the energy of one of them; the hunter. He was mostly in it for the excitement of the chase, and his focused contempt for the children for being weak and stupid enough to be caught was all pervading. The other two men were afraid to stick their heads out but were the more serious and damaging pedophiles.

I was in their thoughts, their depravity, their excitement, and their fear. It was as if I was hovering over them throughout one entire day in their lives. I had originally thought that the hunter had been the previous occupant of this bed, but the memory of my inner child experience yesterday had just flashed into my mind. Had this dream wakened a buried memory from an experience in my own past?

Leaving Portadown I found that the people on the bus were truly friendly. The driver and passengers went out of their way to circle back out of Richhill again, just so that I would be let off exactly where I needed to be. Upon discovering that I had family roots in the area they joyfully embraced me as a long lost friend and traveler. It warmed my heart to be blessed with their eager and happy help, and I felt that I was indeed being looked after. Everything that I had experienced in Ireland, with the exception of last night, had flowed so easily and with so much grace that it felt surreal. I had absolutely no itinerary other than my time with the Caroline Myss tour, and seeing the homestead. Leaving myself totally open to the wind and to my soul had gifted me with an immense sense of freedom and joy. I had allowed my heart to set the direction and choose its own pace; more importantly though, I had opened its doors to hear the voice of spirit call its name.

I found my relative's house with the help of his neighbours and over a table full of delectable food we chatted and casually checked each other out. We warmed up to each other nicely, but he had to get back to helping his neighbour and I needed to travel back to Dublin. There had been no time to see the homestead this day, so we talked of getting together again when I came back this way. We said fond farewells and I walked into Richhill, glad we had met.

August 24th

This morning I took my time getting to the Westin where I would be staying for the next two days. In this section of Dublin the international vibrancy felt invigorating, and it was a pleasing contrast to being on the land. As I arrived at the Westin though, the doorman politely asked me if I would be staying there. He must I suppose, not have been used to seeing one of the multitudes of people carrying backpacks, entering this posh hotel. A couple of minutes later I could not help but smile. As I was standing at the check in counter I caught sight of the doorman scanning the room until he saw me. I just smiled at him and nodded, he walked away satisfied.

I joined Caroline's tour and our first destination was Glendalough. My impressions of Glendalough though were of not feeling any resonance to it at all. I felt no sense of energy. However, outside the old entrance portals were two headstones that I was drawn to, almost as if I recognized whoever had been buried. I lingered a few minutes, and then moved off. St. Kevin's cross was the most prominent landmark but I never paid it much attention. In fact I had started to walk by it, ignoring it completely, when I stopped abruptly and faced it. Wham! I was hit by its energy and knew that I had stood here before. It was totally unexpected and powerful. As I became fully present to this experience I noticed a huge amount of energy under this cross. The energy was less, though equally noticeable under two gravestones near to it. My curiosity was piqued. What was this energy? Why had I not even sensed it until it hit me so powerfully? What was it trying to tell me? What exactly was buried here? It had felt more than just a buried person.

Back in Dublin we had the night free so I walked Grafton Street. I watched the sidewalk artist working with his pastels, then wandered along and listened to a couple of buskers. After enjoying a few tunes I left some euros and continued on, only to stop again to watch a gypsy couple dancing the tango. Eventually I made it to St. Stephen's Green. I wandered, sat, wandered some more, and just relaxed. I needed to get used to hustling around with the large tour group and being on a tight time frame. My energy when I was out on the land where I had just allowed myself freedom had expanded and I was finding myself having to rein it back in. Part of me, wished I was back on my own.

August 25th

Ah, the Trinity College library! Old, old books and they were truly amazing! The books of Kells and Armagh alone were amazing in themselves. When I entered the vastness of this library my heart and soul were trying to jump out of my chest, yearning to embrace all the knowledge here. I did not want to leave.

By afternoon we had visited St. Patrick's Cathedral and I found that I was not really impressed, neither was I impressed by personified monuments of their affluent patrons. To me the prime focus seemed more about wealth, prestige, and the power of the church. What I experienced on the land and within my own life since I had started to heal and open was much more spiritual to me than any of this. I must speak my truth as I relate to spirituality. We all relate in our own ways.

We had free time so a few of us explored the museum. I found the bog men exhibit seemed more like a creation that David Cronenberg might have dreamed up for one of his movies, than the remains of actual people. I found them disturbing. The remains of these men were being displayed within three separate enclosed areas, and it was the third 'man' I came to that hit me the hardest. His spirit was still present and he was tormented by a massive amount of grief. He felt that he had betrayed his chieftain and let his clan's expectations down. He desperately needed to make amends, and his traumatic energies were flowing erratically all around me. I was alone, so I sat down and eased his emotions, telling him that he could enter the Light if he chose. I told him that his chieftain honoured his courage and what he did do for him, and that it was OK to leave. That seemed to be all he needed to finally go guilt free into the Light. I called in Michael and the Light Beings and his spirit was free. I was however, totally drained emotionally and physically after the intensity of his trauma. I needed time to recover, so I was grateful that I remained undisturbed.

Eric Dilworth appeared during Caroline's workshop tonight and gave a presentation about what he was doing in Ireland. There was something about him and his spiritual centre that intrigued me. I mentioned that I would like to drop around for a day or two after the group left and it made him happy. He had a deep heart energy that I connected with. I felt that another door had just opened. Once again, I sensed that this chance meeting was spiritually orchestrated, and that I just had to be open and aware enough to flow into it.

August 26th

We traveled to Mellifont Abbey and this site held amazing energy. I found a quiet place away from the group and sat absorbing its peacefulness. I felt as if I may have lived here.

Stopping later at St. Brigid's Well at Faughart, I noticed that there was a special energy with this water and rested my hand in it.

Tonight we arrived at the Slieve Donard hotel in Newcastle and I needed to go off alone. I had been feeling increasing agitation and anxiety since we arrived in the vicinity of Slieve Donard. I was not sure if it was because I needed space from the tour group, being close to Slieve Donard again, or whether there was something here that I truly needed to connect with. I did not know, but I felt compelled to be alone. I turned down invitations from tour mates to join them for supper and instead found a fast food place and a bench overlooking the bay. The Mourne Mountains, with its mysterious Slieve Donard were over my right shoulder.

There was something pulling at me. I did not know what it was and I could not shake the anxiety. The tide was out so I walked along the water's edge back towards the hotel. I spent half my time looking for seashells and the other half watching the sun set over the mountains.

August 27th

As far as today's tours went, Navan Fort was the only thing that held interest. The group moved off quickly but Don, Mary and I lingered a few minutes more, all drawn in our own ways to something deeper. The story we were told of its origin did not make sense, so it became one more mystery to be curious about. There was a connection between Mary and I, although we were not sure what it was. This had been the first time we had taken note of each other. She appeared more tuned into the earth than most other people that I had known, but there was something that went deeper. We arrived back to the buses a bit late but such is life. Tonight we were staying in Armagh.

August 28th

Today we traveled through small towns and stopped in Derry; or Londonderry depending on whether you were Protestant or Catholic. Every town that we passed through today, especially this one, still held onto a fair amount of tension. The British military surveillance compounds were being de-commissioned but were still noticeably operative. Our tour guide, when asked how he could handle being constantly monitored replied that compared to the way things used to be, they were now much better. Some of us found it claustrophobic and hard to breathe here.

August 29th

On today's travels we stopped at the full court tomb at Creevykeel, dating back to Pagan times. Immersing myself within the energies I could feel the connection the people had to the Earth.

Arriving into Sligo, we made a special trip to the Tobernalt Holy well. As we walked through the gate I felt deep joy when I sensed the presence of nature spirits. I realized instinctively that this was what they were. I had always been fascinated by the fables of nature spirits and faeries, and actually coming into contact with them was an amazing blessing.

This well was old, very, very old. As I held my hand in the water its infinite age, awareness and healing properties washed over me. No wonder its water was considered Holy. I entered a deeply quiet place within, connecting to this water. I was drawn to it in a way that spoke to every fibre of my being. We came from the same source.

Still in this deep meditative state, I was drawn further up the hill. Beyond the wall was a huge concentration of nature spirits. After spending time with them, I was pulled to continue up the path and became spellbound. I stood silently, in wonder and fascination. Faeries. Their energies were distinctly surrounding a tree ahead of me. This was the first time in memory that I had consciously come into contact with the faerie folk. It was a beautiful connection and I was mesmerized. It was hard to describe how I felt. My body seemed to instantly drop the weight of the world. All of the rigidity I had held in my body for years disappeared in the whisper of a breath, and I felt immersed in deep peace, happiness and awe.

Once more I was drawn to continue up the path and this time I could not believe it. I was more than open to the existence of faeries, but this left me shocked. I had never believed in the stories about leprechauns but here they were, more than I could count. They were sitting throughout the limbs of a massive tree over-hanging the path, looking down at me and smiling with joy and amusement. I stood there with my mouth hanging open, and after a minute of stunned silence, I thanked them and the faeries for showing themselves. As I walked back down the path I nodded my head in farewell to the nature spirits.

On my way back to the bus I met Caroline's assistant. He seemed relieved to have found me but also annoyed. It appeared the bus had been waiting for me.

August 30th

Stopping in Westport for a stretch, I came to a sudden stop in front of a store. I entered and went straight to a pendent. Talking to Derek, the store's owner, it turned out that he was a craftsman and energy worker, and had made this pendent. It was Irish silver with a universal energy symbol, almost serpent like, engraved on it in gold. Without hesitation, I purchased it and placed it around my neck. I felt that Derek had become another significant connection, and that this necklace of Irish silver and gold, with this symbol, was somehow important to who I was becoming.

Further down the road we came to Kylemore Abbey. Peaceful, serene tranquility permeated this Abbey and its grounds. The energies felt instantly soothing, and the nuns I saw all had a spiritual glow about them. The Abbey sat at the base of a mountain, and with the fine rain and mist immersing us we felt serene enchantment.

August 31st

During the ferry ride to the Aran Islands Mary and I stayed on deck. Experiencing the open sea with the wind flowing through our hair felt refreshing and invigorating after spending so many days confined inside the bus. It felt like freedom.

Everyone felt more alive on the island, remarking on the difference in the energy here. There were smiles everywhere. The landscape reminded us of a giant jigsaw puzzle with all the stone fences, and with each fence looking about three feet wide it was pretty amazing considering all the work involved. Observing the polite but reserved islanders, I had to admire them.

We traveled by mini bus to Dun Aonghus. I recommend this place, but to reach it and get inside you needed good legs. Dun in Gaelic means fort and at first it gave that impression, but I sensed that its real purpose was much more.

Walking up the hill with friends we noticed that the perimeter walls held awareness. Discovering this, we stopped and looked at each other. Yes, we were all feeling it. With growing curiosity we continued climbing. The closer we got to the walls, the more we sensed the increase in the energetic resistance flowing towards those coming up the hill. As we reached the walls though, the resistance stopped. This fort was on a steep hill, so most people trudged right on through without seeming to notice anything unusual. Awareness in the walls; what was its purpose? Who had anchored this awareness in, the Druids?

Reaching the top many of us could feel our spirits expanding in amazing ways as we gazed at the limitless horizon. All that could be seen was ocean. I realized what some of the significance of this site was as I stood on the stone platform on the edge of the cliff. Our on-site guide, Padraigin Clancy, mentioned that historians and archeologists had been wondering if there might be some connection to an island directly out to sea. Well there definitely was a connection as my whole being could feel it. The energy channeling between these two sites was strong, and in my mind's eye I could see the energetic bridge. Some places are situated on planetary ley lines that are directly connected to other significant sites around the world. I wondered if Dun Aonghus was one of them. Padraigin and I recognized that we knew each other from somewhere, in another time. She had published 'Celtic Threads,' a book about her studies of Ireland's sacred sites.

September 1st

As we passed through the Burren area on our way to the cliffs of Moher, a heavy pressure engulfed my heart. The deepening feeling of nausea was not a pleasant experience. I felt sick, and was becoming increasingly paler as acute grief engulfed me. I was not sure if I was picking up energies from the land, or whether something was surfacing within me.

Once we got to the cliffs though I quickly cleared the energies that had dragged me down, and soon felt exhilarated. These were beautiful cliffs and the energy was amazing. I told myself that I would return before I left for home.

Stopping for the night in Killarney we hopped back onto to bus for a fun evening of dinner, dance and music. While there, I was asked a surprising question. Would I go to the front of the bus the next day and tell everyone what impressions I picked up from the piece of paper that had been passed around? I was not sure who originally started it, but everyone had been asked to doodle about whatever inspired them in that moment. I said I would but I was not fully sure why I was asked.

September 2nd

During our day trip to the Dingle Peninsula the tour guide offered me his microphone. I only had a vague idea of what I was going to say, but managed to ramble on for about three or four minutes. Everyone's collective spirits shone through clearly, and there was no trace of anything within it being limited within the confines of a box. This was the message I tried to get across, for them to believe in themselves and let their perceptions expand. I think half the people got something out of it. Not bad I guess for a captive audience. It was a good experience for me though as I was actually comfortable, even if I did have some jitters walking up to the front.

Looking out the window at the land flowing by, I continued to be struck by how powerful the energies of the land were in Ireland. I was so connected with this land and in these energies that I felt immense gratitude. For the first time in my life I was feeling truly alive, and truly connected to where I was.

In the evening Caroline held her last workshop. I was thinking that what was important in my meeting her was to recognize that I need not be a follower. Maybe my lesson in being a part of her tour had been to observe the people within the group who became captivated on her every word, and gave their power completely over to her.

Everyone, if they looked deep enough within, holds the Divine power, and the spiritual and heart wisdom relating to their own life experiences and spiritual journey, as anyone else. Other people can be guides and inspirations, but we are all, regardless of our perceived social status, equal before God. Even the Christ Essence understands this and is showing us the way to remember this connection within ourselves. It comes back to trusting that we are Divine Essence as well, and knowing without a doubt that we are worthy enough to stand, and move along our life's path, within our own Light.

Why has humanity, as a whole, made it so hard for themselves to feel the inner voice, and love of God flowing through their hearts? I have found that we are innately spiritual beings living human experiences; our own, and other peoples ego's like us to believe that our construed sense of identity, separation and power is the foundation of our reality. It is reality only because we have been brought up to believe it is reality. As I journeyed further into my heart, this truth opened before me.

Eric Dilworth showed up again for this workshop and offered me a ride back to Ard Na Ri with him the next day. I stood there thinking about how much this seemed to be a reflection of some form of Divine timing. There was too much synchronicity in this to be anything else.

Mary and I left the hotel and started walking. Our connection was hard to explain, but the bond between us had become much stronger in the last few days. It felt as if it had been orchestrated that we come together, and since that moment when we had met at Navan fort, the energies between us had become more deliberately entwined. I was deeply intrigued, and somehow deeply connected to her.

We walked for a long time and ended up on the grounds of a large old building. Feeling curious, we followed the driveway around to the back, but we felt something unpleasant so we retraced our steps. It felt better out front, so we found a nice big tree to relax under, watch the stars, and talk. These grounds and building had the feeling of an old sanatorium, and we felt a multitude of spirits looking out of the windows at us.

After we left, we walked for about half an hour in what we thought was the general direction of the hotel. We eventually came however, back through the side archway into the same sanatorium grounds. We had come, via a different route, full circle. It was late, we were getting tired, and we had a suspicion that we were being played with. Mary was upset and sent out an energetic block to whatever it might be and we started off again.

Then, not sure how it happened, we found ourselves on the highway outside of the city limits. Mary gave me one of those looks when we realized this and looked at her feet remarking how tired and dirty they were becoming. When she looked up again and looked into my eyes I was stunned. I had recognized a flash of her essence. I knew what was different about her now; she carried the essence of an elemental. The joys of discovery that I had been experiencing since coming to Ireland were continuing.

Thankfully we soon recognized that this was the same route that the bus entered town. We just had to re-locate the hotel.

Along the way, we were drawn to a mound and decided to climb it. Looking around we commented on the unusual energy. There were eight trees, four big ones forming an outer circle with four younger trees forming an inner circle. A strong energy was channeling between two of the opposing older trees. We did not say anything but we were drawn to these trees and leaned back on them. Mary went to the one, me to the other. I told her to place her palms on the tree and as soon as we both had that connection in place things got weird really fast. Three powerful energy vortices were passing through me, the strongest one in my torso. It felt as if the tree was not quite as firm anymore and I was slowly falling back into it.

I heard Mary say "*Oh my God.*" She was looking at me in shock and broke her connection. Ever since we had placed our palms on the trees, I had felt that she had been keeping me grounded. The vortices quickly stopped but I felt very, very different. I soon picked up that I had another awareness latched into my energy field.

Mary was looking at me strange and asked if I was all right. She told me that my head, arms and legs totally disappeared into the tree and it had started freaking her out. I only half heard her. I was slowly looking around and at her because every fibre of my being felt acutely alive as the awareness opened itself to this world. I told her about our visitor and she wanted to know if it was good or bad. This was something that I had been trying to figure out since becoming aware of it, and I still was not sure. All I was sensing was a huge curiosity. I let it stay with me for a few minutes, then walked over to one of the side trees and put both palms on it. Whatever it was, it scampered up the tree appearing from my mind's eye, halfway between Gumby in the old cartoon and a chimpanzee.

I was beginning to take all of my assorted experiences as an everyday part of life. I just thought of the whole thing as fascinating but not in the least bit unusual. We found a portal of some kind, but whether it was between the worlds, or between other realities, we did not know. Coming down from the mound we discovered that cut into the other side was the religious shrine we passed earlier on the bus. The tour guide had spun a yarn to us that concerned some antics around the statue at this site. According to local legend the statue would sometimes shake and people would flock here from all over hoping to witness it. However, the legend was undermined one day when half the town ran to it and found a young boy behind it having some fun. I wondered though, after experiencing what I did, about how much of a co-incidence it was that the church just happened to put a shrine here.

Back at the hotel I asked Mary if she could sense whether or not our visitor left anything in my energy. She tuned in and said that she did not think so, but picked up that I had moved more stuff energetically in the last few weeks than people usually moved in a lifetime. I had not told her that that had been my intent, especially in the last few months. The day was coming when I was going to need to be clear and I planned on being ready. What exactly was coming I did not really know, but I sensed that it was vitally important that I was ready. That meant being healed on all levels and fully in tune with all of who I was.

September 3rd

As Mary was packing to leave she offered me some gifts; a piece of golden Alpaca wool that held a meaning between us, a stone to stay connected, and a beautiful card with a special five leaf clover inside. She had found it a couple of days earlier. Tucked in around this clover was a small patch of four leaf clovers. Mary was the most tuned in person to the natural world that I had known. It would not surprise me if the Earth had offered them to her when she asked to find one. I was deeply moved.

I said my goodbyes and offered hugs to friends that I had become close to, and as the bus left I was swept by loneliness. No matter what adjustments I had to make in feeling confined with the larger group as a whole, I had really begun to cherish this handful of people.

Penny had shared other special sites that I might be interested in seeing during my last few days in Ireland, and MariAnne loaned me 'Mystic Ireland', then pulled out a bag of crystals. A friend had asked her to place them into the earth wherever she found special resonance. She asked me if I would like to plant the rest. I was feeling honoured that both her and Mary had thought so highly of me. With a lot of warmth I accepted and thanked her.

Eric soon showed up and another amazing day unfolded. Obviously part of the necessity I had felt in coming to Ireland at this time was to connect with him. If it had not been for Caroline's tour we probably would not have met, so all things had worked out the way they were meant to.

The more we talked during our drive the more interested he became. I had become sure of myself, and I was radiating a depth of inner peace and calm gratitude that I had never before attained. I may have had reflections of this at times over my life, but for quite possibly the first time I felt the all-encompassing embodiment of it. I was feeling an immense sense of empowerment and joy.

On the way to his place though, Eric seemed to lose his sense of direction. We ended up at the same spot three times, beside a signpost for the town of Birr. There must have been some reason for this, and by this time we were hungry so I suggested going for something to eat. We parked the car by a tall war memorial and as soon as we did, I became almost sickened by the oppressive energies radiating from it. Walking up the street I began to feel like I was turning green. I turned back and called in Michael, the White Brotherhood and all of the Light Beings to deal with this energy. Within seconds they surrounded the memorial and were beginning to clear it.

We found a place to eat and by the time we came out they were well into their task. The energies though not completely clear, were well on their way to becoming so and I was feeling a lot better. This had been much worse than what I had experienced as we passed through the Burren'; there it had been what I assumed was grief reflecting from the land, or reflecting from me into the land. Here, it was different, much different.

We reached Ard Na Ri without any further ado. It seemed that the Earth and Celestial realm had just needed to draw somebody to Birr's memorial that could feel and in a way recognize these particular energies, and then held the knowing to call in help.

I had come to understand that the Celestial realm was fully aware of all energies and all things on our planet, but they would not interfere against our free will. They waited to be asked. If the asking was from the heart and was intended for the highest good of all, they would respond in whatever ways they could.

Ard Na Ri was located alongside Clonmacnoise, a significant Christian spiritual site in County Offaly along the river Shannon. Apparently this site was so significant at one time that Pope John Paul made an unscheduled stop here on his visit to Ireland.

Eric gave me a tour of what he had accomplished, and to say that I was happily amazed would be an understatement. The labyrinth held amazing power and I found it beautiful. Surrounded by a hedge with fieldstone outlining its pathway; it wound its way to the limb of an Irish oak. This limb had been found in the river, so its energies were of the earth, air and water. His meditation room was tranquil but powerful. He showed me a circular stone mounted on the wall inside his house and asked what I picked up from it. The deeply etched design and circular hole were obviously significant, it had a noticeable energy, and it seemed at least the age of Newgrange and Knowth, but I told him that I felt the stone outside the door held more energy. He mentioned a couple of scenarios about what the mounted stone might be but I did not get a strong sense with either one. He smiled and continued his tour. Everything he showed me was geared towards raising the consciousness and vibration levels. Whatever he had chosen to incorporate onto his property had been precisely calculated to be in harmony with an overall sacred geometry. The waterfall with three calibrated metal rods set to the vibrational frequency of Om as the cascading water hit them. A tree with a meditation stand built onto it, meant to represent the tree of Consciousness. The twelve sided dodecahedron, which brought you into resonance with the Ether. The half octahedron, built to exactly replicate the three sacred inner chambers of Egypt's great pyramid. The icosahedron, enhancing Unity Consciousness, and the harmonious and calming feeling of flowing energy within his workshop and throughout his property made me feel welcomed and at peace.

Over a cup of tea he told me about the circular stone mounted on his wall, and of how it related to his property. It originated in Egypt approximately 3,500 BC and made its way to Ard Na Ri in 2002, and was then cemented onto the wall. The energy vortices created by the tree of Consciousness, Leonardo's Canon and the replica Great Pyramid on his property were established after the arrival of the stone. These energy vortices formed an equilateral triangle. The Vesica Piscis, shared by Leonardo's Canon and the tree of Consciousness, ran from the centre of the temple of Transfiguration in his Great Pyramid, through the centre of the Solar Cross, and ended within the central hole of the stone.

This hole was made to hold the cerebellum. It was the mark of Cain, which was also the Ayin, the all seeing Eye attributed to blackness, nothingness: the cerebellum. This was the all-seeing aspect, which perceived Light out of blackness, enlightenment through intuitive perception. Surrounding this was the Rosi-Crucis, a cross symbolizing enlightenment. Eric said that this stone was the exact duplicate of the human zygote, which held our genetic blueprint. It was the stone of Consciousness and was used by Pharoahs, Kings David and Solomon, and more, leading up to King Arthur, at which time it disappeared. According to Eric this, and not the one on the Hill of Tara, was the genuine Destiny Stone. Those who used this stone used it to help unclutter their minds, gaining greater clarity through having their pineal glands stimulated. It had disappeared for over 1200 years until showing up once again on Eric's doorstep. He smiled and said "*Mysterious is it not.*"

My curiosity was piqued but he pretended not to notice, and then with a twinkle in his eye he changed the subject. This may sound far-fetched, but Eric was drawn to Clonmacnoise and Ard Na Ri after opening himself to following his spiritual path. He shut down all but a token of his medical practice in Dublin and ended up here. After he bought and restored what was to become Ard Na Ri, he did not have a clue what he was meant to do next, but he trusted and kept himself open. I have learned through my own personal experience, that when you put yourself into the right state of being the universe will fully support, guide and provide for you, channeling its energies through your intent and your gifts for the highest good of all.

After dark we cut across a cow pasture heading towards the ruins of the nun's church. This church seemed tiny, but it had a nice feel to it. It was a beautiful night and this whole area felt good. We continued towards Clonmacnoise and Eric told me that the long mound we were walking on was the remains of the oldest road in Ireland. This day just kept getting better and better.

Walking through the old, old cemetery, Eric led me to a long gravestone and asked me to stand on the head of it. I immediately felt energy rush up through my body, and after about a minute I took three long deep breaths, knowing full well that I had this spirit's awareness in my energy field. Eric knew it too and this was why he had brought me here. He wanted verification of the identity of the spirit buried under this stone, and he wanted answers. The first night he had come into this area he had slept on this stone, for something within had been calling his soul, and all through that night he had dreams that did not match the name marked on the stone. The feelings would not go away that somebody had been intentionally trying to hide this person's real identity.

Standing there absorbing the energy, I became aware that there was a body beneath a body. The spirit that was almost becoming me, or me her, was a warm, gentle and loving spirit who I quickly felt close to. It was Scota, Pharaoh Akhenaton's granddaughter and the founder of Uisneach. As I began channeling her, Eric asked her many questions, and then thanked her. She gently left. It was a beautiful experience. Her essence had flowed through my heart and I felt that I was falling in love with her already. Channeling her standing on a centuries old gravestone though, especially in an old graveyard at night was rather surreal.

Eric made sure that I was all right and then led me into the ruins of a church. Before I get into what happened next, I must express my inner belief that the church has not, and was not always what it portrayed itself to be. There were aspects within it that desired to keep the masses subdued and they used a distorted sense of Faith to carry it out.

Let me describe this church; one third of it, was taken up by a room with a tall Celtic cross in its centre, while in the other two thirds only a dirt floor remained of whatever might have been there. On the outer wall directly facing the cross was an elongated vertical window. On the inner wall facing the cross was a small window. The light, or whatever else might have shone through the outer window, would have shone through the circle of the cross, through the small window, and then directly onto a small section of the dirt floor. It was not until after the fact that I realized how everything was connected. Eric had asked me to stand on this spot and my feet had instantly become rooted into place. I had connected into something powerful and vast.

There was an energy trapped here against its will, and the energies holding it suppressed were neither pleasant nor totally of this world. My awareness gradually seeped deeper into this maze of energies, all the while meeting with heavy resistance. It suddenly lessened until there was no resistance at all. During all of this time I had felt as if I was standing within a powerful vortex. My arms had been outstretched, palms down trying to maintain my balance. My body had been whipped around like a tree in a storm as I had worked through the energies. However, with the abrupt disappearance of the resistance I feared a trap had been laid. I instinctually felt that my awareness, even my spiritual Essence would become snared within the confluence of its energies. I remained fully alert, and held my awareness back from going further. After a minute we felt the energies shift and a fantastic lightness of being immersed us as the trapped energy flew free.

Eric had a sense that this freed energy was Creative Joy. He smiled, saying that it had been a good night's work. I smiled back, thinking about all of my experiences since I had come to Ireland. I was realizing just how much I loved every moment of it. To me, this was all verification of who I really was. Perhaps Scota and other Celestial Beings were with me as I went through that maze of energies, I did not know, but I would not be surprised if they were. I thanked them anyway, because I was glad that energy was free.

Eric offered me another cup of tea and I could not help thinking of how amazingly expanded my awareness, abilities, Spiritual connection, and vitality had become since I came to this land. I had definitely unfolded, blossomed and expanded into something much more beautiful and magnificent than I ever imagined that I could have ever been.

September 4th

This morning Eric left for Dublin and would not be back until evening so I relaxed and slowly walked the labyrinth; walked over to Scota's grave remembering her, walked to where the energy was trapped and noticed a sense of calm, and wandered back to Eric's to stand by the waterfall. Time had no meaning here. I was just allowing myself to become fully absorbed in the sacredness of presence and grace that permeated me.

I had no idea how long I stood by the waterfall, but eventually I found myself standing in front of the stone of Consciousness. I was not thinking. In fact, as I thought about it later, I smiled because this was probably why I had been able to experience so much, and so deeply. I generally did not think a great deal, not unless I needed to focus on something. Even then it sometimes took a little bit to draw my mind in.

I pulled the Moldavite from my pocket and placed it to the back of the central hole where it would not be seen. I felt that this was where it belonged, connecting the stone of Consciousness to the source of the universe.

My interest in the stone of Consciousness was not entirely without an ulterior motive. Once, as my friends were doing energy work on me, I vividly experienced a sense of connection with King Solomon. I felt that I might have been him in another incarnation. Cheryl, who was much more psychic than I was said, "*No, you had been David.*" When Eric mentioned that David had used this stone I became real curious. After placing the Moldavite, I propped myself against the wall and stuck the back of my head into the hole. Eric came home hours later, and I was still there. A subtle sensation of energy moving, which became more noticeable after I put my hand on my solar plexus, and a few other fleeting impressions of other users were all I noticed.

Eric eagerly questioned me when I told him how long my head was in the stone, but I was afraid my answers were a little too vague for him. He was grateful for the gift of the Moldavite, and intrigued when I explained that it came from the source of the universe and held some rather interesting properties.

In the evening he found me in his workshop hall catching up on my writing. I mentioned how good the energy in this room felt, and that it almost had a faerie or other magically embracing feeling to it. He agreed, saying he did not know what had originally been on this site, but that for the last three hundred years it had been used as a cow barn. He was disgusted as he said this last part. He could not understand how people could so blatantly disrespect the specialness of this site by letting it pile up with cow dung.

I said to him *"What makes you think that the energies of this place did not know exactly what they were doing? Could it not be that it was being cleverly camouflaged until the right person in the right time came along?"* That had not occurred to him and he laughed.

He walked to the stereo and put on a C.D. he cherished, 'The Keeper of Dreams' by Philip Chapman. It was his daughter's favourite C.D. He started dancing and her spirit soon joined him. I started dancing and Scota joined me. Soon Eric's emotions overtook him and he had to leave. I slowly loosened up and began to flow. All of the women I had ever loved, going beyond time, seemed to join me at this moment and my heart burst. I cried as I danced, in sadness, in remembrance, and in love.

Soon my emotions shifted and I felt a sudden rush of joy. I laughed and I laughed, and I laughed, and I felt as light as a feather. I became very graceful and was dancing all over the hall. The energy was absolutely beautiful and I danced for a long time. I could not remember the last time I had felt so joyfully fluid in my movements and it was dawn before I was ready to leave.

September 5th

I spent a relaxing day, just absorbing everything that I had experienced. Ard Na Ri was ideal for this. The energies were so calming, and so quiet, that I became one with them.

I paid another visit to Scota's grave and used my fingers to bury three stones. I buried another stone in the spot that the energy was freed. Then, as I took one of Eric's bikes for a ride, every fibre of my being felt part of this land.

Later, Eric asked if I would like to see the oldest tree in Ireland, so I gathered the broken feather that Mary had asked me to return to nature.

This tree's bottom limbs were outstretched and propped up, but it still emanated a lot of energy. We spent time slowly walking around, spending minutes in each spot resting our hands on it. The awareness of this tree was all around us. I found a hollowed out spot in its base and asked it to accept the feather, then laid it on the bed of moss. I then began collecting a few of its leaves to bring home, though the tree was to quietly express its displeasure when I did not properly listen and picked more than I should have. This reminder to pay more attention, and not take things for granted, with all of my dealings with nature, or any other consciousness sunk in.

There was a beautiful harvest moon when we returned to Eric's so we walked the land. We talked and dreamed of what was to come and could feel the energies already moving to manifest it. I was so tuned in by now, so open, and feeling so alive, that there was no doubt in my mind that all that I needed to do was dream the dream, and anything would be possible.

As Eric left for bed, Scota's essence wrapped itself warmly and gently around me, so I walked to her gravesite to be closer to her. I sat on her stone thinking about our first contact and of the growing closeness that I had been feeling ever since. There was no longer any doubt. I was falling in love with her. After a while I slowly made my way to the labyrinth. This labyrinth held a powerful energy during the day, but under the full harvest moon its energy was phenomenal. I stayed for a long time.

September 6th

Today was a full day of just relaxing, catching up on my notes, walking in meditation, and sitting around talking to Eric. The time was drawing close to when I would have to leave for home. Home? I had always loved Canada, but on a deep level I was not sure if I had ever felt truly connected with it. There were areas I resonated with, some fairly strongly, but none so deeply as in this land.

All thoughts of going off on my own for my last couple of days in Ireland, and traveling solo once again had by this time left. I must stay here. I had, for the most part, been in a deeply quiet state of being since arriving at Eric's. I felt that I was integrating, on deep levels, all that I had experienced since coming to this land. My body needed rest, not more adventure at this time, and Eric's was the perfect place for this. When sound level checks had been carried out throughout Ireland, Ard Na Ri was within the quietest zone.

Tomorrow, Eric said that he would take me to the Hill of Uisneach. Penny and Kevin O'Kelly had also recommended this hill, and without understanding why, I know that I could not leave Ireland without seeing it, especially now that I had learned that Scota was the one who established its significance.

September 7th

Over breakfast Eric told me of the moon reaching its zenith at exactly noon today, and asked if I would join him in performing a ceremony. I would love to. We wrote out the thought patterns and emotions that we felt had brought the present global state of being into manifestation. On another piece of paper, we wrote out the emotions and thought patterns that we felt would raise and maintain the global consciousness levels, and vibrations. We placed lit candles under the stone of Consciousness and the stained glass depiction of the Star of David in the workshop hall; other candles were placed on the tree of Consciousness, in the dodecahedron, and at the base of the waterfall.

At the zenith we stood inside the dodecahedron and read the list of beliefs and emotions out loud, requesting that the universe accept and transform these energies for the highest good of all. I placed this paper over the candle and let the ashes fall into a container. We then read from our second sheet, welcoming the new energies of higher Consciousness into the world. After burying the ashes under the tree of Consciousness, three spiritual seekers showed up.

The women joined us in bringing the candle from the tree of Consciousness into the meditation room. As we placed the sheet imbuing our intent on the Altar, we held a ceremony, holding the intent that the flame burning on this candle, taken from the tree of Consciousness, never go out. During tea that followed, one of the women gave Eric an insight that transformed his life. He finally understood why his life had been the way it had, and it explained in greater clarity all of the unusual circumstances in the setting up of Ard Na Ri. He was grateful, for he had opened himself to following Divine Spirit, trusting, but not always sure where it was all leading him.

Eric and I soon said our farewells to these new friends and drove to Uisneach. The full potent impact of its energy hit me as we crested a hill. I had never experienced this kind of impact before. We were still miles away and my response was immediate. Whatever was happening, I began to change. This energy was rooted very, very deeply into my Soul. Every experience of opening and connection since I had come to Ireland must have been preparing me for this moment. Physically and energetically my bearing was changing, and my voice deepening, becoming fuller with an inner power and authority.

Pulling to a stop at the base of Uisneach I told Eric "*This is why I came to Ireland.*" I left the car like a High King of old, very erect, very sure, very aware. I *know* this Hill. Our energies were in total resonance. Walking up the slope there was no doubt. I WAS HOME.

I told Eric I would live here. He turned to me and asked if he was walking with the guardian of Uisneach? I looked at him not answering, but inwardly I was thinking that I may well be: my heart connection to the Earth in general, my heart connection to this land, to Scota, and now finally to this Hill, along with the change in my bearing and essence that I had just so vividly experienced? Was it co-incidence? Maybe, but I had never known anything with such instant surety of connection and belonging as I did on this Hill.

I could not help remembering, that throughout my life I had always felt that there was something important that I would be doing on a planetary level. Could it be that in my coming here, the energetic heart of Ireland, which some thought to be the energetic heart of the world, that this was somehow related, and that it was significant? Was this somehow meant to have happened during this specific time period? Was this why I had connected with such synchronicity and impact with Eric? What foundation was being laid here? Perhaps this was my ego speaking, or perhaps it was fantasy, but then again, what if what I had always sensed inside was truth and this was real? What if I was indeed someone of this importance? With every fibre of my being, I felt that I was walking unerringly into a vaguely familiar destiny.

On the summit only outcroppings remained, but I had a vision of Scota and others burying knowledge for a future time. Eric marked the spot and said that he would return with a shovel. Everything about this hill and the land surrounding it were deeply fulfilling to me.

Descending the hill we passed a young man. Recognizing his spirit I was filled with joy, though I did not interfere with his ascent. It was not important at this time to establish greater contact. I was just grateful that he had also been drawn back. He seemed curious about us as well, and a minute later we stopped and looked up at him. He had also stopped and was looking down at us. We waved at each other smiling. Eric noted his license number as we pulled away.

September 8th

This morning we were both quiet, knowing that it was my last day here. Tonight Eric was going to drop me off at the airport hotel in Dublin. I was to fly out in the morning. My life in Canada felt like another world. I cherished my family and friends, but I had been only a shell of who I was here. I did not know if I would return to living as this shell or not, but I had come to realize that I could no longer accept not living to my fullest.

Eric asked if I would like to go for a walk to the river, then asked if I had been to the fort yet. What fort? I had not even realized there was a fort nearby, as anyplace that I had wandered it could not be seen. It was the ruins of a Norman castle, which I thought was pretty neat in itself, but then he mentioned that it had been built on top of Scota's original palace. Hearing this, my heart leaped.

Surrounding the fort was a barbwire fence. 'Danger. Authorized Personnel Only' said the signs, but Eric kept walking until he came to a hole in the wire and I was happy to see him crawl through without hesitation. I laughed and quickly followed him. Scota's energy was strong around me, and she was happy, playful, warm and loving. My heart opened with pure joy. By this point I knew I was deeply in love with her. I was thinking how true Cheryl's observation of me was when she said, "*You do not date women do you? You fall in love with them.*" It had become obvious to me that whether it was the essence of a living woman or spirit it made no difference, for me the heart connection was the same.

Apparently Eric spent a lot of time here, feeling his own connection to Scota, but he soon left me to my thoughts. I lay inside the walls for a long time soaking in the sun, the amazing energy around this fort, and Scota who was lying beside me in the grass. There came a point as I was lying there, that my connection to the Earth became so powerful that my body felt as if it was being absorbed. I was fully aware, but my body felt as if it was being transformed into granite; not in physical appearance maybe, but every sense of my being was feeling it. I was so fully present, and so in my body, that all I felt was profound gratitude for this experience. I had loved the Earth, but I had never felt fully connected or grounded to her. After encompassing this experience, I felt deeply accepted, connected and grounded, and I felt blessed and honoured. I buried three stones here. I know that when the time comes that I return, I will be spending the night on this grass.

Eric agreed to go out of his way tonight so that I could bury my remaining stones on Uisneach. We quietly climbed the hill by moonlight, and when I reached the spot where I wished my home to be, I offered a prayer and planted the stones.

A car was coming down the road, still a long way off, but the noise of it had carried and amplified; part of me felt revulsion from hearing the intrusion of it. A voice spoke from nowhere and yet everywhere from the spirits of the earth and sky around me "*Who is breaking the peace of this land?*" Sound carried invasively at night here and it dampened my resolve to place my home where I had chosen, but I will find a way to remain at peace.

As we drove onto the freeways on ramp leading into Dublin I felt Scota pull out of my energy, she was returning to the land. The world that I was returning to was not her world; neither was it really mine. The spiritual and heart expansiveness that I had so wondrously opened to had begun to close in and I felt myself shutting down. All of the heightened awareness and feelings of pure joy and vitality that had brought me so alive were leaving me. My question of this morning had been answered.

As I landed back in Toronto I was a shell again. All I felt was the emptiness of this society and the neglect of the land. My Soul and all that blossomed within me had remained within the land of Ireland.

My family and friends welcomed me back with love and open arms but I yearned to return as soon as possible. The power of the land had uplifted me but it had stayed in Ireland. I set my intent to find and grow into the full integrity of my own power, and my own heart, no matter where I was. It would only be then I felt, that I would have earned the esteem that Eric placed in me. He saw within me the potential to be an integral part of the foundation for a global consciousness shift to happen. Having returned to the shell that I once was, I needed to prove this to myself.

Ireland, and the intimately profound experiences that were so willingly granted me, offered a depth of blessing to my life more than I could ever describe. It offered me new hope, new understandings, and a new life. My experiences within this land had gifted me with the ability to open to the freedom and the love of being the full-realized beauty and potential of all that I was, in full unity and harmony with all that is. I was so very grateful. I love you; I love all that is.

Book Three

Changes . . . and a Symbol

Mary and I continued to stay in touch, and felt that something in Utah or New Mexico was calling us. We did not know what it was but thought that it would be a great adventure to find out, so we decided to become traveling companions as soon as I had everything settled. I no longer wanted to be tied to a home, I needed to feel free to roam wherever I was called, and I needed a fresh start.

Within weeks my residence was gone, and as I stood before the storage unit I realized that I would be getting rid of almost everything that I had remaining. A form of claustrophobia had set in. Material things no longer held a hold over me; instead, they had begun to smother me.

It was October now and I was camping at Silent Lake. I was virtually alone in the park. It was quiet and beautiful, and this was my favorite time of year to camp. This morning I caught sight a calf moose and squatted in appreciation, just watching it. After about fifteen minutes she carefully wandered over. There had been no sign of the mother and this calf seemed completely innocent. She cautiously observed me, and was so close that I could have reached out and touched her. She wandered a few feet away and stopped to face me. I was centered, relaxed, calm, and at peace. I just felt deep love and appreciation towards her. Lowering her head she charged, but ground to a stop about two feet away with her legs splayed. I had not moved and was still squatting down looking into her eyes. She gently appraised me again with growing curiosity and then softly brushed her nose against my cheek, getting my scent. I smiled. This calf had a gentle energy and seemed to be asking me to help nurture her. Soon she wandered off in search of more leaves. Two ladies on holiday from England approached me thinking that I was an animal whisperer, and said that they would send me some photographs once they returned home. I owe these ladies much gratitude, for they kept their promise.

While we were talking the calf came back. One of the ladies went in search of their husbands and soon it began nosing around all of us. Minutes later the park warden approached and told us that she had been hanging around all week with no sign of the mother. He mentioned that it was rutting season and that she had either gone off to rut or had been hit on the highway. In either case the calf was by itself, and if the mother did not come back she may not survive the winter. Our experience with this calf had been peaceful, loving, and exhilarating. We all felt blessed.

After dark I looked into the heavens. The sky had been crystal clear with an extremely radiant, unusually powerful full moon for the last couple of nights. Feeling calmly grounded and connected I slowly absorbed the majesty that was so vividly apparent everywhere around me. Later, I walked to the lake for a leisurely swim under the stars.

Leaving the campground I spent an interesting evening with a friend. She had taken me out to look at the night sky, and pointing up, asked me what I thought a bright light might be. She told me that last night at about this same time it had been in a different part of the sky. At this point the light began to rotate in circular patterns, and then squares. As soon as we remarked that it must be a UFO we felt an energetic beam surrounding us. It felt exactly as it was portrayed in the movies, except that we did not see anything. It infused our hearts and heads with an energy that I recognized, though I was not sure exactly why I did. I felt comfortable with whoever was sending it. They had known we were focusing on them, so it seemed that our thought projections were going out into the universe and were capable of being picked up. Another thought came. We all have our own unique energy imprints. When thought and imprint come together, our location or state of being can be exactly known to anyone, or anything, capable or sensitive enough to tune in. Returning to the car later I found a child's foam star sticker on the bottom left corner of my windshield. I took it off, but then I thought that this was just way too much of a co-incidence, so I put it back on.

The Orchard multi-faith centre had invited me to read my Irish journal. Paula had heard that I had some profound spiritual experiences, but she may have opened the door to more than she bargained for. This was the first public debut of my journal and I felt a little nervous. As Paula and I pulled up we saw a woman sitting on the steps. She radiated a powerful energy, and I felt an instant energetic recognition even though I did not know how I knew her. Stepping out of the car I was caught off guard by just how powerfully her energy hit me and I could not take my eyes from her. Circling around her I entered the building. Who was this woman?

The reading went well and people were profoundly affected. I was comfortable and sure of myself, and Jay, a dear friend, was emotional as she clasped my hands in hers saying that I was on the right path. She left a quartz crystal in my hands saying that she had carried this with her for a long time. She felt that it had to be passed onto me, as I would know what to do with it when the time came. I was deeply touched. People were telling me that they would plan their own pilgrimages, and the woman from the steps handed me a folded piece of paper and said that she now understood why she had been told that it was important for her to meet me. She had written her name and phone number, asking to meet as soon as possible. I was totally intrigued.

I spent the next few days visiting another friend. Teresa and I shared the same energy, almost as if we were brother and sister from the same soul group. We shared many intuitive gifts in common, and when we were together our abilities amplified. A few months earlier we had shared one amazing experience. We were walking amongst some old trees by the creek and noticed many disturbed spirits lingering from the early years of colonization. After we assisted the spirits that were ready to move on into the Light we sat on the bank, but within minutes my back suddenly shot ramrod straight in shock. Two native men in loincloths had walked past us and were kneeling down to get some water. They were from an earlier period, before the settlers, and they were very real. I felt people behind me and as I looked back I saw that we were in a native village. Teresa was validating what I was experiencing.

We were invited to share food in a community gathering and were inside one of their dwellings. There was much laughter, sharing, and a whole lot of subtle curiosity. We had been accepted and were being honoured, though we were not in native form.

This scene ended and another vision connected with these same people years later took its place. They were in turmoil, and running scared as soldiers and colonial volunteers were decimating them. It was obvious that many were in the advanced stages of smallpox. The British commander had intentionally infected blankets with the virus, and with a display of much graciousness had offered them to the people as tokens of esteem and friendship. They were sorely weakened and confused.

One of the women ran to me cradling a baby and held it out imploring me to save it. I brought it into my arms and looked into the woman's eyes saying that I would save this child. She looked into my eyes a moment longer, in the acknowledgement of a mother who knows that she would not survive this day and had done all that she could to ensure the survival of her child. Then she turned and ran. I had known this woman.

I was present for this woman, totally in her reality and timeline, but yet I was not there at the same time. Some of the people recognized me as they tried to flee, but none of the white people saw me and I was not touched by their bullets. The chaos did not seem to affect me any more than if I was only an observer who was not fully in that reality. I was in physical form, yet I was outside the periphery of the white people's perception. Even more, bullets went through me as if they, and I, were not real. It was surreal, poignant, and different from anything that I had experienced before. I took the baby into another world of reality, and knew that there was an aspect of me that stayed with him until he had grown into a man, a man who could also walk between the worlds. I found it interesting that I experienced all of this within only a few minutes of our time; time and realities really are fascinating mechanisms. Is time really linear? I am finding that it is not. There is no time; there are just different aspects of reality of what is. What fascinated me most of all though, was that I had no idea how I did all of this.

The same natives that were involved in the vision now surrounded me, as I am writing this, in spirit form with love and nurturance. I knew that it was time to bring us all further into the Light, but in receiving this knowing my heart suddenly burst open and the tears flooded from my eyes in remembrance. Within seconds I sealed my heart in protection from the intensity and acuteness of the emotions that had been unleashed. I had not been prepared for the onslaught of this, and I had not known that I still held onto so much pain from this memory.

I thanked my body for letting me know what it was still holding within. I was not yet at the stage where I could easily express this kind of deep release, even in front of myself. I had always held my more powerful inner emotions pretty tight, and basically, sealed off. I was too scared actually that they may potentially overwhelm me and that I would be exposed as vulnerable. I had come to understand that this was a journey that I must go through, because that was the only way to really bring healings to the divine mother, the divine father, and the divine child within. Even through healing the acute intensity of emotions that I had suppressed in my own life, it would have a quantum beneficial impact on the Earth and the mother aspect of all creation.

In not honouring the fullness and full expression of our emotions and sense of selves, we deny this part of creation. Emotions and experiencing them as they happen, and learning from them as we live our truth are the Divine's gift to us to experience the full range of life. They are just as much a part of us as anything else.

I was still afraid of letting this out because I quickly sealed it back in. It might not be the intensity of the emotions themselves that I was afraid of, but during the power of their release I may lose my semblance of control. I had denied this full aspect of my-self because it was not really acceptable in front of society as a whole to express it. I felt that I had to appear to be in control of myself at all times to maintain the typecast masculine image. I have come to realize that full empowerment and wholeness, and for that matter becoming *truly alive as a creative thriving human, meant accepting and allowing this to happen.*

Women in general have more innate power than men because they recognize this and are more tuned in to all aspects of themselves and the world around them. I am choosing to find the full emotional, spiritual, mental, and physical breadth of all that I am. I will dance my own song in harmony with the songs of other dancers that have also found harmony, and, I choose to allow my vulnerabilities to show. Limiting myself behind pride, image, and societies boxed in acceptances was losing its power over me.

I had originally planned on spending only a day or two with Teresa, but the Beaches area of Toronto where she lived caught me happily by surprise. It pulsated with Wiccan energy, and I recognized elves, dwarfs and more that had manifested into human form. Their distinctively elemental imprints overlapped their human auras and I noticed that many of them were not totally in synch.

I have since discovered with amazement that elves can choose to flow through family lines. I met one family in particular who carried the vibrancy of elf energy through its generations, though if they were aware of it they kept it amongst themselves. I suspect that this decision to manifest within extended family lines also applies to most, if not all, of the elemental realm.

The energy that I experienced radiating from some of the trees in this area reminded me of Ireland, and I felt that I could easily live here. The trees reminded me of how aware they really were. They even take turns going into a sleep cycle, with at least one always remaining fully conscious to its surroundings within any given area. As we walked through a park I was drawn to two majestic trees. They were majestic even energetically as they possessed regal masculine and feminine energies. Trees really are amazing. If people could only allow themselves to see, honour and appreciate them enough to realize that they were sentient beings as well, and started connecting with them, they would find greater peace in their lives. They are here to assist us if we could only remember how to ask from our hearts, and then of course, remember how to receive their guidance and knowledge as if we were children opening to daydreams.

People have such a feeling of reluctance in our world to truly open themselves to allow in and receive, that connecting with other Divine aspects of creation becomes in many ways difficult. Through the millennium humans have learned fear, and have closed themselves off in order to feel secure, or to survive. They lost trust in their innate instincts and increasingly separated themselves in multitudes of overlapping ways. That is why young children remain so much more open, heart based, accepting of others and connected to all that is around them, they have not yet been cultivated into 'learning' to view or perceive things differently. They still possess the ability to see, sense, feel and comprehend in ways that go beyond the barriers that we adopted along our way to becoming adults.

We eventually came across an old tree stump that as we put our hands on it, took our awareness deeply into the earth. We had found a portal. This area of Toronto really was magical.

Teresa later showed me an unusually shaped stone that she called a shaman's stone. It appeared to have been rolled in the palms of the hands and then left to harden. This stones energy was powerful and I felt it taking me into deeper layers of awareness, while at the same time I felt channels opening into astral traveling. At one point, the shaman's awareness surrounded both of us and I could sense him looking through each of our eyes in turn. Teresa and I were facing each other and I knew that he was memorizing our faces. I slept with this stone in my hand that night.

The next night, October 15th, Teresa mentioned a re-occurring dream that she had been having since I arrived. In her dreams she was shown a symbol, and she was told to offer it to me. She looked at me curiously, and then began drawing it in the air. As she began, the power of it distinctly unbalanced me. The energetic power of this symbol was opening me on some very deep levels. I had not been prepared for this. Breathlessly I asked her to wait until we are alone before she completed it. She did not understand, but agreed. I did not fully understand either. All I knew was that I was experiencing an acute reaction, and I did not feel safe enough to have my energy field opened where we were. We were in a restaurant amongst other people, and I could not be opened up there, not like that.

As we walked it became apparent that bringing this symbol in was going to be a significant and important moment for each of us. We felt humbled and honoured, and returned to her apartment to prepare ourselves. Putting on warmer clothes we gathered a candle, sage, crystals, our special stones, and anything else that we thought appropriate.

It was well after dark when we arrived at the beach and found the perfect location, an open area amidst a stand of trees. After smudging ourselves to clear our energy fields we were ready. Teresa began drawing the symbol, and as the exact sequence and placements channeled through, we were being taught. My body in general, but especially my bone marrow rapidly heated up. This was a powerful attunement. I felt my posture strengthening and felt more grounded. By the end my awareness and perceptions had also increased, but as she taught me the symbol, I showed a surprisingly slow grasp in learning. Eventually however, and with a great deal of patience and disbelieving laughter from both of us because of my seeming ineptness, she was attuned.

I added an interpretation at the end that I felt anchored universal heart energy, as well as the heart energy of the person channeling, with more loving focus into the heart energy of the one receiving. My experience while in the energy of this symbol was that it connected to the One Divine Heart, and that on the human scale; heart essence to heart essence fulfilled its intention.

We felt the presence of a great number of spirits, angels and other beings, and waves of joy from the Earth, trees and water enveloped us. It was a special moment. Standing back to back we playfully drew the symbol in each of the four directions, Teresa intending to impart the feminine energies and me the male. Kneeling down I buried another Moldavite, some other stones, and the Chinese Gratitude and Dragon necklace that Terri had given me on my Irish trip as an offering. I sensed that the blessings Terri imparted to me in its original gifting were now meant to be passed in turn to the Earth. I felt immense gratitude for having received the symbol, and as I stood the universe reciprocated. Going to the water we placed our hands in, and then Teresa picked up a stone and threw it in, honouring the feminine energy of night.

Before I left the next day we returned to the sacred spot where we had received the symbol to again draw it in the four directions. Then, going to the water, I pulled out the crystal that Jay had given me, explained what she had said as she gifted it, blessed it, asked it to help transmit all of the incoming energies from the Divine throughout the world, and threw it into the lake. As it hit the water unlimited joy engulfed us from all directions. Looking around I experienced all around me, and expanding out into the universe, the Celestial, spirit, nature beings, and even the Earth herself celebrating in unbounded joy. Thank you Jay, I felt that this was the right moment. The ceremony now felt complete.

In time, I came to understand that in receiving this symbol, it deeply transforms, heals and reconnects people spiritually, in its fullest sense from our core levels. In receiving this symbol, aspects within our DNA become re-awakened, and in time, will allow us to experience a fuller sense of reconnection with our Light bodies. It also allows us clarity with the Divine awareness that flows through them. The inherent energies re-integrate our body, mind and heart, with the consciousness of the universal body, mind and Heart. It enhances a deep inner calm, greatly expands and heightens awareness and perceptions, and brings you closer to the state of being where you live fully from a place of love and your own truth. Teresa and I realized that I was the first human since ancient Egyptian times to receive it, and that it was connected to the Eye of Horus and the Sun portal of Akhenaten.

I learned that for anyone choosing to receive this symbol, it was a decision not to be taken lightly. It was to be offered only to those people who had chosen to walk within the full commitment of the higher spiritual path, in all ways.

The awareness flowing through this symbol was calling out to the initiates of old, and to those who were now ready in their own ways to assist humanity and the Earth. Its purpose was meant to go beyond personal benefits to the receiver. It was a sacred and powerful symbol that would unlock doors that had been closed for a long time. It would open and prepare the receiver for specific frequencies of vibration that would be channeling through their energy fields.

In agreeing to receive this symbol, the receiver would be agreeing to a spiritual and Divine level agreement and sacred contract. If a person had not yet begun their inner healing journey, had not yet taken responsibility and accountability for their life, and was not yet ready to move away from limiting patterns and illusions, they may not be at the stage of being where they would be able to handle the frequencies as they channeled through in the coming years.

The purpose of these frequencies was to assist in bringing in specific levels of vibration to release lower density energies from within the collective human and Earth energy fields, so that higher vibrations of Light could anchor in from multiple sources and dimensional realms. The intent, wisdom, and power of the awareness behind these frequencies were geared to the highest good of all life.

I was curious as to why I was the one chosen. I felt that I still had suppressed beliefs and emotional turmoil to heal, so we asked. It seemed that on a higher spiritual level I had been ready, and had agreed to it. I had been expressing my desire to people that I knew, but especially to the Divine since returning from Ireland, to travel the world seeking out spiritual experiences and other spiritual people. This symbol was to be shared globally with anyone who sincerely walked the spiritual path and possessed a level of deeper heart awareness. Religious and spiritual are not necessarily the same. Not all who are religious walk the spiritual path, and not all who are on the spiritual journey, are religious. I was honoured, grateful, and somewhat stunned and awed by the enormity of all those beings that were trusting in me, and I felt fully competent and small at the same time. The universal depth and intricacy of how much everything was involved around humanity and the Earth was much bigger than we ever imagined.

I returned to Peterborough and set up camp. It was a beautiful but cold night, and I spent a long time appreciating the lake and watching the stars. I felt whole.

A little later I met with Maureen, the woman that had so intrigued me the night of my journal reading, and what a meeting this turned out to be! Our connection was so strong that the energy bounced between us well into dawn. As she had pulled out her knickknacks my amazement just kept growing. When she showed me the ancient pre-Aztec high priest or shaman's ring, with a diamond motif signifying human DNA, I instantly felt a surprisingly familiar power, and as I tried it on I could feel my cellular structure changing. That experience in itself was eye opening, but what I found truly amazing, was that as soon as I put it on I knew that I had worn it before. I could not believe the synchronicity in having it somehow come into Maureen's possession.

Her ancient Inca healing stones and condor feather were equally impressive, but it was her downloading of the Mayan Light language into my energy field through her intent alone, that put the icing on the cake. If she could do that, I decided that I could do it as well, and so it was with only partial surprise that I did. With focused intent, I downloaded all of the energies that I had connected with in Ireland and anything else that might be beneficial to her, into her energy. Then I gave her the symbol that Teresa had channeled to me.

Maureen was one of coolest women I had ever met, and we both felt that our connection was not meant to be over. We felt that we had been brought together for a reason, but whatever it was, it now had to wait. I was leaving for the states within the next two days, so with only a couple of hours of sleep I was off to Peter and Raven's.

They showed me to the source of the spring with the oldest Earth wisdom and granted me permission to sleep alongside it this night. After we talked about many things I walked into the woods. I lit candles to surround me, immersed my staff in the water for the night so that it could absorb its essence, sprinkled water over my drum, drank some, and honoured all that was around me. Then I had the best and deepest sleep that I had ever had.

At sunrise I felt pure invigoration as I bathed in the water. Its essence had washed over me all night and I was feeling vitally alive. I woke up sensing more inner power, and a greater depth of knowledge. The water and earth had graced me and I was deeply grateful.

My connection to Raven and Peter had deepened. Raven's gentle but powerful energy was bringing back remembrances of another time, and another place when we had known each other. Peter and I had talked about the blue star and of the eight other pure water sources on the planet, and I could sense that I was beginning to consciously connect with them. He also gave me a vial of water, saying that if I attached it to the intake pipe of any water supply wherever I stayed, it would transform the water into a vibration of love and purity. He then offered me a jug of it to drink on my journey, and Raven handed me some fresh homemade food. I was most grateful.

At midnight I crossed the border with ease and was off to Connecticut.

Book Four

The Southwest Beckons

As I entered the area surrounding Kent I seemed to pass through an invisible barrier, and it caught me totally by surprise. The sensation I experienced was of subtly flowing through the wall of an energetic dome, and it did not feel natural. I was startled but curious, and my mind automatically flipped to science fiction stories.

When Mary and I re-united we felt mixtures of uncertainty, joy and excitement. It was good to see each other again.

As we explored the area we came upon a magical and fascinating sight; a stone bigger than a person's head had been lifted into the air and delicately encircled by the slender roots of two trees. We felt that this was an amazing gift from nature, and the anticipations and hopes for our upcoming journey grew.

I had mentioned the energetic barrier that I experienced entering this area but she had not noticed it. She wondered if it had anything to do with Henry Kissinger, an ex-secretary of state who lived in the area. My mind drifted. There were many stories, especially those written by Arthur C. Clark, a respected physicist, which revolved around known and tested principles. Discoveries that were not public knowledge yet, government officials who could be relieved that they would be safe during certain contingencies, and more, were scenarios worth pondering. I could only speculate, but I wondered how people in the area were being subtly influenced on cellular and energetic levels when this energy field was operational.

There was one other thing I noticed since crossing the border into the states. It seemed to permeate the air I breathed, as it took just a little more effort for my lungs to expand. The overall energy felt subtly tenser than in Canada. The people that I met were truly friendly, but at the same time, there was a difference in their level of inner ease. Reflecting, I sensed the reason, the fight or flight reflex was being finely played with on a subconscious level. This unease made sense to me now. Throughout American politics and media the undercurrents of fear, glorified destruction, us against them mentality, and power were given more in your face prominence then anything heart centered. Regardless of how much good news there was, fear and destruction captivated and anchored into people's psyche to a much greater depth. Constantly having the survival instinct triggered was keeping people off balance and reactive.

We left Kent during a heavy rain, driving north. I had convinced Mary to travel around the Great lakes from the Canadian side before we journeyed into the southwest. This way I could introduce her to my own family, Canada, and to some of my favorite places.

I had arranged with Maureen for us to stay and she had welcomed us with open arms. She joined Mary and I on a visit to Serpent Mounds, and we arrived just before the most beautiful sunset that we had ever seen. After awed silence, Mary left a cocoa leaf offering for safe and blessed travels. As the sun set the spirits of these mounds gathered, curious. I lingered awhile, waiting for something. Perhaps it was just to meet these spirits. Maureen and I felt that we had other incarnations of ourselves buried here.

Returning from the mounds a friend of Maureen's joined us, and as she arrived my heart felt as if it was being torn from my chest. Whatever connection her friend and I had in past lives we had been very close. I now felt a powerful yet uniquely different connection with all three of these ladies. There was something special about the four of us being together. We all felt it, so we began a ceremony. We felt as if we had been the Disciples of Christ, and as we continued our ceremony powerful Presences filled the room around us.

As Maureen overlaid her eagle and condor feathers, intoning when south meets north, there was a massive energy shift in the room and its abruptness startled all of us. The feathers seemed to affirm a pact with the Earth, and by Maureen voicing what she had, something awakened. Whatever it was, we felt that something significant had just happened, and that if there was a prophecy somewhere about this the time for it to re-manifest was perhaps on the verge of being realized. We later drummed and shook Maureen's shaman rattles, and once again she brought out her ring and healing stones. It was an enjoyable night.

Leaving Maureen we traveled to meet Teresa, and like our experiences at Maureen's, an energetic power was generated amongst us. It would be interesting to get the five of us together. I was left with the feeling that having all of us come together as we did was somehow significant, and was meant to have happened.

At Lake Superior Provincial Park, one of my favorite parks, it was beautiful, sunny and noticeably warmer, so we walked the trail into the Agawa rock paintings. We found beautiful formations of crystalline ice formed from the water's spray, and one looked remarkably like an Angel. Whether this was another sign indicating that we were being watched over or not, its fine and intricate beauty mesmerized us. As we had begun this journey, the feeling that there was more to it than we understood had underlain our hopes. This feeling had been increasing, and with this, our sense of being watched over and protected had also increased.

That night we were to have many dreams. We were observing a native community and sensed earth spirits welcoming us. This was followed by an Angel vision, and then a vision of Egypt and the Eye of Horus. We shared a vision of the mist on the Lake Superior shore, and felt the thunderbirds' presence watching over us. Colours, and the energies of crystals flowed around us, and the pure white energetic light of the diamond was immensely powerful.

We woke feeling well rested and grounded, and Mary prayed for continuous attunements for the remainder of our journey. I wholeheartedly agreed. We felt relaxed and in anticipation of something special about to happen.

An hour after we left Wawa I spotted a moose carcass in the long grass. Approaching it we found a crow feather and stopped, wondering what its significance might be. That it was somehow connected to the moose we had no doubt. Stepping closer to the moose its spirit gently acknowledged and welcomed us. Her hide covered her head and legs but her ribcage was exposed and empty. After a few silent moments, we offered tobacco in appreciation of her life. Her spirit responded, and she gifted us with a rib and a hoof each. As I reverently removed them, I knew that we were not to take more. We felt that she had honoured us, and that we now had a shield for swift, safe and sure travels.

Life offers messages and communications in many ways, and Ted Andrew's book, 'Animal Speak' would become well used on this trip. Animals, birds, and the rest of the natural world can become effective messengers from spirit, and the earth. Study their habits, their natural way of being, and how they move, eat and communicate. If anything seems a little more unusual, or they focus on you or come closer than usual, these may all be signs that they are seeking to communicate something to you.

Returning to the car we noticed how much more empowered and grounded we were feeling. Moose energy had integrated into us and I could sense it creating a subtle difference in my perceptions. We became aware of a faerie mound nearby, but after having experienced the quiet power of the moose we were content to leave it in peace. We felt that we had created a sacred space in our honouring of the moose, and that she had created a sacred space around us. Everything has its time and place. In this moment all we wanted to do was quietly integrate the experience that we had just shared. The spirit of this moose, a bear, and then more, travelled with us until we reached our next gifting in Neys Provincial Park. We found the almost fully intact remains of a young bald eagle. Mary was ecstatic, and we felt blessed that the natural world was lining up with us to enhance our journey. As I safely stowed it in the car I could not help but contemplate how much more attuned and connected I was becoming to what was around me.

At the American border we were questioned. They did not believe our story, as there was no record that verified that I had entered the states to even meet Mary. After verifying her U.S. citizenship though, they could not deny her. However, they had serious doubts about my intent and about how much stuff in the car might actually be mine. It did not help matters when they asked for my address and place of employment. I no longer had either, nor did I have any cash in the bank. They considered me transient, and without hesitation the sergeant 'Red flagged' me so that I was on their computer system as a possible illegal immigrant. Great, I was filled with joy. I had not planned on staying more than my request anyway, but now I needed to be conscious of the possibility of being pulled in and questioned.

Crossing the border I had a vision that my headlights were shining on a cow moose. She was walking on the left shoulder of the road and looking intently into my eyes, and as I drove by her gaze never left me. The vision switched to a buzzard intent on its prey. Once again it switched to a close up of an owl, and even these eyes were focused intently into mine. I felt that my guardian spirits were intending to warn me of something. Then again, perhaps it was just my inner fears of being watched over by big brother that were surfacing.

We stopped to hike along the Lake Superior shore and noticed a great sense of Earth power here. It permeated the rocks and water, and the air radiated with it. I breathed it in and consciously immersed every cell of my body with it. In these energies I felt amazingly connected to the earth, and amazingly alive.

After a while we were drawn to a circle of trees that radiated its own amazing energy, and discovered a large mossy faerie mound surrounding a fallen tree's exposed root. Surrounding this root was an unbelievable mixture of dragon and unicorn energies, and it had been this that had drawn us here. Moving closer we kept sinking into the knee-deep moss, offering sincere apologies to the faeries for disturbing their sanctuary, but we had to physically connect with that root. Recognizing that we had been called they did not stop us. After a long while, we gave our appreciation and thanks to this special grove for drawing us to it, then followed deer tracks until we came to a path that went to the road.

Later, we quietly ate a thanksgiving supper. We were missing our families.

In the days that followed, Mary needed to confirm that I really wanted to go on. I had not been the talkative, lively company that she had been hoping for, nor was I particularly good at analyzing and debating spiritual teachings or experiences. I did not experience spirituality in that way, and it did not really interest me. We possessed two different personalities, complementary, yet contradictory, and we subtly agitated each other. Her question brought my mind back into this journey. As we had travelled through Ontario my loss of family ties had begun to hit pretty deep, and for some time I had remained quiet. I sat reflecting. I had seen great underlying gentleness and strength within Mary. There was deep beauty inside her, and deep wisdom, and I loved her enough to know that if I were to do this type of journey with anyone it would be her. On the other hand, I was much more introverted, and prone to absorbing and just allowing myself to experience, and deeply feel my experiences. I was searching for, opening to, and refining all of who I was becoming. There was much that I sensed lay deep within, and my understandings had deepened enough that I had learned to follow the quiet voice of my heart. I had come to realize, that as we drove mile by mile I was on just as much an inner journey as I was the outer one. All this being said there was still enough between us to continue. Perhaps even more importantly, we were both aware that there seemed to be a higher purpose for this journey, even though we did not understand what it was.

As we left Aberdeen the land was covered in ice, and there was a strong wind that seemed to want to tear through everything. The road was quiet. All that we saw for hours was tumbleweeds whipping by, and only occasionally, a buffalo.

We were driving to Sitting Bull's monument. I had realized the night before just how important it was that I go there. As I had looked at the map for this day's route I suddenly bent forward with focused intensity, my heart flooding from my chest, pounding towards the symbol of his grave marker. I knew I had no choice but to stop. Something about this monument was intimately connected to my spirit.

The wind was still frigid and fierce as we reached the monument, but as I approached it my spirit stirred with heart filling recognition. Standing as protected from the wind as I could get; I took my gloves off. My hands instantly went numb, but I had to lay an offering. With my fingers frozen and fumbling, I left tobacco and buffalo jerky. I said a few quick words in acknowledgement and respect of Sitting Bull and drew my hands away. Then, out of nowhere, I began channeling a native song. I did not know the song but my voice was strong and it carried the energy of this land. Whether this was one of my guides or my own past memory, or even Sitting Bull himself I did not know, but I felt honoured that it came through.

Standing in the open wind I turned to look around in all directions, absorbing a feeling of deep peace from this land. I felt comfortable and at home here; comfortable on a soul level that is, for I was by now utterly frozen.

On the other side of the river I saw a pair of Great Horned owls. I felt sure that this was a sign that was somehow connected to the experience I had just had at Sitting Bull's grave. Then we saw two deer. A little later a dozen wild horses crested a hill not far away and ran towards us. They followed the fence as we drove, and slowed down and stopped to observe us as we slowed and stopped. They then kept pace with us until they were blocked from going any further. We could not believe it. These horses had seemed to purposely come to us and had consciously tried to connect. We were deeply intrigued, and so very grateful. Joy filled our hearts as we drove away.

The following day I was being drawn to Mahto. Curious to see if this was somehow connected to my guide, or whoever else came into my energy at Sitting Bull's grave, I decided to drive through it. We left again though, not knowing what had drawn me there.

We arrived at Bear Butte, outside of Sturgis before dusk. This Butte must be sacred to the native peoples. There was a power here, and significant native presence. We were alone, but multitudes of spirits had gathered on its slopes to observe, honour and welcome us. Prayer tassels and sacred offerings were hanging from every possible branch, and the air vibrated with the feeling of reverence. We had been accepted, but as we climbed the trail we felt out of place in these white man bodies. Two hawks circled the butte, and at one point one of them dropped close overhead to check us out. It was after dark when we returned to our car, but we left feeling honoured and energized.

Feeling that we were somehow going to connect with the native community in South Dakota, we chose to spend more time here and to cover a much broader area. We looped back east again towards Chamberland. Passing Bear Butte from this direction we saw what looked like the image of a giant bat carved into its upper face. It gave the distinct impression that it was either guarding the butte or watching over the land. Soon after, a bald eagle just sat calmly on a fence post and watched us as we drove by.

In Chamberland, we were to have a profound experience. After we visited the Akta Lakota museum's Dances With Wolves exhibit, we were told about the tapestry of the native Christ in the chapel next door. Intrigued, we went to see it. I had experienced Christ's presence before but this was the most powerful and unexpected. As I stood quietly before the tapestry he came fully into my body. The tears flowed from my eyes as my heart cried to open, and I lingered for many minutes. I was not religious, but the continual culmination of spiritual experiences that I had had since my time with Feir, were reaching with such increasing depth into my soul that I could not help but change. Mary mentioned that something within her had changed as well. We could only offer our heartfelt gratitude and love.

A couple of days later we passed a golden eagle calmly watching us. This was the first golden eagle that either of us had seen and it was magical. Everything that we had experienced, even the earth that we passed over was holding a deep spiritual, heart, and energetic significance to me. In truth, I never really felt this way before I changed so profoundly in Ireland, but now it had become my way of being. I connected easily with things now. There was a sharing of awareness with everything and I know that it impacted on my energy. I did not analyze it; I just absorbed it, expanded into it, appreciated it, and allowed myself to grow. We felt increasingly blessed that the birds and animals, even within our dream states seemed to be watching over our journey.

We arrived at the wild horse sanctuary outside of Hot Springs, looking forward to some peace and quiet amongst the horses. This must be about the most arid land that I had ever seen and wild turkeys were everywhere; yet, it felt like a blessing after weeks on the road. The tranquility here permeated our souls. We leisurely connected with the horses in the corrals and then wandered back to relax on our veranda. The full moon was rising fast and beautiful into a clear sky, and somewhere in the distance we heard a coyote yowling happily. We melted into the peaceful serenity of the moment.

The next day we arranged a tour, and after introductions to the domesticated horses, Barb drove us to the corrals where two wild stallions had just been brought in. These stallions came from the other side of the river, the free side. It was on the other side of the Cheyenne River where the mustangs were allowed to roam totally wild. Humans rarely entered that part of the sanctuary. My heart surged towards one of the stallions as soon as he came into view and I could not take my eyes off of him. He was a beautiful tall and muscular dark brown and tan paint, and I cannot describe the feelings that he was pulling from me.

As Barb continued to drive past, this horse and I linked eyes and the soul connection between us was intense. I quickly implored her to stop and went to him. He automatically rested his head on my shoulders and then on top of my head. We had greeted each other like old friends and I was filled with elation. When he lifted his head from my shoulder for the second time he brought his eye to within an inch of mine. For what seemed moments insurmountable, moments that went beyond time, our souls connected on a deeply intimate and spiritual level. Glancing over at Mary and Barb I saw them looking at me in surprised joy. Barb mentioned that this was definitely not characteristic of these horses. Mary now walked to the second stallion and established a connection with him, and Barb became doubly surprised.

During our drive to the range she told us that she would give us more freedom than tourists were generally allowed. We felt honoured and happy because we did not consider ourselves standard tourists. We experienced things in our own ways, and in our own timing, and we liked to wander off the beaten path.

This sanctuary was huge, but Barb eventually spotted a few mares. The rest of the herd was grazing on the other side of the gorge and we could only see them from a distance. These horses appeared more accustomed to humans than the wild ones, but they were still skittish and wary of people they did not recognize. Once again though, we were in for an unexpected surprise.

While we mingled with the mares, offering them biscuits, we felt the ground start to shake. The mares on the other side of the gorge were stampeding towards its lip, and then down its slope; all that we could hear was a steadily increasing rumble. Within seconds the front-runners had crested our side of the gorge. There were over a hundred of them, and as they stampeded they had formed a column five wide. Their manes were blowing in the wind at the speed of their gallop and it was an amazing sight to see, an amazing feeling to feel. Before we could bat an eye they had circled us, still running, and they did not break their formation or turn inwards until we were totally surrounded.

After they closed in some were kicking at each other, others were rearing up on their hind legs, and yet others were trying to butt in close to get a biscuit. Hooves were flying up just a couple of feet away but I was in such a state of awe and grace that I felt as if I was in perfect surreal harmony with them. I let out such a purity of laughter that it arose high into the heavens. I slowly turned in a circle with my arms raised to the sky, just absorbing and feeling the fullness and the beauty of this experience. In that moment in time I was beyond words, I was beyond anything worldly. I was in my body but greatly extended from it at the same time, and I felt in full communion of spirit with these horses. As I walked towards Mary and Barb I was radiating pure joy, and I could see the same radiating awed joy as it flowed from them. We felt dazed and stood looking at each other in silent wonder, and then Barb whispered that this had never ever happened before, and began appraising us with even more curiosity.

Our next stop was to a site where the Anasazi Indians had left pictographs, and I was struck. The snake etched into the rock face was identical to the kundalini or snake symbol engraved on my pendant. There must be a connection. Alongside this site was the cave, probably not more than thirty feet deep, that sheltered the first two families of homesteaders during their first winter in this area. These early settlers were hardy folks indeed. The Anasazi had learned how to survive on the land, but for these newcomers it must have seemed despondingly bleak at times.

A short distance away we were shown the remnants of a pony express drop off point. I felt strange. It was not until I saw this that it seemed we were in the old west at all. After having experienced the wild mustangs, Bear butte, and Sitting Bulls grave, this still seemed to hit home more, and it felt surreal. Barb told us that movie scenes for Hildago and Crazy Horse were shot on this property, and took us to an overlook where we looked down on a remake of Fort Robinson. This was the fort where Crazy Horse had come to talk of surrender, but was eventually murdered instead.

Barb's impression of us had grown significantly over the day. She was not native herself, but she had earned their respect and trust so she felt that permission would be granted for her to take us to a sacred sun dance circle. During the time of ceremony no, or very few, white people were allowed. Mary entered first, barefoot and reverent, while I remained outside. After she laid her offering and left the circle, I entered, also barefoot. The energy of those who had danced around the cottonwood pole was strong. I touched it in reverence and said a prayer of gratitude; then looked to the sun and the star families, touched the Earth, laid an offering, and left. Barb had remained outside, observing, leaving us to experience our own experiences. Our knowledge of the preparations and teachings that led into this ceremony was vague, but we heard that the native communities held the people who danced in honour. Mary and I felt as if we had just been honoured as well, and entering this circle had transformed us. We knew the sacredness of what this circle meant to the indigenous people. I offer our apologies to the people if boundaries were overstepped.

What is interesting about the cottonwood is that instead of it showing growth rings, it shows a five-pointed star. It is the only tree in our knowledge that is like this. I feel that the native community understands their connection to the Earth and stars to a much greater extent than what we, in our disconnected culture have been taught.

Back at the cabin we showed Barb what the natural world had gifted to us. As we pulled out the moose ribs and hoofs, the young bald eagle, and the intact hawk, she showed increasing amazement. In appreciation, we offered her the left wing of the hawk. It was only now that we found out that in the United States you were not allowed to have any part of a bird of prey in your possession unless you were of aboriginal blood. This caught us by surprise. We felt that since we had disturbed the hawks resting place, that in order to release its spirit properly we had to honour it through ceremony. I had not realized until now, that we forgot to do this before we scooped it up. As far as I was concerned the young bald was gifted to us on Canadian soil.

After dark Mary and I had everything ready. We carried berries, water, tobacco, and sage to a rock that made the perfect Altar. We gently laid the hawk on the sage and blessed each offering as it was placed around it. The ceremony was beautiful, and during it I felt a deep sense of inner communion and peace with everything around us. Then, as if Divinely orchestrated and timed for the exact moment that we finished, the full moon broke free of the clouds and shone with vibrant radiance. It had only seemed a minute had passed since it had crested the far side of the gorge and it was magical. In perfect synchronicity, two owls literally started singing to each other. I cannot fully describe this moment, but it was fantastically surreal, and we were captivated by it. We felt as if we had moved into the land of wonder. The owls singing was melodic, and in perfect harmony. We looked around in silent amazement, and all we could feel was that the ceremony was being acknowledged and honoured by the universe. We felt humbled and elated at the same time with the way all aspects of the Earth, nature, and the Divine were coming together to help and honour us on our journey. We offered heartfelt gratitude and blessings in return.

Earl and Andy, the sanctuaries ranch hands took us out to the range with them the next day. Standing outside of the truck, we watched as they slowly circled the field spacing out the bales of hay. It did not take long before the mustangs ran in from all directions, totally ignoring us; they were intent on their food. Unlike the magic of yesterday's encounter with the mares, we realized that during this particular encounter it was not a good idea to get between them and their food.

On our return to the cabin we checked the Altar and were stunned to find that it was exactly as we had left it, nothing had been touched. Owls or some other birds or animals normally would have taken and eaten the hawk by now, so this was completely unexpected. Mary threw her hands up and said of course! She had forgotten to break the circle of power that she had surrounded the Altar with. I was still watching and learning, so it was not until the next day that I understood the true significance of what she was talking about.

The next morning we prepared to leave the sanctuary, but as I glanced across the river I noticed that a herd of deer had come down to the water's edge to drink. As I stopped to admire them, my heart leaped with surprised delight. I saw the herd of wild mustangs working their way down the slope of the escarpment directly across from our cabin. This was the first time that we had seen them, and from what we had been told people rarely saw them. Both herds were large and they drank side by side. Mary and I wondered if they had come to honour us with a welcoming goodbye. It felt like it, and we graciously thanked and honoured them in return. They stayed the whole morning grazing.

The hawk was gone. The ring of power that Mary had put around the Altar to create a sacred space had protected it from anything that might have disturbed it. To me this was another realization of how intent, and knowing that it would manifest, could work. I was reminded of the wizards of old and realized that there was much that I still did not understand, and there was still a whole lot about Mary that I did not yet understand.

Before leaving we said our goodbyes to the stallions. I did not want to leave this horse. It felt as if we had been separated for a long time and had just found each other again. I wanted to claim him for my own, though I knew that he was his own master. I would have dearly loved to ride him bareback as he ran with untouchable freedom through his own domain, a domain not fully of this world, a domain without boundaries. He sensed that I was leaving, and as I turned away he rose up on his hind legs and pranced around agitatedly, all the while never taking his eyes off of me. We looked back as we rounded the corner and the stallions were still standing against their fences watching us.

We drove into the Black Hills and stopped alongside the road to look into Crazy Horse's monument. This monument was still a work in progress, but it will be amazing when it is complete. I was not sure what the dedication plaque might have said, but I assumed it intended to represent the spirit of the aboriginal people. To me it represented the spirit of all people. To me, it represented the highest potential for people to achieve the Divine power of their true essence, and then to stand tall in it as empowered humans. I found it appropriate that the foundation for this monument was the horse, for it depicted that man was inter-connected to life outside of himself. It reminds us that we were not alone and that all was part of the whole. Life sustains life.

From the moment we entered the Black Hills my soul longing for something that lie within them became overwhelming. A huge part of my spirit seemed to be here. There was an Earth awareness, and sense of connection throughout the entirety of these hills that my heart and spirit were responding to, much like they had with Uisneach in Ireland. I have heard from different people that this place or that place was the heart centre of the Earth because of their associated energies, but I had come to believe that this heart centre goes way beyond our concepts and that it was inter-dimensional. I also believed that there were many conduits into this heart centre and that that was what people were picking up on. Any areas where heart energy became enhanced and where there was a sacred feeling associated with it, was potentially a conduit. I felt that these hills held much heart energy, and sensed that there was much here that had been honoured with sacredness. An incredible sense that these hills were alive and breathing surrounded me. I know that I had to return one day and enter these hills on foot, and then go wherever my spirit leads. The quiet voice of my spirit seemed to be whispering that this would become a journey that would go beyond time, almost a shaman's journey.

Eventually we made it to Price, Utah, and toured the 9-mile loop. As I listened to Richard Warner's Spirit Wind and Quiet Heart during this drive, the combination of the music, the colours of the rock, their formations, the sky, the energy, and the very air I was breathing seemed to draw me right into them. My spirit expanded so much within this combination that I felt as if I was intricately enveloping all that was around me. I loved what I had seen of Utah so far and I felt part of this land. My soul felt free here.

Well before dawn we entered the Arches State Park. We were hoping to get some good sunrise photos and experience something that we never had before, and we found both. I highly recommend visiting these arches in person, for the feeling becomes much more encompassing. It felt like pure enchantment. We watched the sun rise through the large single arch and it felt as if it was dawning on primordial Earth. The air was cool and fresh, the sky clear, and the land pristine. It was magical seeing it, but it was equally if not more so, profound in another way. I felt my spirit stirring from its slumber and expanding into the morning sun with an awakening expectation. It held a knowing that the sun was not just the sun. There was a sense of recognition and inner connection with something much more, something vitally intelligent and aware, a vast Being of much purer Light that was flowing within and through the sun. I could feel its awareness probing with its particles of Light, I could feel its essence, and both my spirit and the earth's spirit were rising together to meet it.

No, the sun is not just the sun. It is sentient and holds its own awareness, and it is both within a symbiotic relationship to us and to that which is much more. At the moment my spirit rose to meet it, I realized that the sun was also a portal to that which was much more. Was it God that was flowing through? Who really knows, but to me it is a being much closer to the knowing of whatever God truly might be than I am. I still carried a lot of inner struggles around the concept of a God. Maybe though, this is what my journey had now become, not just healing what I held inside and opening to and experiencing spiritual experiences, but becoming the journey and finding my own way back. All of my life I have felt a deep inner yearning, and a sense of deep separation and emptiness from something that I vaguely remembered. Becoming attuned to healing energies and having the spiritual experiences that I have had, have all touched on this remembrance. Looking back, they had all been guideposts. I had walked away from religions, so maybe I was truly returning to God in my own way.

After sunrise we looked to the abutment beside us and were surprised to see the image of a Neolithic face carved into its top corner by wind and rain. It seemed as if it was an earth spirit set to watch over the land, and in our inspired imaginings we felt as if we were being observed.

Words do not fully encompass what happened next. I do not know how they ever could. When I sat on the highest interior junction of the double arch, my heart was flung open to the depths of its core and became one with the Earth. I felt cradled by the Earth's loving awareness and knew that deep healings were happening. Deeply buried levels of grief, sadness, and many other emotions were being gently lifted away and transformed. Not just this lifetime, but it felt like many lifetimes worth. I was so choked up by the emotions of this experience that my tears welled from my heart in waves. I felt as if I was sitting within the Earth's womb and the double arch over my head was the vulva. The inner child and perhaps even the Divine child aspect of whoever I was, were being re-awakened and nurtured, and I sensed the same, though less powerful, rhythmic heartbeat of the Earth that I had resonated so powerfully with before.

This experience was totally unlike, and yet much deeper than anything that I had ever experienced. The stone that I had embraced within the Ballynoe stone circle being the exemption. Feeling my heart surrounded and embraced by the focused energies of the Earth in such a way made the magnitude, and awed beauty of what I had experienced truly a Divine experience of connection and wholeness. I now understood in a way that I never had before, that I truly am the Earth's child.

It felt like pure magic sitting here, as if between worlds. Looking over either my left or my right shoulder was like being invited through windows into different times and realities, as even the terrain was different. Mary crawled up and sensed the womblike feeling, and the windows going into other worlds, but nothing else. I told her about my experience and then sat reflecting. Apparently this healing had been specific to me, so I was more than grateful to the Earth. I realized that in ways that went far beyond being human, she really was our mother. I know that one day I will return here, for I have a knowing deep inside that I can return the favor, but, for now, we focused our attention on Colorado and stopped for the night in Cortez.

It was in Cortez that we began to feel that we had entered the area where our hearts could find deeper truths. Our hearts were yearning for understandings that went much deeper than what we had been taught. There was an intrinsic feeling that seemed to permeate everything around here with ancient knowledge, and we wanted to become immersed completely into it.

At Mesa Verde we found that the people were pretty ingenious about surviving in a cliff dwelling community. I remembered learning about Mesa Verde in school and not feeling anything more than idle curiosity. Being here in person was definitely more rewarding. This site impressed us, but we were impressed even more by what we saw on the six-mile loop. Sunken cliff top habitations, other cliff face communities, but most of all, it was in seeing how perfectly aligned the Sun Temple was that caught our attention and admiration. We arrived just as the setting sun was striking it and its impact hit us head on. There was an amazing sense of power reflecting off the Temple, yet at the same time I could sense it absorbing the sun's rays. These people were far more intelligent and aware than history books gave them credit for.

We reached Taos in a snowstorm with hope, anticipating that it would be either here or Santa Fe that we would settle. We had no clear idea as we began this journey of what to expect in New Mexico, so we had based our decision on the reputations of the communities and the opportunities that could open up. The reputed energy of this area was already noticeable.

We found boarding, and after hearing the landlord's stories of the Taos Pueblo, their sacred Lake, and of them being outside of Federal jurisdiction and a law unto themselves, we found that they were performing a deer dance ceremony Christmas day. The inhabitants of the Pueblo had a reputation for strictly enforcing their privacy, but for this ceremony they were allowing the public to watch. Mary and I had jumped at this chance, and as we stood atop a mound of snow overlooking the ceremonial grounds we were absorbed by the power of these people and of this dance. This was a powerful experience, especially when the dancers were lined up in front of us in procession waiting to enter the circle. All of them, men and boys from toddlers to the elderly were wearing the complete hides of elk, deer, moose and buffalo, including the racks and horns. They all appeared as if they were deep into an altered state.

There was another group of men wearing feather and grass headdresses running up and down the procession line. These men were aware and observant, and obviously knew that they held a position of responsibility during this ceremony. The women were dressed in their regalia and had already formed a circle within the bigger cleared circle of the dance, waiting for the drums to start. As these drums started to beat the heartbeat rhythm you could literally feel the whole Earth responding to it. I was overlooking the procession line, and as this drumbeat started the dancers started shuffling back and forth and moaning. The hides alone carried the spiritual energies of these animals, but once the men started shuffling and moaning, with really low intensity, the energy amplified many times over. As their trance deepened they transformed themselves into merging completely with these animals, and as they did my spirit left my body and was absorbed completely into these people, into this heartbeat, and into this land.

At a certain point within the rhythmic beat the men moved in. The women opened their circle to accept them, and the men began dancing as the animals that they had spiritually transformed into. The women re-formed their circle and danced to their own beat. As a few of the male dancers began to succumb, those with the feather and grass headdresses picked them up and carried them into one of the buildings. It was not until the dance ended that I came fully back into my body.

Something within me had changed; something deeply moving. I had become these people; I had become this land. The procession line had formed and moved past us only feet away and it was not just the energy I felt, but the smell of the animal hides had permeated my soul. I had become this experience. Blue Lake, their sacred Lake, was calling me and I turned to face it. My spirit was yearning to go to it but I knew that that was forbidden. The close-knit ceremonial and intricately entwined community atmosphere amongst these people had been refreshing after our own experiences with mainstream society. Mary and I both felt at home here.

Days later we arrived at Bandelier monument. The scenery on the drive into it had been beautiful, however while still miles away I started becoming deeply quiet. With each passing mile that we drew closer, the deeper I went within. This area must have meant a lot to me in another life. Bandelier's impact on me was greater than what I had experienced at Mesa Verde, and it reminded me of the energy at the Taos pueblo but in a different way. I was not sure how, only that it was different. On first impression it looked like the cliff face was covered by a huge array of ant holes, and it was hard for me to imagine people living in them. We were allowed access into two of these though and my perceptions quickly began to change.

This pueblo was situated on the site of an ancient volcano that had last erupted over a million years ago. In fact it had erupted twice within a short span of time, and each of the eruptions, were six hundred times more powerful than the Mt. St. Helen's eruption. The ash fallout grew to one thousand feet deep in places and any forms of life living in this area would not have been able to get away fast enough to survive. Through time, as people settled here, the porous cliffs created perfect accommodations because the ash was so easily carved out.

As we sat inside these cliff homes and looked out, it gave us a greater sense of these people. It felt peaceful and somehow calming, and we had impressions of them milling around the commerce area in front of us. We waited until sunset to leave the cliffs, and the magic of the sun's light shining through the valley was enchanting. The spirits were gathering around us as we walked and we felt welcomed. They seemed to share a great deal of contentment and community spirit.

We experienced many emotional ups and downs during the weeks that we had been here. The job interviews were coming in for Mary but she no longer cared. Neither of us felt happy or grounded in the tourist focused, congested, and chaotic energy of Taos. Intending to find out if Santa Fe would suit us better, we found that it did not. We only spent a few minutes in it, and that was all it took for us to know that we could not deal with its city like atmosphere. The peace and expansiveness of the open roads was still with us.

Mary wanted to go home. She could have forced herself to fit into this community and had found that she could get work, but she understood in her heart that she would not be happy unless she was close to her family. She was tired of having to keep up appearances. She wanted the people in her chosen community to be genuine, and she wanted to be able to relax into her art. I could not blame her. Regardless of the energetic reputation of this area we had observed superficiality and underlying currents of discouragement about this town. I was happy for her and my heart shared her knowing that she had made the right decision. We decided to leave within the next two days. However, we were invited to attend an authentic native sweat in a week's time and became ecstatic. I had been yearning to go to one for years but lacked the confidence to approach anyone in the native communities back home. My heart and soul were there, but the rest of me felt like a naïve and bumbling outsider.

I wanted to be closely involved with the people and their culture, but I could not express how I felt from that level of soul connection. I had helped my family and others to believe in themselves and grow, but I held a deeper level of personal confusion that had hindered my own ability to grow. I had a lot of insecurities about believing in myself and feared rejection. In a way, I did not feel worthy enough to connect. I was empowered as a father, a husband, and a provider for the most part, but on a human level I was far from it. I yearned to be accepted into the native culture as I resonated much more to their original way of being than I did to modern society. To have been invited to share in this experience was very important to me.

Kim, the owner of the house where we were staying, taught us how to make medicine pouches and we met her friend Kay. It had been Kay who had invited us to the sweat. As I reflected on how we were guided to rent space in this house, I realized that we would not have known about the deer dance, Bandelier, or been invited to the sweat if we had not taken a room here. When we considered the experiences that we had, and were about to, living here had become a blessing. I really felt that we would not have experienced these if we had not been led to Kim. I thanked the universe for having led us to her.

Tracy, another of Kim's friends arrived and did past life regression work with us. I had asked these questions going into it *"What situation in this or a past lifetime caused me to put such a thick wall up, and, is there some knowledge from that lifetime that can benefit me in this?"*

These were the visions that I received: I was standing on an ocean cliff and a dolphin and native man appeared before me as my guides. My vision shifted and I saw myself working in the desert. I was North African and my skin was neither dark, nor light. Mixed races of people were toiling around me and I was in Egypt during the time of the early pharaohs. Looking over my left shoulder I saw the Sphinx, and sensed that it had already been here a long time. My name was Akman. I was thirty years old, and part of the work crew that was building with the big stones.

Tracy guided me back to when I was twenty years old. I was walking in the woods wearing a garment that reached half way down my thighs. Wherever I was now was not near to where I was at thirty. I grew up in these woods. My mother and father were now both dead, I had an older sister, and I had a crush on Iwanna, a friendly and pretty girl who sparkled when she smiled. I felt swept with happiness thinking of her.

I was taken back to age ten and there was fighting in my village. We were in battle with people from another area and the village was in an uproar. My Dad died in this battle and I was hiding with my Mom. We did not know where my sister was. The scene changed and I was now eleven years old and the man of the house. I had gone through a ritual, in a way, but it was not the regular ritual. Animals were roaming freely through the village. Our huts were made with branches and mortar, and the Elders ruled. My mother was now constantly sad.

At age five, I saw the people working, happy, and curious. My father was a trader and was somewhere in the neighboring villages. I spent my time playing with the animals, and my older sister was learning how to become a woman. My mother, during this point in time, felt joy in life. After a villager had a successful trade the community danced and feasted, and we ate meat, fish, plants from the woods, and fruit. Overall I felt happy, but I held a lingering sadness inside. I loved my family but I was not sure that I wanted to be a trader like my father. He was tall, strong and agile, but we were not the same.

I was taken back to find out where the sadness stemmed from, and I had a vision of being outside on a beautiful sunny morning when there was a sudden brightness in the sky. It filled the sky like a giant prolonged lightning bolt. Some people were afraid but I felt drawn to that light. As people gathered in wonderment, confusion, and fear, I was thinking in my heart that the light was Home. My mother silently communicated to me with her eyes about the flash, but my father kept his opinions to himself and went with the prevailing thoughts of everyone else. Other traders spoke of it whenever they came into our village as well. I felt heavier and curious after that flash of light.

The scene changed and I was in my early twenties and almost drowning. I was in a boat and fishing with a couple of friends, Ahmed and another, when we were swamped by a bigger boat with masts and sails. The people who pulled us out looked like Persians and there was a feeling of death on board. We were thrown in with the other prisoners; both black and lighter skinned and had no idea where we were going. Eventually we pulled into a port, but the friend whose name I could not remember was already dead. The attitude of our captors was that if you did not survive, you did not survive. Ahmed and I were separated and sold, and I never saw him or home again. In time I was re-sold to the Egyptians.

We went back to when I was thirty years old. As long as we worked hard we were treated and fed well, and some earned their freedom. We lived in canvas-covered buildings and ate meat and vegetables to keep us strong. There was a close-knit bond between us for as long as we were together. Tracy asked me to send my vision to Iwanna. I saw that she had married another. I never had the chance to earn my freedom and marry in this lifetime, for when I was thirty-two years old I was crushed and died. We had been working with pulleys and building a different building this time, a regular building. Some of the stones were as big as I was and some smaller.

Asked what I had learned from that lifetime I erupted into laughter as my impish side came out *"Watch out for falling stones!"* but then more reflectively I said, "*It was to observe people from all angles to enhance my awareness, and to learn what it was like to be a prisoner.*" I regretted losing my friends, being taken away from the trees and the water, and my heart's flame, and, I regretted dying so young.

The scene shifted unexpectedly and I was standing amidst mist and sparkles. I was curious and could sense other essences, other presences. Someone approached, and I recognized one of my Celestial teachers from the last time we had met, before my last incarnation. This was the same place and I felt comfortable and happy. He was human, in form, but I sensed that he was more.

"What was that big flash of light?" I asked.

"It was not them," he said, *"it was not from the Angelic realm. The light originated from Beings from another dimension. The Angels talked with them about not interfering with the Earth and found that they were in a good way, and had just been curious."*

The lesson I learned as a result of that lifetime was to feel at peace in any situation. During it I had developed a fear of being confined and molded. I asked what I could do to start breaking down the walls I had assumed, and it was requested that I learn to love myself, so that the walls of fear would be seen from a place of heightened awareness and fall away.

My teacher kept shifting between male and female. The awareness came immediately that gender held no relevance here; the totality of our Essence is the same. Our spirits are innately the perfect balance of both.

It is my understanding that our spirits choose what our genders will be before each incarnation, and we come in with either more of this or more of that to learn to find balance, or to not find it. It is all part of the journey of our spirit. We grow through the understandings achieved through all experiences. Ultimately the journey has nothing to do with whether we are male or female in any particular life. It is in what will best serve us in fulfilling our desired experience within that life frame. It is in what we will learn during that life from that particular perspective, and how much benefit it will be within that life, or through repercussions into future lives, it will be to the collective consciousness of humanity and other sentient beings on Earth for us to assume those roles. It is through sharing our understandings gained through these experiences, and through the empowered expression of that which we truly are, that humanity will blossom.

Days later we were at the sweat, standing outside of the lodge barefoot in the packed snow. The women were wearing skirts and the men shorts. We were allowed a blanket or towel as extra accessories and these were wrapped around our shoulders to keep us warm. A formal ceremony was taking place for those who were requesting clarity on a life issue or a healing from the spirits. These participants wanted to prove their sincerity through courage, so one by one they had voiced to those gathered, and to the spirits, their pledges. As the words left their lips, they had their upper left arm sliced open by a knife. It was carefully packed with a mixture of herbs and berries, and sealed by a compress that I did not recognize. These people were held in high respect by the Sioux facilitator and those gathered.

After this ceremony, first the ladies, and then the men entered the lodge on our knees and crawled around left to right until we were all in. My understandings were that when a tepee becomes used for sacred ceremony, as the sweat lodge is considered, or when a significant meeting is called, it becomes a lodge. It is whatever the intent is that underlines its function. There were about twenty of us, sitting two deep around a low fire. Our facilitator and his doorkeeper had obviously taken part in the sun dance ceremonies, as the scars of their piercing were on their chests and backs. I felt that these men were genuine, and I sensed that they were more authentically native and closer to their cultural roots than anyone that I had seen outside of the Pueblo. As I sat observing those around me I felt doubly honoured to be in this sweat.

The sweat lodge ceremony is considered private, and I respect that. I can only tell you that each time the stones were brought in a lesson and healings were involved concerning a specific direction of the medicine wheel. During this sweat though, there had been enough fire remaining within the stones that the spirits had requested another round.

As the ceremony ended and I walked out into the cold air, it became apparent just how much my face had been burned by the steam. The coolness felt refreshing after the intensity of the heat.

We were invited into the host's house where we reformed into a circle and a spirit food ceremony began. Amidst their individual teachings, bowls containing cranberries, raisins, kidneys, and cornmeal were offered to us. As each offering was shared we offered a prayer to the spirits. The pipe ceremony followed, and as the pipe carrier passed it to each of us the feeling of acceptance from those gathered surrounded me and I came more into myself. During the feast and social time that came after, Ben, from the Taos Pueblo introduced himself to Mary and I and asked if we would like to take part in a sweat being held at the Pueblo the next day. We were ecstatic. Yet we were equally intrigued and amazed when he told us that a Japanese monk was to lead the ceremony. We were honoured and grateful, and felt that doors were opening into greater contact with the Pueblo. As a token of her gratitude for the experiences of this night, Mary gifted all with an Amethyst tear of joy.

We had heavy snow overnight and Ben did not make it to our rendezvous, so we returned to the house to prepare our car for the road again. We would be leaving Taos the next day.

We decided to visit Chaco Canyon before driving east, and noticed, still a half hour from the canyon, that its energy was already hitting us. As soon as Fajada Butte came into sight we became aware that that was its source. It felt sacred. We discovered to our dismay that access to the Butte had become restricted. It had been closed to the general public due to tourist damage. Instead, we had to settle on watching the PBS documentary 'Mystery of Chaco Canyon' to find out about it. I was thankful we did, because it was excellent and I highly recommend it. These were no ordinary people. How they had buildings for miles around in such perfect mathematical alignment was awe-inspiring.

On the eastern topside of the Butte there is an astronomical calendar consisting of three large perpendicular stone slabs, with one large and one small spiral engraved into the wall behind them. During the summer solstice a ray of the sun's light, called a sun dagger would shine in top to bottom cutting the larger spiral in half. At the time of equinox, this dagger would be two thirds of the way in from the right side, and a smaller dagger would slice the small spiral in half. At the winter solstice, two of these daggers would perfectly hug the outer sides of the larger spiral. A lot of careful study and astronomical awareness went into this and my admiration for the people grew.

We felt a sense of lightness, a distinct vibrancy to this canyon that permeated the land. The Butte itself seemed to be a generator to it. We recognized that we held memories of this area and felt comfortable and at home here. The friendly community essence of the people still surrounded us as if time was not real, but while we explored Chetro Ketl I began to feel an unexplainable unease. I experienced the presence of the people coming and going, but though they appeared joyful I was not comfortable. In fact I did not remain long. I went outside and started walking past the outer wall at the back. It was there that I understood my discomfort. There had been a massacre here. The people had been lined up against the wall and killed. I could feel myself trying to run away but was hit in the leg by a bullet, then bayoneted. I had a sense that my incarnation in that life was Navaho, and Mexican soldiers were slaughtering us.

As I realized this, I could feel everything as if it was the present moment. I felt the pain and emotions of everyone around me, and I could feel the distinct awareness of the Earth and surrounding life as they were witnessing it. The birds, animals, insects, and the Earth itself were all psychically and empathically absorbing all that was happening. It was not a good feeling being here.

I felt that I was shown this vision to clearly remind me and to demonstrate just how much life truly was inter-connected. I had become one with each of them, and I was living the experience of each of these aspects of life as they absorbed the trauma. My awareness had projected into their awareness and I was looking out of their eyes; I was feeling their sensations. My experience of the Earth was different, and heightened. I seemed to see and experience from above, below and all around. It became apparent that everything that happened to one on this world affected all other forms of life in one way or another. The intensity of the fear, pain, and sense of betrayal that had engulfed me and knotted my insides still felt as if it was pushing up into my throat as we moved away.

As I was transcribing these journal notes I had an experience that though not from this moment in time, was directly related to this moment in time. I will share with you a glimpse of where my journey is leading me.

I was emotionally triggered as I recollected this experience, so without thinking, I instinctively opened myself to traverse time and place. I was amongst them, within them, and above them. I experienced each of their experiences as if they were my own, yet I was removed from them at the same time. I was forgiving the soldiers from the essence that I was, and yet still am. My energy was focused over my body in the perfect resemblance of it. I was standing in the body that was, yet it was lying at my feet.

My awareness rose above the scene and I called on Quan Yin, the Lady, the Angels, the Earth, and my guides to bring unconditional Love to all that were there, including all other life surrounding that was being affected. As my heart opened Divine Love flowed through and around me, and all of the people, whether still living or in spirit form began to look up.

There were now others around me. We were all sending Love and Light, and healings were happening. Forgiveness, Love and higher understandings were sinking in and the people and spirits were becoming free. They were looking up with wonder, awe, and appreciation, even the soldiers. On the inner spiritual level they had given themselves permission to heal the trauma from this incident, in all its forms. All of the traumatic energies were flowing into the Light, and the Light of new understandings shone through their eyes. I could feel it deeply within their hearts, and I could feel the gratitude of all other life in the area as they too became freed of the energies.

I had moved myself completely into the energy of the experience, focused my thought, asked for Divine assistance, and allowed myself to just be the inter-active observer with the intent to heal. After it completed I moved back into my 'present' moment to bring healing to any residues that I still had within from this or related experiences. I was changing. I was no longer who I used to be, and as this journey continues I am growing into deepening spiritual connection and heart awareness.

As I walked along the base of the cliff these feelings began to subside, and I heard Mary suddenly gasp as she looked up. A hawk was watching us intently as it hovered just feet over us. It lingered for a few seconds before rising to crest the top of the ridge again. We were stunned. Giving Mary credit for the hawk's appearance I looked at her and smilingly gave her a spiritual name, 'She who soars with hawks'. She laughed, turning away with her new name. Feeling joyful we moved towards Pueblo Bonito with a sense of growing recognition. My mind moved off in a tangent and I reflected. I had felt a definite reluctance to draw a full breath in during my time in the eastern states, I found it easier to breathe traveling through the mid-western states, and easier still since hitting Utah, but in this canyon, especially as we were approaching Pueblo Bonito, my lungs and breath felt a depth of freedom and vitality that they had never experienced before. Soon, we felt a growing certainty that we had once lived here. We had much more of a bounce in our steps and happily explored inside and out, for that lifetime had been a happy one. Everything seemed familiar, the look, the smells, and the feeling.

Leaving Pueblo Bonito I must have entered Peter Pan's never never land; the land of imagination and possibilities. I found myself suddenly walking beside 'me' as I walked these same steps in that other lifetime. I could see every detail, smell his aroma, read his thoughts, hear our footsteps, and feel his happiness and contentment. I could sense that he was aware of something different around him and was turning his head curiously, but he could not see me. He shrugged his shoulder then carried on. I was dumbstruck with surreal amazement, and I will not even try to explain it. Most of my spiritual experiences had been through feeling them so empathically that I could virtually see them. I did not usually hear, I did not usually smell, and any words spoken or heard were telepathic. However, this one was strikingly different and much more enhanced. I did not know how I did it, and I did not know if I would ever be able to repeat it, but I was feeling more than blessed that I experienced it. What if, in areas where energy was amplified around the world, as it was in this canyon, the possibility for these types of occurrences happening, especially if we had a lifetime within that energy, would also become amplified? Before we left we offered tobacco and sage, hoping to return some day.

We had been driving east, and were approaching a giant cross outside of Groom, Texas. There was much spiritual energy here and the statues were amazing and a beauty to behold. The statue of Christ at the last supper was the one that held the most impact for us and we lingered for a long time with it. We both felt as if we had shared this meal with him.

In contrast, hitting the Pennsylvania state line was like being hit in the stomach. After weeks in the southwest where we had opened to a sense of energetic expansion, the density of the energy that we were driving into was hard to adjust to. The land itself was beautiful, but there was a denser energy and a greater underlying tension in the air that permeated everything. We must have energetically expanded just as much in the southwest as the land itself. This would be our last day on the road, and by evening we would be back in Kent. Mary was excitedly anticipating her homecoming.

It was only now that we began to contemplate the totality of our journey, as up until this time we were always caught up in the movement of it. I thought that it would be a while before we fully understood or absorbed it all, but it really had been amazing. I looked at Mary, thinking that no matter what the undercurrents were between us, I loved and appreciated her for being who she was and I would travel with her anywhere. We both had strengths, weaknesses, and foibles, but there was also a great solidness between us. I valued her as a friend and companion.

In a sense we had been propelled to be together. First by, seemingly, random chance in Ireland, then our growing sense of connection, our 'feeling' that there was something drawing us into the southwest, and then our journey of discovery. We had been almost constantly together since we started this journey, so had basically stayed within each other's energy fields. Perhaps our combined energies assisted something along our way, or perhaps it took our combined energies, and agitations, as well as our combination of experiences to facilitate deep level openings and healings within us. We did not know what the meaning or purpose behind our being brought together had been, or what may have been accomplished because of it. I realized however, that it was because of it, that I had grown and was stronger within myself.

Mary and I were spending a lot of quiet time together since returning, knowing that we may never see each other again. In these days we drew very close as all of the dust of our travels had fallen away. I was soon to leave for Canada and our hearts were heavy.

About a half hour or so north of Bennington Vermont, a red tailed hawk flew ahead of the car for about thirty seconds, and then veered off to land in a roadside tree. It did a full landing spread and its beauty filled my heart as its entire upper side spread out in full view. It was beautiful and amazing, and I thought that this was a promising sign for my future. There was also a part of me I had to admit, that wondered if Mary had shape-shifted and it was actually her blessing my journey. I was returning temporarily to Peterborough, and Maureen had agreed to rent me a room.

Book Five

Akashic Records

I would like to take an opportunity to point out one or two things that may reflect on how you as the reader relates to my experiences within this segment of the chronicles. There were experiences that I was about to have within the Akashic Records that reflect a more abstract frame of reference. There would also be experiences that I would have, or would share with Maureen that had no reference points with anything that I have known. Much of this segment in many regards can be viewed as experiences or communications within. That is how the knowledge and the experiences within the Akashic Records come through, awareness-to-awareness. Your inner world, the world of your Essence and inner wisdom, takes precedence over your intellect. Your inner experiences take precedence over seeking experiences outside of yourself. You go within to expand. There would be times where I would be just asking questions, but the answers may be relevant in one way or another to humanity as a whole. I ask you to join with me as I share the telling of this part of my story, for I enter much more into the realms of the Divine. Not all of these questions may have relevance to you, as they relate specifically to my journey. Skim over those ones that do not and linger with the ones that do. You may find them to be guideposts on your own journeys.

Within a day of arriving at Maureen's I crashed from exhaustion. All of the remaining reserves of vitality that had kept me going in the last few years were now gone. After the almost constant travel, life changes, and deep healings that I had gone through in the last few months I was totally depleted. I walked through the house vacant eyed and listless, and could offer little real company to Maureen. I mostly slept, ate, and sat on the recliner, empty. I did not usually even have enough energy to think, let alone think of leaving the house to look for a temporary income. In fact I recoiled just at the thought of going back into a job. I needed to cocoon. Maureen recognized my need for quiet space, and slowly, her nurturing friendship helped me to recover.

Weeks later, Maureen and I were offered a chance to learn how to go into the Akashic Records, also known as the Book of Life or the Book of Remembrance. Despite my continuing exhaustion, I felt that it was important for me to be able to do this. Divine synchronicity seemed to be at play once again in aligning this up, and I was not wrong. I experienced openings in my understandings that set the course for other significant life changing experiences; all of which would eventually lead me closer to truly experiencing God as not just a concept.

A pre-requisite for this course was that Eileen, our course facilitator, opens the door for the Celestial realm to work with our body awareness in the integration of the archetypal energies most prevalent in our lives. My archetype was Lancelot. While he was standing before me Archangel Michael appeared, and I became aware that they were one and the same, in their physical and non-physical manifestations. As they merged and integrated I could sense their strength, focus and gentleness becoming part of my own Essence. It was not until twenty-four hours later that I sensed that the integration was complete. Once it was though I felt more inner surety than I had felt for the most part throughout my life. I felt more peacefully whole and complete.

As the course began Eileen told us that people could open themselves within the Records to be used as surrogates for healing, and then looked startled, saying that she did not know why she had just said that. I felt without any doubt, that that message had been intended for me.

I sensed, as I opened my Records for the first time, a feeling of pressure in my head, the awareness of different beings around me, and deeper levels of energy focused around my torso. I was experiencing a deep expansiveness of spirit, but I was visualizing myself standing within rows upon rows of bookshelves stretching into infinity. Every shelf seemed full of books, scrolls and manuscripts. Librarians were gathering around me, curious, as I was not asking anything. I stood there experiencing this new place, soaking it all in, and only observed. I did not really know what to ask.

Eileen had us ask the emanations "*How are you here to help serve me in this lifetime?*"

They answered, "*What is my request? What do I want to experience?*" Initially I felt curious and confident when I asked this question, but with their straight to the point response I suddenly became unsure and shy.

I felt slight anxiety leading into my next question. "*Is it in my highest good to find a standard job, or do I offer my services as I am?*"

The Librarians replied, "*Be who you are and they will come, options are yours. We will help you with whatever decision you choose.*"

I then viewed scenarios. "*What steps should I take?*"

"*Finish preparing and let people know who you are and what you offer. Improve health, feel joy, release doubt, relax, be focused and trust.*"

"*Show me what being in the place of witnessing is,*" and I was able to get a deeper understanding of the inter-relationships between all, not just human. "*Show me how to assist from the vibration of Peace and witnessing.*"

"*Be an example as you live this vibrational truth.*"

The following questions were first asked outside of the Records and then again within the Records. The aim was to compare the depth of our experience and the extensiveness of the answers received.

I asked, *"Can I have guidance on becoming the clearest channel that I can be?"*

Outside of the Records the answer was to *"Feel joy and become,"* but with the Records open it became much more of an experience. A powerful Presence was standing before me and I was no longer in the Library, or in the Hall of Records that I had first experienced. I sensed this presence to be Kryon. A gentle but powerful energy began to encompass me, and as it continued I was connecting with dolphins, apes, and the water essence. I felt myself opening as all of my chakras were coming into greater balance. I saw Jesus and others standing alongside me, and Michael was assisting in the integration of energies.

We were next asked to focus on a potted plant and I could feel its soothing energy. As we continued focusing I felt its vibration increasing from our combined attention, and a faerie appeared from amongst the stalks and looked at me with vibrant happiness. My heart and soul flooded open in glowing joy. This plant was aware, and it was speaking to me. It said that it liked the way that its pot was wrapped but its roots were getting cramped. It was telling us to open our hearts to accept that all plants were aware, and that they were here to share and help life on our home. That was a pretty vivid communication for me to receive outside of the Records, so I was assuming that my senses were heightened due to all the focused attention in the room.

That same focus within the Records generated the following response. *"Form is an illusion, but an interesting mode of learning."* There was more information coming but my mind was not picking it all up, so I asked if they could send me this information through my heart. They were happy with this and the information came in much clearer, though unfortunately I did not write it down.

Self-limiting patterns of thought, unworthiness, and the fear of fully opening and exposing my creativity and love were shown to me. I could easily relate to it. I felt that if I opened those doors all of my weaknesses and vulnerabilities would be at the mercy of others. I was to find out though, that those patterns had been imprinted into me from an outside source; another soul. I asked Michael to clear them and I began to feel lighter.

We were told to look into an imaginary mirror and ask the emanations of Light how they saw us. I experienced myself as being an energy imprint, with space and stars in the background. I was a thought pattern, a flow of swirling and spiraling inter-dimensional energies. That vision was a bit of an eye opener, and I looked at my body and around at this room, the other people, and this reality with new awareness.

I asked, *"How can I live in my life with joy and peace?"*

"Trust, be free, and open."

Finally, *"Is there anything else that you want to say to me right now?"*

They replied, *"Welcome, we love you. Honour yourself and all that is, and then allow yourself to flow and grow."*

The Healing prayers included with these teachings are valuable and I will share them with you. I have however, revised the wording of the Prayers into what I feel reflects greater resonance with the vibrations of the evolving human consciousness. I have also revised and elaborated on the underlying concept of the Forgiveness Prayer, into what I feel reflects greater spiritual understanding.

These prayers are said alone or in combination with lightly touching certain Grace Points. Perhaps I should take this chance now to explain these points, as they add a powerful compliment to how encompassing the Healing Prayers can potentially become. The Grace Points I refer to are specific integration points on our hands where certain energetic meridian pathways, that run throughout our bodies touch the surface. Each meridian, or energetic super highway, directly corresponds to, and plays a major role in how harmoniously or healthy our lives play out.

The Grace Points are a physical point on our bodies that become a reference in taking a physical action to stimulate movement of energy on other levels of the human being. These encompass physical, emotional, spiritual, conscious, unconscious and genetic levels. The Divine had positioned these energetic access points so that humanity had a physical, experiential means to return to a place of alignment and inner peace with Divine Will. This process, of gently touching specific points on our hand while focusing upon a specific intent, supports us in attaining our highest potential.

The Grace Points were offered to humanity in order to assist us in three ways: gaining clarity, releasing that which no longer serves our life, and integrating that which does serve our highest good.

Using the Grace Points with focused intent, while being 'present' creates an opening to higher consciousness, or if you prefer, to God, and to your heart's wisdom, body awareness and higher self. Using the Grace Points gives us the ability to obtain a higher source of insight or clarity, and opens our energy pathways, in a way giving our bodies permission, to release all that is not for our highest good and imprinting all that is. If you turn your hand palm up you will find the Grace Points in the soft tissue areas; you can follow your instincts to determine which hand to use. I will describe their locations but you may need to slowly and very lightly feel around to determine the exact spot for you. Use your fingertip, your body and your inner guidance to guide you. As you feel a little surge of energy, or what you think is an itch or a tickle, you are on the right spot.

Number one or the Main Grace Point is in the exact centre of your palm. It connects directly to your heart awareness and clarifies information being received. It helps to release any issues, emotions, beliefs, judgments, etc. that concern the soul's evolution, past, present or future. It also releases resistance and integrates new insights, creating positive reference points to move on in your life.

Number two or the Body Release Point is on the outer edge of your hand, almost directly opposite the V between your index finger and the base of your thumb. This point clarifies information from cellular memory and releases limiting issues, judgments, beliefs, emotions, etc. that are held in your cellular memory. It allows integration of new insights which enhance your well-being.

Number three or the Genetic Lineage Point is at the base of the V between your thumb and index finger. It clarifies information received from an ancestral source, and releases issues, judgments, etc. which had been passed down.

Number four or the Higher Self Grace Point can be found at the inner base of your two middle fingers. Slide your finger lightly along the inside edge of these fingers, the soft tissue at the base is what you are looking for. This connects you to your Higher Self and allows you to access wisdom, compassion and truth that relate to the past, present and future of your soul's journey.

Number five is the Heart Grace Point. This point is in the same location as number one, as all evolves from the heart. It clarifies information coming from your physical heart. *Your physical heart generates an energy field that encompasses your body and all of your other energy fields, or energy bodies.* It releases limiting issues, judgments and beliefs from the mental, emotional, and physical levels. It also integrates information and Divine Grace from your Higher Self and Body/Creation Grace Points.

The Heart Grace Point is in many ways similar to the Main Grace Point, but where you are coming from as you approach it creates a huge difference in what becomes encompassed. Are you feeling with your heart as you encompass your intent and speak it? Are you letting the energy of your focused heart awareness and love flow into how you experience your intent being fulfilled, or are you speaking this intent as if it were a mental exercise? Encompassing the use of this point from your heart allows what is released and received to become much more encompassing and experiential in its scope. On my journey I found that following my heart awareness was always more important to me, and rewarding than following mental impressions.

The final one, the Body/Creation Grace Point is located at the centre of the base of your hand, about half an inch up from your wrist. It clarifies the information held in your body, and when applicable from the Heart of Creation. It releases issues from the emotional, mental and physical levels, and connects the body's awareness to the Heart of Creation.

These last three points can work together, and when all three are held at once with awareness and intent, there is a connection from your heart, through your Higher Self, and into the Heart of Creation. This allows for greater insight into releasing old limiting patterns and allows the integration of new beneficent ones. Follow your intuition as to when these points are to be touched alone, together, or in what combination.

If you are seeking clarity, use your 'intention' and gentle touch to redirect your conscious mind to the information that you are seeking. In asking for clarity, it allows movement within the consciousness to open to new awareness or truth. When choosing to release that which no longer serves, use your intention to release limiting conditions, patterns, false beliefs, judgments, etc. to allow the movement and transformation of any stationary energy. Releasing limitations allows a shift in consciousness that replaces a contracted memory with an uplifting one through bringing love and heart awareness to it. This expands your comfort zones, and allows greater balance to integrate into your inner state of being.

While integrating that which serves your highest good, use your intention to integrate new information and insights that will facilitate the imprinting of positive experiences and greater awareness into your being. This includes all information that brings you into a deeper place of love, joy and Divine awareness.

Using the Grace Points creates an opening to whatever our concept of a God source is. They open us to consciously receive Divine Blessings, and they show our willingness to transform into a vibrant state of love, peace and health. Using the Grace Points with intent gives us the ability to release all that is no longer in our highest good and imprinting what is. As much as possible be in a calm and restful state of being, and take a few slow deep breaths to ground yourself before stating your intent. This way you can bring greater focus, clarity, consciousness and 'presence' to your intent.

By lightly touching these points as we say the Prayers, it allows their intent, healing abilities, and the encompassment of your experience to become heightened and more far reaching. Select your desired prayer and repeat it as many times as you feel a need, *but a minimum of three times*, taking a deep centering breath after each repetition.

The first prayer was originally called the Forgiveness Prayer. In my experience, forgiveness is a concept which has become misconstrued throughout time, and has now become self-limiting.

I have felt people's emotions, both those offering and receiving, as this word and its intent are used. I have noticed that with the vast majority of people, any emotions or beliefs held deeper than the superficial level become conflicted. People generally are not truly forgiving, and they do not feel truly forgiven, as a result, a deep-seated sense of powerlessness begins to take hold. Over the generation's people as a whole have become so separated from themselves, and so separated from the state of being where they could really incorporate this energy, which originally was a Divine gift to assist in our understandings during the timeframe it was given, that we are just throwing up veils.

People have been taught that this is the way to achieve inner peace and salvation, but on deep inner levels they do not feel 'seen' and they are not 'seeing' the other. People have forgotten the inter-connectedness of spirit. People have forgotten that we are all Divine beings, all aspects of God mirroring what we, collectively or individually, is experiencing. Whether it is in what we are holding within that is asking to be recognized and healed, or what we are holding within that is yearning to be expressed. Everything that we experience, or agree to bring into our perspectives resonates with a vibration held within us. In forgiving another God aspect, in the way that most people do, it disempowers everyone. We do not know what anyone's ultimate spiritual journey is destined to consist of, let alone our own. What lessons are the collective souls of everyone directly or indirectly involved, wanting to learn? What exactly is being shown to us? How is this opportunity a chance to open into deeper levels of heart awareness and understandings about our own-selves and what we perceive? How has it become a guide for us to move consciously into greater spiritual connection with the Divine? How has it allowed us to open to, and understand compassion? In the end, all of this becomes a blessing.

Being willing to accept from this place of awareness is the key that opens the floodgates into a greater awareness of Divine Love. By accepting from this place of being, we are moving deeper into our spiritual power, not away from it. Accepting, does not mean that we, or others, can walk away from taking personal responsibility and accountability for our actions; or the thoughts or dramas that we allow ourselves to focus upon. All we need to do is open the door through intent and desire. If we feel that we are struggling to accomplish this, all we need to do is ask for Divine assistance. It will become easier the deeper we are able to encompass and understand compassion and non-judgment, and it will become easier the deeper we move towards the God source.

Whatever the situation is, or was, we do not need to know the root cause, or to be drawn back into its associated dramas. We only need intend that the healing energies of the prayer flow to the source. The original source is almost always, much deeper than we think it is. We need to be willing to accept and allow our self, and others compassion. Become the neutral, unattached observer and the witness. If we feel love and gentleness towards ourselves as we say this prayer, and bring nonjudgmental compassion to the intended recipients, or situation, then the power of this prayer to affect all around healings becomes limitless.

I am choosing to refer to this prayer as an empowered 'Acceptance Prayer'. With this prayer, a greater potential for transformation exists if we state our intent from a sincere place of unconditional love and compassion, and, as if we are focusing on a present time event. Please understand that 'All past, and all future, is observed and experienced only from wherever we are, whatever state of being we are in, in the Present Moment, and they are held within our energy fields with equal power.'

*If there is anyone or anything that is hurting me **now**, knowingly or unknowingly, I accept it for what it is and release it. It has no power over me. If I am hurting anyone or anything, including myself, by suppressing, holding onto, or projecting limiting energy patterns, either knowingly or unknowingly, I accept and release it for the highest good of others and myself. I am Grateful that this is so.*

The healing power of this prayer is limitless. Our past consists of anything prior to 'this Breath.' If it is spoken at the end of the day, it clears all the negativity that builds the walls of separation within us. It is not necessary to know the root cause; we just need to be willing to open ourselves to bring in higher understandings of our heart. Seen through the eyes and understandings of this level of love and awareness, we come into the state of being where true forgiveness and acceptance unfolds.

The Prayer for Releasing Outside Influences can be used any time that one feels a sensation, physical, mental or emotional, that may have been emphatically or inadvertently taken on from someone else. Emphatic absorption is done on the spiritual or emotional levels in an effort to understand or relieve the burden of another. This prayer is to assist the person, animal, or other aspect of life, and/or yourself to release all to God.

If what I am experiencing is not mine, may the Divine Emanations of the God Source, be aware of this energetic pattern, surround, and release whatever it may be to the infinite Love and Light of Creation for the highest good of all. May the place or places where this energetic attachment had been, in any time, space or dimension be filled with infinite Love and Light. I am Grateful that this is so.

The Prayer for Loved Ones, other Souls, and/or other curious or interfering Energy Patterns can be used on a personal level to release any energy that is interfering with the evolution or harmony of our own spiritual, emotional, mental, or other subtle energy body layers. A Soul is the energy of another spiritual essence that may be seeking some form of completion with you, or has not been ready to, or understood how to enter the Light and has been drawn to your spiritual Light for comfort, or in some cases, manipulation. An energy pattern is another energy form; thought pattern, mental projection, other form of consciousness, etc. that has been drawn to you because you hold either, consciously or unconsciously, a similar magnetic resonance with it, or, you have unconsciously allowed it in through gaps in your aura.

I ask that the Emanations of Love and Light surround this energy pattern or soul with Light, gently remove it, and send it into the Light to continue its spiritual evolution for the highest good of all concerned. If there is anything that I hold onto that is masked, hidden, transparent, or cloaked in my conscious or unconscious knowing, including any judgment, I accept and release it. I am Grateful that this is so.

We open our hearts as a natural part of who many of us are, but as we do our energy fields open proportionally and energies become attracted. I would not have it any other way. It is easy to release these influences, or attachments. I open my heart and feel enveloped in immense love, knowing we are all one in God, and then I allow these energies to flow gently out of my energy field. I do not judge, and I do not get hung up in feeling that something may be good or bad. While I am in the heart essence, I feel only compassionate and loving neutrality. This is how I handle the scenarios encompassing these last two prayers now; a gentle breeze of love carrying all that does not belong to me into the Light.

As I finished the opening prayer to access the Records the following day, I saw myself standing before a panel of Beings that stood in a wide semi-circle around me. I was curious why they were around me, waiting and not speaking, but I just started asking questions. *"Is it important for Maureen and I to connect to Ireland together?"*

"Yes, you will assist in re-awakening and re-activating the Divine feminine."

I asked, *"Are we also meant to do something in Peru?"*

Now Higher Beings joined the semi-circle and answered, *"In time."*

I then asked if I was connected to the White Brotherhood and they answered *"Yes."*

Curious about who and what exactly they were, I asked, *"What is the White Brotherhood?"*

"They are multi-dimensional beings coming from all galaxies and universes who protect and assist planetary civilizations to grow into higher states of consciousness." This sounded remarkably like the intent behind the Jedi knights in the Star Wars movies. I wondered how much of this was co-incidence?

My mind drifted into another direction and it became apparent why I had such an illustrious crowd gathered around me. Eileen's mention of becoming a surrogate within the Records had just re-entered my mind. I began opening myself for the Burren; the area in Ireland where I had been struck by such a sense of grieving on our way to the cliffs of Moher. The beings that stood around asked me if I knew what I was asking, saying that I might experience possible discomforts, and then asked for my agreement. They were happy and honoured me when I gave it.

I said the Acceptance Prayer three times slowly, and then three times again. The energies on the land were beginning to open up. A powerful, vibrating beam of intense brilliant white and gold light lit up the centre of my chakras. It extended from above my head to below my feet, and it moved ever so slowly out my left side. I could feel the hum of its resonance throughout my body, and felt myself arch abruptly as soon as the beam commenced. All of my senses were acutely aware of it. I had become one with the land and could feel it as it was being healed, and I could feel it lifting itself up as if being released from under a heavy weight. I said the Prayer to release any lingering souls and called in the Light and Angelic help to assist. Many souls flowed into it and I sensed the land beginning to breathe with a sense of peace. It was only as this peace set in, that my body began to relax.

I was physically exhausted leading into this, but now my heart and soul were so vitally pumped with joy and adrenaline that I wanted to bring healings to the world. I knew that my body was strong because of how much it had endured over the years, and I was convinced that I could continue, but all I could feel around me were gentle smiles and impressions of gratitude. They told me, "*That is enough for now.*" Yet deep inside, I could not understand why they were stopping so soon.

Of course they were right. No matter how much I had felt exhausted before, for the next forty-eight hours I could barely crawl out of bed; my body needed to recover from the intensity of that beam of Light. As soon as I felt strong enough to open the Records again I asked about my connection to the mustang stallion.

They replied, "*You share the same soul. It is a powerful connection and the link has been accomplished. It is not necessary to meet again.*" Oh but I still wanted to, and needed to.

I asked for the teacher, and asked if I could have my energy patterns adjusted so that I could receive perfect clarity. I felt myself being led somewhere. I was standing at a metaphysical centre in Dublin Ireland and was told that I could work here. "*Is there anything that I need to do before I make contact?*"

"*Organize yourself and have focused clarity and intent. Believe and have faith that all is possible.*" Well I did not have focused clarity or intent yet, but I intended to.

I asked more questions. "*When I see somebody radiating an Angelic presence is it because they are a manifested Angel, or is an Angel with them?*"

"*You are sensing the Angel that is with them, though all life carries seeds of Angels.*"

Curious about broader ways of channeling energy, I asked, "*When channeling non-specifically directed energy, what is the best way to approach this?*"

"*Set your intent, the energy will follow. We will take the energy where it is needed.*"

I asked, *"In time, will I have access to more layers of understandings within the Light?"* I then received a powerful download of brilliant Light that radiated throughout my body.

Downloads can come as an energetic pressure behind the upper nose, in the forehead, around the temples, as a circular bead around the head, pressure at the base of the skull, or a combination of all of these. They may even come as surges of whole body energy rushes akin to what we feel after a sneeze, followed by a sense of knowing. We do not know what the information is consciously; we just understand that the knowing will come into our awareness at the appropriate time.

Jesus came and put his hands on my shoulders and the intensity of the Light increased. I watched, as if I was viewing in 3-D, as the inside of my body opened and responded to deep healings; my whole being flushed with gratitude.

I had one final question, *"Is there anything more that I can do as a surrogate for the Burren area of Ireland?"*

A Lord of the Records came to answer this. He told me, "*Yes, drink more water.*" I could feel his humour as I got up and did, and told him that it was good to feel it. I felt awash with it in response. As I sat back down, the left side of my head began to feel a great deal of focused pressure, as if someone was trying to unscrew something. Within seconds it felt as if I was undergoing psychic surgery, because there was a beam of Light going through the upper left side of my head and into my neck.

Remarkably gentle energies were surrounding me. I felt that they were trying to pull something out, but my mind soon drifted off to Eric and other people I had known and loved. Minutes later the probing stopped and the energy lifted. I was not aware of anything in particular that may have been healed, re-balanced or removed, but I felt total trust. I understood that on a spiritual level I was in full agreement. I sensed that I knew whoever was doing the surgery, and had total trust that my highest good was being honoured. Beyond having my curiosity piqued, I took it all in stride.

Jesus was still with me and seemed to want me to open in some way. I stood there unsure of just what or how I was meant to open, so we started walking and many levels and doors were opening. I called in all aspects of myself from all incarnations and dimensions that I existed in, so that they could merge with me now. I asked them to integrate fully and to open for healing. I also asked that Ireland open herself for healing and felt a deep sense of peace flowing from her in response, and, I asked for healings for all other energies that needed healing.

We continued walking through layers of corridors until we came to what seemed to be one final door. It was closed and we stopped in front of it. I asked the Lords of the Records that if they thought that I held anything remaining inside that still needed to be cleared or healed before I opened this door, could they help me now. My incarnations and other energies began flowing into me and I went increasingly deeper within, but my awareness was expanding proportionally to how deep I was going. I felt that I was transitioning through a major shift and was changing. Is that why this door had been closed? Was it important that I integrated those aspects before going further? It seemed so, because the door was beginning to open and my awareness began expanding in multiples.

Minutes later I woke out of a deep trance like state, not remembering what had lain beyond that final door. Healings had taken place on many, many levels and dimensions, and all with the most gentleness that I had ever experienced. I thanked this Lord of the Records and all others, and he told me once again to drink more water, be good to my body, and rest. Jesus then guided me back and I closed the Records.

Maureen and I visited the rock and gem show and many stones called out to us, but one stone in particular did something unique, it chased me down. I had the Ilmenite resting in my palm for a minute feeling its essence, and then I replaced it. As I moved away though, the vender purposefully ran up to me asking if I had seen the Ilmenite yet, and held it out for me. I almost broke out into amazed laughter. There had been many people around the table while I held it and the vender had been looking the other way. Obviously the Ilmenite and perhaps even the universe had influenced him to pick it up and chase after me, eager to tell me the story of its finding. OK I said with a smile, I would take you home with me. It was not until I approached a friend and asked her to look the energetic properties of this stone up that its true significance emerged. We were virtually shocked. Thank you universe!

Days later as I went into the Records I was surprised at the depth of telepathic communication, empathy and sharing that I experienced with the stones that we had brought home, and I feel a need to share this. Stibnite was the first stone that I asked about. As soon as I had walked within its range I had started to astral travel. *"Do I need to be in contact with Stibnite during journeying?"*

The Beings within the Records answered, *"It would help at this time. It will help you focus your awareness to communicate with Celestial Bodies and beings."*

I asked, *"Can I use Stibnite to assist others?"*

"In time, Stibnite is important."

Another question, *"What is the importance of Sphalerite to me at this time?"*

"This essence can help you to maintain focus on your centre and stay grounded. It is a shield stone that assists in connecting to the faerie realm, marine life and to solar flares."

When I focused on the Flourite I was surrounded by a gentle feminine presence, but before I could ask my questions I received a surprising eye opener. Maureen had just entered the house and I felt this awareness project its focus to the side entrance, verifying the identity of who had come in. Maureen was not in line of sight, yet this stone essence had recognized her energy and acknowledged that she was now in the house. After witnessing this level of awareness and consciousness from it, I talked to it directly. *"Is there a specific way that I can use you while offering energy work?"*

She answered, *"Yes, hold me over the 3rd eye, heart and lungs. My essence can help set you free. I work with the physical heart and spleen."*

I asked her, *"Do you have anything else that you want to tell me?"*

"Transmit love and kindness. Do not presume or assume anything about others. Recognize your frailty and the frailty of others. Know that Earth responds to attuned energies and separated energies in kind. Flowers are Earth's gift. Rejoice in your ascension, it is time to open. Have faith; the words you search for will come through compassion. The stone friends are assisting in re-activating DNA and RNA codes within you. These codes are in all physical forms, but activation can have the most profound effect on humans because of their degree of separateness from Source energy." This particular conversation was the first time that I had coherently communicated directly with a stone essence, and I felt pretty blessed.

Celestite was the next stone that I communicated with. *"Why have you come into my life at this moment?"*

"I can purify bowels to increase receptivity and awareness, and I am here to remind you to drink more water. I can clean your aura and increase your awareness to other stone people. I open portals into the Celestial and elemental realms. I can assist you to bring calm, gentle but powerful focus. I imbue the

focused intent of the Angelic realm. I work with the diaphragm, bones and muscular structure. I can remove contaminants from the blood, can purify water and air, and can help others during energy work. You must make a conscious choice to open for receiving the full benefit of what all stone manifestations have to offer. We are life forms that are here to assist in your understandings." Thank you, I now had deeper respect, understandings and appreciation.

Garnet was next, *"Garnet why have you come back to me?"*

"I can help ground you. I stimulate red blood cell growth and can help clear energetic blockages from your pineal gland. I help relieve organs of their toxins. I can imbue a golden protective energy through and around the body as I am held." I felt Archangel Michael's essence channeling through as this was said. It continued, *"I cannot tell you more until you release all doubt."*

Reaching for the Scapolite, I asked, *"Scapolite why have you come to me?"*

"I give warnings. I am a guardian to protect against low vibration Extra Terrestrials and others of low resonance. I am an Earth guardian and provide access to deep communion with the Earth. I offer balance and strength, and I am connected with the Amethyst and Green stone."

"Do you have anything else to tell me?"

"Truth reflects your being" I got a huge energy rush when this came through.

"Remember your truth, your Light, your Essence, and your song."

The final stone I was curious about on this day was Maureen's Green stone, so I asked, *"Green stone what is your significance?"*

"I ground and balance energies, and enhance joy and awareness. I anchor the energy of Light into the earth plane and work in co-operation with other beneficial energies. Lake Superior and the faerie realm await you. Nanticoke needs you. Be free and open." This last remark made me curious. Was this the earth around the coal plant that was asking me to assist it? As I projected my awareness towards Nanticoke I could feel a lot of dense energy there.

Eileen dropped around for a visit later so we did a combined opening of the Records. I asked about Nanticoke, and we learned that the Earth was concerned for her children. These children were not children in the context of human perception but they were still children, and they had taken on an unwarranted amount of density. These are energetic entities in a symbiotic relationship with the Earth, and their structure allows them free movement within the surface. Their original purpose was to assist the Earth in her evolution as a Celestial body, but for varying reasons many had become almost cancerous.

There were many pockets of these children, some small and independent, and some very large as a result of many of the smaller ones merging together. These entities were meant to be independent, but when the energetic density set in to a certain level they started to attract each other. This density was usually a result of either condensed and localized levels of human disregard, or mass psychic trauma. These children carried thought pattern constructs that were set in place when the Earth was young, but, because of their growing density they were unable to fulfill their symbiotic role. As a result, the Earth's ability to grow as a Celestial Being able to absorb and integrate higher vibrations of Light had become subtly, or not so subtly, compromised.

I was being asked to assist in re-awakening the old constructs within these children, channeling new templates into their awareness, so as they fully awakened, they would channel Grace and the higher energies of Love and Joy into the Earth. I was being asked to become the channel to transmute this density into Love. I understood why Nanticoke was brought to my attention. There was a large accumulation of these children there and they had reached critical mass as a result of the coal plant. I felt that I might need Maureen's help with this one.

I had a great sense of inner peace, clarity, and right purpose after this. The information flowed through the three of us and it all felt so right. This was much more of a reflection of who I was, and this was what I was capable of offering. I was meant for much more than the confines of a paycheck.

In the Records later, I was told, *"Remain open, go outside near water and be quiet. Receive, explore, and glide."* In perfect synchronicity, Maureen phoned, asking if I would like to go for a walk to the lake when she got home.

We started out at sunset and the colours in the sky were amazing, but as we reached the lake we were guided to continue on. Arriving at the dam we realized that this was where we were called to be. Our walk had been a bone chillingly cold walk as we pushed through the ice-encrusted snow to get here, but standing here, we felt ourselves beginning to warm up. We opened ourselves for channeling, feeling that this was why we had been called, and we asked the water's essence to accept the energies and carry them to all waters that it touched.

We stood side by side, beginning to channel, but soon Maureen was guided to stand behind me to act as an antenna, focusing and concentrating the energies through me. Not knowing that Maureen was focusing on my heart chakra, I felt a desire to open my heart and send love into the water. Minutes later, I opened my eyes and saw a water spirit hovering in the air before me, looking at me curiously. Around her the energies were all in flux. As far as I could see the water was literally sparkling with starry brilliance as the portal into the elemental world was opened. I turned to Maureen, telling her about the water spirit and the portal, and that I thought the channeling was finished. She came back alongside and we stood quietly waiting for whatever was to come next.

I was drawn to look up and spotted a UFO. My perceptions just seemed to be tuned in that way, so I asked them if they were here to help. There was no answer but I felt them tune into us. We identified them as Pleiadeans and said that if they were not here to help, then we would focus our attention back on the water. I felt a download starting at the base of my skull and knew that it came from them. I ignored it, and returned my glance to the water, only to find that water spirits now surrounded us.

They were curious, and moved in to touch us. Eventually they moved back and Maureen received a powerful channel. I had the impression of focused violet beams of Light shooting out of her eyes and into the water. I watched spellbound, the water was becoming subtly turbulent, then increasingly so, until its essence suddenly shifted as it became transformed into a higher vibration within the Light. Wow Maureen that was real cool. Vibrant joy now erupted amongst the water spirits and they were radiating a great sense of lightness. Looking around, the trees and riverbanks were full of them.

After spending joy filled moments with our new friends we set out for home, but I stopped and turned back to make a request. I asked that they help us to remember the many ways of fun, as in the man world many of these ways had been forgotten. I felt their appreciative smiles, and knew that they were willing to assist. An escort that seemed almost elfish supported us back up the hill, and I could not help observing them as they walked. The snow was knee high and crusty, but they seemed to float along its surface without leaving any imprints, even as they helped to balance us. Maureen and I in contrast sounded like huffing cows as we kept sinking in.

Curiously as soon as our escort fell away, though they were keeping pace with us from a distance, the bitter cold set back in. We had been standing almost motionless by the water for about an hour and a half and had been perfectly comfortable, now we hustled as fast as possible to maintain any semblance of warmth. We were to become overjoyed and surprised once again to find that our friends had followed us home. They crowded into the kitchen with us, and they were still with us when we went to our beds.

Looking at my reflection in the mirror the next morning I was surprised, well maybe not too surprised, to find that our elemental friends had integrated into my energy. I felt joyful but surreal acceptance. I loved their energies, and if I merged with them my life could only move in a direction that I had always been drawn to anyway.

Within the Records again I asked about my remaining stones. However, I was caught completely off guard when I heard the response to the Ilmenite's significance in my life. *"This is disruptive to your energy. The original composition has been altered and it is now radioactive. There has been a lower energy Extra Terrestrial influence in manufacturing this stones current state."*

Feeling stunned, I asked, *"Is this the reason that I have not been having a good sleep since I put it on my night table?"*

"Yes."

I set the Ilmenite aside, unsure what to do with it, and continued onto Sodalite.

I asked, *"Sodalite what is your purpose in my life?"*

"I enhance purity, inner balance, harmony and joy, and I am a connection to water and air spirits. I resonate with, and enhance the movement of fluids within the body. You are still dehydrated. Your fatigue, joint pain, and loss of concentration are all a result of not enough water." This repeated message to drink more water was really sinking in. *"I can also, once spiritual and heart oneness is established with my consciousness, take you further within inter-dimensionally. I can release some forms of energy attachments and other cellular toxins, and I can form a subtle protective function working in resonance with cyclic lunar waveforms. There is more, that in time you will understand."*

The last stone that I questioned was Tourmaline, *"Tourmaline why have you come back into my life?"*

"I assist in healing blood and bone disorders. I offer a re-connection to your chakras and heart centre. I remind you to keep your intestines purified and to honour your feet and body temple. I remind you to stay connected and enjoy."

After Maureen returned home, I asked her to verify the information that I had received about the Ilmenite. It was through trusting her nurturing instincts while talking to this essence that the true value and gift of this stone came through. There was confirmation to the information that I had received, but when she asked it directly if we could help it return to its natural state sincere gratitude washed over us and it opened its doors to reveal all that it was.

This became a most valuable lesson and reminder for me to go deeper into my heart at all times, so that my perceptions, responses and questions to anything that I encountered in life came from a place of greater heart awareness. I had forgotten to offer it nurturance. In fact to be more concise, I had not even considered offering it to a stone essence. Due to the passion in the Ilmenites response my inner doors opened to embrace an even greater sense of heart and soul connection.

Maureen asked the first couple of questions, and then we jointly asked. *"Tell us about yourself."*

As it responded, we could sense the depth of joy it felt in connecting with us. *"I am bare and discarded after the experimentation at the research facility. I have qualities that have remained hidden, even from the experimenters. I can cleanse and clear chakras and can raise body energy with a blast. I may also be life-saving with intention. My power can be modified to align with your energies without disrupting you. At this time my volume is turned high. I can take your energy, through intention, and focus it back amplified. You are honouring me by asking to work and co-operate with me rather than what the experimenters tried to do."*

Maureen said, *"You are safe now and we are asking for your assistance and knowledge in teaching us how to work with you."*

"Yes!!"

She continued, *"If we ask you and set our intention, can you moderate what has been done to you?"*

"Yes."

"Do you need John and I to assist you to heal?"

"Yes."

Now we asked our joint questions. *"Were you altered?"*

"Yes, the experimenters were trying to use me for amplification, and the underlying intent was not for the highest good of this planet. Humans performed the experiments but were influenced by lower energy Extra Terrestrials."

I asked, *"Are you here to help us change the constructs and install new templates into the Earth children's awareness?"*

"Yes, I can amplify your energies for this work. I am part of the key, as you are, but first I must return to my original integrity. My resistance during experimentation distorted my energetic structure." Maureen laughed, saying that she was a trauma therapist and that the Ilmenite had come to the right place. It continued, *"You can assist me to heal by focusing your pure intent*

and integrity into becoming open channels to source energies, and then within the Records have those energies channel through your hearts. Have both of your palm chakras in contact with me during this channeling. My origin is the source of the universe, and I can work together with Moldavite and other stones to assist you but not until I am fully healed."

We asked, *"After you are fully healed can you help us?"*

"Yes, willingly, that is why I am here."

I said, *"That is why we are all here."* We thanked this Essence and I thanked it again for influencing the vender at the gem show.

During a full lunar eclipse I set the intent to include the Earth in any dimension that it may exist in as the intended focus of my channeling. That was powerful, but two days later I had a more intense and profound experience that was to last over two hours. I called in Sai Baba's spiritual energy to assist in this channeling and the stones around me amplified his, and all of the healing energies greatly. I received many downloads during it, and as the waves of energy flowed through me I shifted into the higher vibrations.

I had a vision of dark trees blowing in a storm, and then the scene switched to an energetically dark male presence sitting on a throne, focusing on me. As if his will was projecting it to happen, the throne moved rapidly towards me. I felt him literally radiating intimidation and fear with focused intent, intent upon suppressing me. I told him *"You are who you are, and you have no power over me."* His expression changed into confused fear, though this time it was genuinely his, not an emotion he was trying to project in order to dis-empower me. With this, the whole image quickly dissolved. I had acknowledged his presence and right to exist, but at the same time I did not fear him, nor did I try to overpower him in return to protect myself. I had stood in the knowing of my own Essence, my own power, and my Light, and that was all it needed. I knew that he could not impose himself onto me unless I allowed it. Throughout this channeling I had stayed within the higher vibrations, and it would take me a long time to come out. I thanked the universe.

Days later I woke from a deep sleep at four in the morning knowing that I was opening myself to channel. I had not consciously made this decision, but obviously on some level I had agreed to it; also not seeming with conscious choice, I went into a deep meditative state as powerful energies started channeling through me. These were far more powerful and different than what I was used to. I could feel them spreading out like a veil as they encircled the world, and I could feel the Earth opening herself to receive.

During the next four and a half hours these energies continued channeling. It felt as if I had become a powerful yet subtle generator of rhythmic waves of energy. I felt honoured that my spirit and body had been willing to be the conduit, but I was now more than ever feeling the awe and wonder about exactly who or what my Essence truly was, to be so capable of being used like this. I had felt the nurturing gratitude of the Earth as she began receiving the energies, and once more it significantly enhanced my sense of her as a living entity.

In the coming days more specific awareness' came through: Malachi, Esther, Obadiah and Zephaniah. With surprise I sensed that I had known them.

I spoke to Malachi first and asked what the significance of his coming into my life was. *"I bring in Truth and lift distortion, opening your perceptions to greater discernment, self-esteem and balance. I help you to stand tall through self-knowing and love, and to hold your convictions. I remind you that your greatest strength is through an open heart and remaining centered. Have courage, faith and a joy of knowing."*

I asked him, *"What is important for me to know right now?"*

"You are of the Light of God." Hearing this I repeated it aloud three times. 'I am of the Light of God. I am of the Light of God. I am of the Light of God.' As I spoke each repetition, its resonance within my body and soul did quantum leaps, shifting and strengthening my energy. I felt more whole.

He continued, *"Get your message across through the quiet grace of God. Do not doubt the power of the Light channeling through. Your strength is not through confrontation but by opening your Essence. You carry the Christ consciousness. Absorb and transmute negativity, it has no power over you. Let it slide through leaving no trace or residue. The vibration of the lower energy will pick up some of your Light."*

Curious, I enquired, *"Will you be willing to give me your full teachings?"*

"Not all at this time but yes. Much that I spoke has been lost over time, and of what remains, there is only a glimmer of what was."

"Do Esther, Obadiah, and Zephaniah also wish to talk to me?"

"Yes."

"Are there others?"

I felt his smile as he replied, *"There are many, many others."*

I said, *"I open myself to whatever you need to say to me at this time."*

"Run with joy. Speak, and people will respond. You will amaze yourself thereby becoming free of old patterns. Speak and the door you seek will open wider. My voice as well as others will flow through you. Learn to sing; it will

help to open and balance your chakras. It is not 'your' fear that is holding you back; it is an energy imprint very deep down." I called in Michael to surround it with Love and Light and asked that it be transmuted for the highest good of all. I then called in the Light Beings to fill this spot with Light and healing energies.

I sensed myself being immersed in green, then greenish gold light, especially in my heart, diaphragm, and intestinal areas. Many more hooks and negative attachments became apparent. I called in Michael and the Light Beings, White Brotherhood and the Lords of the Records. As I felt their presence I asked for the healing vibrations of sound and colour to go to those places affected.

I asked if I had any spiritual contracts with any of these attachments that still needed to be honoured; *"Yes, there are some."* I said that I would honour any that were still relevant, but I asked to be released of all others that were no longer for the highest good. I felt things stirring and re-adjusting within, and I seemed to have a bit more focus. My pineal gland seemed to have opened more as well.

Malachi nodded and said *"Enough for today,"* then moved back. Thank you, Malachi.

I asked Esther to come forward and asked her why she had come into my life. *"Love. Remember Love and the ease of Forgiveness and Compassion; for it all helps to open the heart. There is truth through love. I open you to companionship, the animal kingdom, and greater nurturance with the Earth. I free emotions and help you rise above illusion. I am also an aspect of Sophia. Remember, heal through remembering and forgive."* I said the Acceptance prayer and could feel all that had gathered around me respond and go through healings.

Maureen brought up the forgotten ones and I brought up the ancient ones; the ones who were here before the onrush of people pushed them into the hills. They were one and the same. Their energy flowed into the room and we sensed their power. We felt that we were all re-uniting. We had felt their presence before, but the connection between us had now become more powerful.

Maureen was given the word Host, so I asked if this was Solomon's Host. *"Yes, but it is much more."*

"Is the White Brotherhood included in this Host?"

"Yes, the Host is inter-dimensional and encompasses universes. You are the only awakened keys at this moment, though there will be many more awakened amongst the crystal children."

I said, "*Esther, do you have anything more to say to me?*"

"*Live with peace and thank you.*" Thank you, Esther. She had surrounded me with a deep, all-encompassing and embracing love since we had begun our talk, and it warmed my soul. The immense loving connection I felt with her reminded me of being immersed in Scota's energy, but she said that they were not of the same essence.

I had one final question, "*Am I, as Eric Dilworth referred to, the guardian of Uisneach?*" I received a huge energy rush as I asked this.

Delighted, I heard her say, "*You are one of the guardians.*"

I was intending to close the records at this time but Zephaniah rushed forward.

I began receiving images of multitudes of books and sensed that it was important to begin research, though I did not know about what. I asked the librarians, teachers, and the Lords to assist me and I felt them gathering information. I could sense that on some level, I was reading and absorbing everything that was being brought. I thanked them for allowing me access to these records.

Jesus and others began gathering and formed a circle around me, but once the circle was complete, they did something that amazed me. Those within the circle did not move or change their positions, and the circle remained intact, but it began flowing in the motions of a mathematical sine wave before it flowed into different geometrical shapes. After this, I was told to honour my body temple, eat all natural foods to help flush my body of impurities, and raise the vibrational level of all food that I consumed. I found the vial of water that Peter had given me and attached it to the water intake.

"*Zephaniah, is there anything more that you would like to tell me at this point?*" "*No, all has been accomplished, go in peace.*"

"*And to you my brother,*" I said.

Before he left he showed his appreciation towards the stone friends that lay before us, and the stones were pleased to receive his attention. I closed the Records, thank you to all.

Maureen and I were to experience another multi-layered visitation. It began with her desire to lower her walls; she wanted to come to the inherent knowing of her own power, her own Light. The fear based walls that she had put up to protect herself over the years, as I once had, were an illusion that kept humanity unbalanced and disconnected from Source energy. We asked Michael to assist her to understand the power of her true spiritual strength.

She was having a hard time trusting this, so her spirit helpers came to assist and guide her. Minutes later a powerful energy filled the room and I turned to see Quan Yin, in fact only her head, looking at us. I was awestruck. Not so much by the fact that it was Quan Yin, but it was in how proportionate her head was to the room. It was strikingly, though with emphatic awareness filling one quarter of the room from floor to ceiling. She did not say anything but seemed focused on holding the space. Archangels Raphael and Ariel appeared and channeled healing energy into us. Gabriel also appeared, though she stood quietly back, observing.

Our feet were touching already, but we were led to hold hands to form a circuit. As the energy looped and surged between us it increased in intensity until it flowed powerfully within us, forming three figure eight's. Maureen inquired about it, but I laughed at the human need to always understand. I felt Raphael's amusement.

After many minutes they left, but within seconds a more powerful energy filled the room and Gabriel returned, this time bringing in Kryon. Michael now appeared with others. They acknowledged us but remained in the background. None of them appeared to have come to talk, though they seemed intent on a purpose. We were suddenly buffeted as wave after wave of energetic downloads washed through us. Was this why Quan Yin had come in first; so that she could buffer the energy that Gabriel and Kryon were bringing through? Was this what Raphael and Ariel prepared us for energetically? The energy rapidly intensified in our bodies and I visualized myself being separated into finely diced cubes. They maintained the integral structure of the whole, but as I watched they expanded and spread apart. I sensed that within each cube the energies knew exactly what to do, and I felt as if my cells and other minute particles were being altered or re-programmed. I could only assume that we were being energetically and physically re-aligned. I felt surreal awe from the experience, but total trust.

This encounter seemed to last minutes and left us in a bit of a daze, but as it finished I saw the happy gratitude of all those who had gathered. One by one they stood before us, bowed in honour, and left. We felt blessed, honoured, protected, and as usual quite intrigued by it all. Soon after, elemental beings appeared to assist us to re-activate and tune into memories that we had once known.

Days later I re-opened the Records and asked, *"How am I connected to the Elohim?"*

"You are a vehicle of the Merkabah, a gateway, a soul star shining. You are as Gandalf, a wizard, a star seed. You are Morpheus brother of Connaught, you are indigo."

As I heard this some of my pent up frustration from not moving forward as fast as I thought I should surfaced and I asked, *"What is holding me back?"*

"Memories are holding you. Believe in your core essence. Open your heart to love all that is, and trust." Another download began. *"What you thought was solid or real will fall away to reveal your true Essence. You will see Light pathways, other dimensions, and beings. You will be the Overself body of Light."*

My mind drifted and I thought of Maureen's healing stones. *"Can you tell me more about Maureen's healing stones?"*

"There is a higher being connection with them. Their work is separate from yours but of mutual benefit within the Light. It is your choice if you choose to open to them but they are beneficent beings. Trust your heart and intuition in any dealings with them or any other beings."

"Is there anything else that is important for me to know at this time?"

"Yes, stay open and receive. Do not doubt. All will be. The Keys of Enoch and Urantia books are important."

I called in Malachi for more clarity and he said, *"Remember. Research hidden archives and read. Look for Keys. Open your soul."* I opened to Jesus and felt pressure in my head. I could feel him looking through my eyes, but more than this, I sensed him looking out through the entirety of my awareness. I opened to fully and consciously become part of the One, and as I opened to the merkabah I gave up all need to hang onto my ego self. I felt a huge energy rush.

Maureen and I signed up for the 2nd level of the Akashic Records and it was to open us to a dimension of understandings that broadened our awareness immensely. Through learning the 1st level we had learned to open specifically into our own Records to gain greater information and understandings about our own lives. In this 2nd level, we were to learn how to access the Records of other people, animals, and more, so it was to be a much more in-depth level.

In the days preceding this course, something happened that intrigued us all. Eileen was still in shock as she recounted her experience. She had been approached by an extremely high vibrational feminine energy, an energy that was much higher than anything that had shown itself in the Records before. Initially she could not handle its vibration, but since, this energy had moderated itself to come into harmony with the human body. She felt that it had come in specifically in time for this weekend, and that it was important. She believed that because this energetic presence had passed through them, the Akashic Records themselves had taken a quantum leap forward in evolution.

Eileen asked us to collectively bring this energy into the group, and as we did, we felt an immensely powerful awareness. We sensed that this awareness held an unlimited expansiveness of perception, and agreed that it was way beyond any of our previous concepts of a universal being. She radiated a distinct sense of intelligence and purpose. We wondered just how much she must have had to moderate her energies to even come into this universal dimension. We sensed only a glimmer of her entirety, but felt the nurturing warmth that she radiated; yet there was also a feeling of indifference.

We felt that her presence at this time in the Earth's history was significant. People within the last few years had become increasingly aware that lighter vibrations of energy and Light were flowing into the Earth, and transformations were happening. Many have termed this as transitioning into the New Earth, where Heart awareness and joy become the new state of consciousness. I was not sure at this point, but I sensed that she had come to observe and possibly influence which direction humanity decided to go. Our choice seemed to be whether we collectively chose to move towards higher consciousness and love, or towards ongoing separation. It seemed that either way she would be assisting the Earth to evolve into a higher Celestial state of being. Humans may just be placed somewhere else if we unconsciously chose to continue living our lives within lower vibrational patterns.

We felt that this was the feminine aspect of the Divine emanations of the God Source itself, or at least as much as this universe could handle. We passed through a range of emotions; honoured that she seemed to have specifically chosen to come to us, awed, full of curiosity, but also greatly humbled, as we felt very small compared to her. She quickly honoured us in return, grateful that we had opened the door for her to come into our awareness. The date was March 23rd 2007.

We decided to call her Beatrice, though she seemed beyond the need for a name. Her gentle acknowledgement and appreciation surrounded us as she scanned its meaning. It meant the 'Blessed voyager through life'. Eileen felt that she might be a new archetype, so we honoured her as Lady Beatrice.

We learned that it was important to always verify any information or presence that came to us in any spiritual form, and that it was in direct alignment with the Christ consciousness. A good way to verify this was to focus our thought, surround whatever it was with Light, and then say out loud, '*Are you, or is this information aligned with the highest Light of the Godhead and the Christ consciousness.*' Say this three times. If it is aligned it will maintain its essence and integrity; if it is not, it will not be able to hold its form and will begin to dissipate by your third repetition.

I must note though, that if you are not grounded and centered, and the underlying energy that you are projecting with these words is fear based, the power of them becomes empty and you will just be going through the motions. You must believe in yourself, your own power, and your own right to equal existence. You will find that if you come from your heart, truly from your heart, as you say these words, the power of them becomes amplified many times over. It is a gentle and compassionate power. Imagine it as being able to move a mountain with only the gentlest of breezes.

Beatrice informed us, "*Re-define your limits to perception. Allow yourself to expand into realizations not limited by previous belief structures, for there are no limits.*"

I opened my heart to her and she gently and respectfully entered all levels of my being. It seemed that the groups' opening to her and allowing her to integrate into our energies was her most important goal at this time, as she now withdrew a little so that we could carry on. She was now anchored into human consciousness and manifestation, and could draw or channel her energy through us as we were ready.

As we entered the Records from here on in, we were to enter them with the intent and the knowing that these were now the new Records. The new Akashic Records hold the same resonance of vibration as the New Earth vibration that we are moving into. They hold the resonance of the Divine Heart, and all humanity, as they come more fully into their own hearts will automatically have access. Eileen asked us to enter the Records both ways to see how we related to any differences, and there was a noticeable difference to all of us. In entering the new Records there was a far greater feeling of expansiveness, possibilities for a higher level of information, and change. The new Records are connected to the unified field and we were strongly advised to enter them as a blank slate, with no pre-conceptions.

With the new energy that the Lady brought into this reality, humanity had the ability to evolve their spiritual contracts into a higher frequency of being. In many ways, because of the third dimensional reality that we had embodied, the potential for consciously experiencing full spiritual growth had been stunted. We have achieved, in the Divine scheme of things though, a great deal of spiritual growth. To humanity as a whole over the millennium our experience had felt more as if we were floundering. The third dimensional reality had been our choice. I can base these statements only on what I have learned, but we had agreed to partake in it to experience the full range of separation from Source. In a sense we had created this reality to be a training ground, with many opportunities to learn, and finally, to make the decision to return to higher states of consciousness. We need only allow the knowing that all possibilities are now truly possible. Through intent, taking responsibility and accountability for our lives and choices, inner work, and making the firm commitment to move fully into our hearts, we have the opportunity to integrate the full creative potential of our spiritual or Light bodies into our physical bodies. Beyond that, we have the greater potential to make room for the higher vibrations of the God Source itself to flow into our lives. We have been given the opportunity to return consciously into the higher vibration of the heart. If we choose to step in this direction, we will literally move into becoming the Christ aspect of our self on Earth. We all carry that seed. This will raise our vibrations out of the third dimensional vibrations. Our choice is individual, and collective.

When Eileen began opening the new Records for the group as a whole, my body awareness eagerly tuned in and focused with joyful anticipation. It had recognized that something special was coming. Perhaps, it was remembering a long dormant ancestral memory, from a time when we were harmoniously connected between body, heart and Divine spirit.

We were to live within the new Records with the spiritual authority of having recognized, accepted, embraced, claimed and anchored in our spiritual power within this physical manifestation.

This power is our Divine birthright. This ultimate permission, which the Lady Beatrice is relaying, about claiming and anchoring in our spiritual power, is intended for humanity as a whole to encompass. Much of humanity feels, and/or believes that they, for one reason or another do not have this approval, or that they are not worthy enough to receive it. Encompassing this will allow a shift into experiencing empowered spiritual freedom, and will open humanity to the experience of greater joy, and the comprehension of fuller understandings.

Eileen advised us to call in the Archangel that was assisting us the most at this time, and we were to ask that we be handed a mandate. As the Archangel stood before me I envisioned him holding a golden scroll radiating a golden energy. He reached forward to hand it to me, but I found with surprise that my first reaction was a deep-seated uncertainty and I was reluctant to accept it. Was I truly capable of fulfilling what they ask of me? I did accept it though, and as the scroll unfolded an all-encompassing golden Light surrounded and immersed me. I began to remember that I know this Light, and a sense of inner peace and comfort flowed from my core.

I asked how to embody the guidance of the scroll and the Archangel replied, "*Love. Have deep love and acceptance for your own Essence. Trust in the truth of your Divine Self. Know that you are safe and we are here.*"

Eileen suggested we ask our Archangels for more clarity about the new Records, "*What are the new Records for me and how can they be of service in my life?*"

"*Feel the experience. Thoughts are not important, only awareness and focus. Flow with the current of awareness. Be one with it. Decide on action, then use focused intent to manifest it. Honour self. Honour all that is. Be humble but in your own power. You are the one who sees, who opens, and who is. You can blend into any new higher vibrational patterns by tapping on your heart or body to assist the coming together of spirit and matter.*"

"*Is there a new mandate from my body?*"

"*Yes, LET GO and BELIEVE.*"

In many ways this was what my journey had become; really letting go of the old limiting thought patterns, beliefs, fears, and way of being. I was fully aware that they were holding me back. This letting go may be a continual work in progress, and there may be many layers to it, but at least it had begun. I could not, and would not turn back.

I felt a joyful excitement about that weekend's course, and a growing curiosity, especially since Beatrice was introduced. I asked the Archangel, "*What is the most important thing that I need to learn during this weekend?*"

"*Continue opening and expanding your heart awareness and feeling its interpretations. Heart awareness takes precedence over conscious awareness. Be aware of ego and honour your instincts. Share, grow, and spread your wings. Do not hesitate by doubting, you must learn to thoroughly trust and respond to intuition. If you feel any resistance, no matter how subtle, hold your Grace points and send the intent that they help ease the resistance. Then breathe in peaceful energies.*"

"*Who am I in the new Records?*"

"You are a winged one, of the bird tribe. You are pure heart awareness. You have clear inter-dimensional and universal sight. You have scrolls available to you that contain immense openness to knowledge. You breathe fire energy, the energy of transformation and change."

"What is my reason for being in Peterborough?"

"It is to anchor a pillar of Light. It is a time of transmutation of your soul's unfolding into joy. A book is to be written here. You can connect your awareness anywhere through the trees and winged ones. You are within a Divine matrix of Light. It is all around, above, and below. Recognize it and claim it. Refresh this knowing everyday through your breath; I AM THAT I AM. Become an integral part of this Divine matrix. Create a field around your house, yourself, your loved ones, your animals, and everywhere that you go. Be aware of your shadow self."

We then separated into pairs so that we could practice going into other peoples Records, and Maureen and I eagerly paired off.

My question was, *"How do I go into the deepest layers of my Essence to heal all that needs healing?"*

"Your intention in its purest form will accomplish all that you set forth to accomplish. Be aware of the daily patterns and issues that arise as they will be your guide to go deeper within. Your guides and helpers from all realms will support you in awakening to those aspects that need to be cleared and healed. Be patient with yourself as you race ahead." Maureen laughed as she was shown an image of me and me and me, racing against me and me and me. She finished by saying, *"Turn your patient and loving heart towards yourself."*

We had brought Maureen's healing stones so I spoke to them, *"Do you have any advice from your level of awareness?"*

"Feel your connection to manifestation and learn to honour it. You are not stagnant beings but must learn to understand the ascension process of physical planes of existence. Honour all steps along the way and all who help you. The Earth nurtures, if you have difficulty feeling this nurturance, allow yourself to open your heart to receive."

As we paired off with new partners, my question was, *"What is it that I need to know about my issue with myself?"*

Barbara's reply was, *"So deep is this river."* She was shown a panoramic vision of a Shamanic no man's land; a field of plain and earth, a land of lost souls. More specifically, she understood it to be a place leading into a journey of darkness, a journey that went into the dark night of the soul.

She continued, *"This is a descent that you can make. This is a journey into your fears. The depth of your descent into darkness will determine exponentially the extent of the Light that you will move into at the end of it. You will need help in this place of lost souls to retrieve something that was stolen from you. It is a symbol or emblem of your power and is part of your spirit. The person who can help you is a person of deep heart, an ancient Shaman of the heart. This is the spirit of the one supporting you now, but there are other teachers on earth. A dialogue is needed between the Shaman and yourself within the Records to find the person of heart most suited.*

This is a private journey and you must fast first. This is medicine. Your gifts are great but you must regain this missing part before you can move forward. It is important to let go of your past emptiness. When you go there is a river, and its water is sacred for you. Retrieve some of this water to hold the part of your spirit that has been lost. If possible, immerse yourself in this water. If you cannot find the river, ask the Shaman for a vial of it. This container of water will facilitate your rebirth. You will be a different person and great secrets will be returned.

Say the prayer of Light five times daily to fully integrate it into your Essence before you start your journey. As you move into the darkness the stars will remind you of the Light. Bring around yourself all of the supports that you can and if possible, create an Altar with what calls."

The Prayer of Light mentioned was my version of the Centering prayer that Eileen had given as part of her teaching. I revised it in a way that I resonate personally with, though I have made spur of the moment adjustments to it. This prayer will work best for you if you phrase it in a way that you can feel its resonance within your own spirit.

I bring my attention to my heart, to the place of my Divine eternality, the place that is all Loving and all Knowing. I ask this 'Light' of my eternal nature to embrace the Light of all that I AM, in all times, places and dimensions.

I feel the resonance of the Divine Light of the New Earth's awareness and of the Source of Creation within my own Light. As I become aware of my breath, the Light fully enters my heart and flows through the entirety of my Essence, enhancing my experience of Divine Love and Peace as it brings all into harmony.

I ask this Light that is my eternal nature to flow outwards into the infinity of the Divine, and as I bring this Light back into my heart, I become the conscious knowing that I am fully inter-connected and One with the uniqueness of all that is Creation. I am the manifested expression of Infinite Love and Light. I AM THAT I AM and I am Grateful.

Hearing this message through the Records I began feeling trepidation as to what was approaching. I yearned for the fullness of all that I innately was, but I think that I had equal fears between coming fully into my Essence and power, and continuing living feeling half empty. Truly being happy, creative and fully out there, and succeeding at anything that I desired, knowing that there were unlimited possibilities was still hard to grasp. My ingrained fears of all that had ever negatively impacted onto me felt almost more in my comfort zone than exposing myself unrestrainedly to the world. This place of inner fear was afraid of change, no matter how much better my life would become. I had survived so far with this, and all of the unknowns of fully claiming my power were stirring up a lot of stuff, stuff that was turning my insides into a quagmire. My heart in my boots, and with some genuine surprise, I determined to continue to move forward to be all that I was. This time, with much more poignancy, I placed my trust in the Divine and the still expanding place of knowing within.

I had an experience a while later as I walked through the woods. It was a disturbing lesson on awareness, and how to be more discerning of situations we might walk into that are best to avoid. There had been a deep fog surrounding the sanctuary as we arrived, and we sensed a feeling of distortion everywhere. The person I was with and I looked at each other in curiosity, commenting on how unusual everything felt. As we started our hike the fog and air began to pulsate in waves from the ground up. The more that we walked, the more agitated, nauseous and unbalanced we felt, so we had to cut our hike short and leave. It felt as if we could almost reach up and touch a UFO.

I came back later with Maureen, and though the fog and distortion had lifted, it still felt unusual. As we walked Extra Terrestrial beings came around us that carried a much lower energy than us. We called in the Light Beings to keep us safe and continued walking, and soon left them behind. They had not been heart-centered beings. Shortly after, wood sprites greeted us with playful joy and I sensed one going into Maureen's energy. It began looking out of her eyes, and as Maureen spoke I realized that she was channeling this sprite.

I asked her about the Extra Terrestrials and what they were doing here.

She responded, "*They have been coming here a long time and are using the mineral formations underground to refuel. They suck up the essence they need energetically. At first, before we knew how to respond to it, they caused severe disruptions to the Earth. Over time we have learned to modulate exactly how* much they can receive. If a situation ever arises that a critical level is reached we now have an ability to totally shut them out. Earlier, you were caught in a time/space distortion caused during their siphoning of the energy."

I went into the Records later to get greater clarity on the encounter with the Extra Terrestrials. *Is there a way to protect ourselves in the future from walking into a similar experience?*

"*Yes, listen to your inner voice so that you are aware as you are approaching a situation that may be best avoided. Surround yourself with a protective cone of Light. Intend to remain centered, balanced and protected. Allow your energies to match the frequencies of the surrounding energies, but maintain your intent that they retain their intrinsic structure. Flow with the energies; do not fight against them. We are all one. Allow the energies to pass through knowing you are one. Intend and know that as these energies flow through they can leave no trace or disruption. Learn to believe this, there is no room for doubt. Doubt leaves an open doorway to disruption.*

This is like the Matrix movie, but with differences. You are a vial of Light. All outside will try to take you away from your centre and push you into the abyss. You can observe the abyss for what it is. Do not feel above or caught into it. You just ARE. All else is a kaleidoscopic projection. Observe. Seek out the source, both within and without, and heal through loving acceptance. Come from a deep place of love and stillness. Allow compassion for yourself for holding these images. In awakening to new understandings within the Light, it will help raise you to a higher vibrational tone."

I asked for the ancient Shaman within the Records. He approached and said, "*Help will come from many sources, many unexpected. We honour you. You hold much pain and emptiness. All this can be healed within the Light.*"

I requested his guidance to prepare for my inner journey, and asked for higher dimensional awareness to show me how to pass through my layers of fear and pain. I understood that nothing within these layers had power to intimidate or harm me unless I gave them the power to do so. I had no desire to harm them.

I asked Beatrice a question "*Is there anything else that I need to know at this point in time?*"

"*Feel free and breathe. Feel joy, get rest, exercise. Read, prepare, and remain open. The Lady Gabriel will help. Connect with nature and its spirits. Strengthen your body, mind and spirit, and learn to focus with precise intent. It is important to empty your mind and follow your inner guidance, for you cannot see the whole arena. Your mind will diminish your effectiveness if you are not clear. Center and ground your essence. Remember that your body is* much more than you have assumed. Your body is your body temple and is the living organism of Light and Love that houses your spirit."

Reflecting on this in a slightly different way, we are the living organisms of Light and Love that house our planet, and our planet, Gaia, is the living organism of Light and Love that houses and nurtures us.

I sensed myself as a Light Being in a symbiotic relationship with both my body and the Earth. I felt sincere gratitude in thanking them for supporting, carrying, and protecting me in this manifested world until the time came when I had grown enough to understand and support you. I was now in real communication with my body and cherished the feeling of mutual honour and joy. As I spoke these understandings, Gaia embraced me as if she was cradling me in her arms, expressing the deep emotions of a mother who was witnessing her child open its eyes for the first time with awareness. She was radiating the love and gratitude of knowing that another Celestial Being had just awakened.

Beatrice continued, *"Fear is sabotaging you. It is not real but it is hindering you from seeing your worth. Feel gentleness and love towards yourself and it will diminish the hold that this illusion has on you. Honour your core Essence and all Celestial help. Know that your ego is tripping you up by thinking that lower Angels and guides are not worthy of your attention. You must work on becoming clear in all ways. We love you but you must not lose sight of all who can help you."*

I asked, *"Is it in my highest good to do my soul journey in the coming weeks?"*

"No, you are not ready. Drink lots of fluids. Feel yourself living within the Light constantly. Fill your lungs and body with as much fresh air as possible. Eat nutritional, balanced and high vibration meals. Strengthen your rapport with the heart Shaman, and wait for the coming together of another heart presence. You carry fear within your cellular and karmic memories that is continuing to cause you to stumble. Gabriel can assist you."

"Is there anything else that I need to know?"

"Show Gratitude and be humble and sincere. Offer the purity of your heart and discern the intentions of everyone around you by feeling with your heart. Ask to open more into your own heart. All energies you can learn from. Think of it as classroom learning. Surrender to the experience and open your arms to all that is. Believe fully in your own Divine Essence and become a compassionate observer, without fear or judgments. Focus clear, unencumbered thought and channel it into your being. Trust, relax your mind and stop dwelling on lack. Visualize prosperity and Light immersing you at all times. Abundance is created through giving abundantly with an open heart. Have joy; all will be as it is

meant to be. Jesus will help you retrieve that which has been removed from you but there is also a feminine energy that will help. I will help prepare you and will watch over you on your journey.

Learn. We will guide you in the birth of a new creative Essence. Open your heart and sing a song to embrace this living creation. The resonance will help it grow within your heart. Love and nurture it. Balance your awareness between an empty mind and focused intent. It is detached mindfulness. Channel healing love and bring it into manifestation. Rest, drink water, and then drink more water. Eat vegetarian or pure organic non-compromised foods of high vibrational vitality. Flush the toxicity from your body. Make a conscious choice to purify your vibration in all ways.

Read Seth Speaks and other Seth books, read the Kryon books, Urantia, Children of Light, Right Use of Will, and others. Peter and Raven and the Light School Body in Peru are important. Let go, we will catch you. We have primed you, and you are now ready for the re-birth of the Divine child. Honour thyself. This fragment feels your resonance and is agitating to re-unite. Intend it, visualize it, embrace, honour, cherish, taste, and hold it. Envelop it within your loving Light. Your Light is leading you and we are coming to assist. Your Essence is strong and becoming stronger the deeper you go. Others are channels of Light and Love for you. Kryon and Gabriel are aware and assisting.

The means for abundance are manifesting around you. Teach yes, but through example. The Ilmenite is ready. Other stones await your clear focused desire, and will help you manifest through them. The elementals will help you go to deep places. Call upon your soul horse and the animal realm. Call upon Horus. Find the silence. Become the silence. Speak, create, play, sing, and love. Focus your desire from the foundation of your Light within. All will flow into place.

Continue meeting and integrating with other dimensional aspects of yourself. You are all one being experiencing multiple and ever expanding levels. You may call on all other aspects when greater clarity or understandings are needed, as you will be able to tap into their awareness.

Remain open, clear, and pure of heart and intent. Continue inner healings. Continue attunement with the Earth realms. It will deepen your inner Light and conviction of truth. You will become a lighthouse. Acknowledge, understand, and release fear for what it is. It is a separation from, and a distortion of Divine Light essence. Created reality is what you focus upon. Remember your Essence is Light. Darkness is only overlapping layers of separation and density. Do not focus through fear, but through knowledge of the connection of your own Essence within the Divine Light. That is why healing of self within all *layers is permanent. You are one within the Light within your own cellular Essence. Remember this truth. This directly affects the minds perceptions and reactions. Become fully present in the Now."*

As time went on I came to realize that I had a connection to the Blue Flame. I could feel its presence expanding in my energy, but what exactly it signified I did not know. I asked for verification and clarity.

"The Blue Flame is a living aspect of the Blue Star. It is inter-dimensional in its scope and originates in a higher vibrational consciousness field. Through you it brings joy and hope. You are a forerunner, an anchor. Become the embodiment of it, and transform and evolve into new life energy. The Blue star vibration alters cellular structure, breaking up density. Combine this vibration with the vibration of Divine Love and see all from the heart."

As I absorbed this, my mind went to Ireland. *"What is important for me to complete here before I return to Ireland?"*

"Believe in yourself and open to your hearts' song. Permit abundance to flow in and through you. Release fear and judgment of self. You hold onto the feeling of unworthiness. You hold onto the fear of opening and expressing the full creative, empowered and loving Essence of who you are. Sing, feel joy, dance, play, and write."

I was unfortunately, still all too aware of my fear of fully expressing myself, so this message had hit deep. I set the intent to keep working on this, and then changed the subject. *"Can my staff be used to balance chakras?"*

"Anything can balance or clear chakras through intent. Think outside the box. Think outside of physical manifestation. Become a co-creative force within the Light. Flow with the energy. Do not try to contain it. Focus your intent into a moving spiral of energy, and then release it so that it may carry out your desire.

Ease your concerns; answers will come as your heart opens. Mindfulness will help. Exercise and cleanse. Eliminate toxins; they are affecting your clarity and vitality. Drink water, you are still dehydrated."

I had another thought, though I would not be surprised if this thought actually came from my guides. *"Will Sacred Geometry help in raising these vibrations?"*

"YES!!"

"Do I already have the Sacred Geometry symbols in my energy field to accomplish this?"

"Yes, call upon them."

The first time that I had met Maureen at her house, she had downloaded these symbols into my energy field as part of the Mayan Light language.

I discovered that I had harbored an underlying doubt that it had actually happened. Receiving this verification became another sign that focused intent and knowing that it will happen, works; I called upon the symbols and sensed them at work within my energy field. Through this simple re-enforcement, of sensing them at work within my own energy field, it became a valuable lesson in removing any doubt associated with my own ability to call upon them.

The following week Maureen and I were at Silent Lake again, and the energy was perfect for setting the stage for the Ilmenite. We determined to leave the Records open for the duration of our stay; we wanted this time to be experienced entirely within the energy of the Records. It would turn out; that after these few days, we would never leave the Records again, they would always remain open.

Late one night, under a perfectly clear and starry sky, Maureen and I sat on the rocks by the beach and let ourselves be carried away by the display of northern lights. There is something soothing, even primal, about sitting beside a quiet lake and looking into the night sky.

In the daylight hours to come, we intended to hike to an island on Bonnie's Pond trail that we felt ideal for performing our ceremony. As we arrived at the trailhead though, a thunderstorm had set in. I called on the air elementals, asking their help in creating an opening in the storm. They immediately responded, and with surprised joy I instantly communicated with them and was informed that the storm would soon pass. I sensed many elementals, both air and land waiting around to join us.

We waited until the rain had almost stopped and stepped out of the car, but were told that it was not safe yet, so we climbed back in. A few minutes later, under blue skies, we started our hike with our new friends surrounding us warmly. I had been on this trail before, but I never had certain things stand out to me as much as they did now. There was a sense of vibrancy in the air and it felt as if we were passing through standing stones. I wondered if the expanded perception that I was experiencing was related to consciously being within the Records. After we passed what appeared to be a sentinel stone, I was drawn insistently to a large rock outcropping whose energy reminded me of Ireland. I explained to Maureen that there was something here that we were supposed to find.

Curious, she jiggled the loose fragments at a juncture of cracks and I knew instantly that that was it. Whatever it was that called us was hidden behind those fragments. When we pulled them away we found an almost flat, clean, and smooth interior rock face. We understood with certainty now that this is what had been calling. As I placed my palm on it I knew that it was a teacher and Maureen confirmed it. She angled her walking stick and I angled my staff into the opening, crisscrossing them. A surging flow of energy started channeling both ways; from the teacher into us, and from us into the teacher. We were not sure if we were downloading something to it, but it felt as if something was being pulled out of our energy fields.

After it finished we thanked the teacher and took one of its stone fragments to help us remember the experience. As soon as my foot touched the path I was pulled back to the sentinel stone and guided to place the fragment onto it. I was instantly engulfed in a wave of energy and transformed into a deep altered state, and had to lean on it. I became one with this stone, and for what seemed minutes; I felt its waves of energy clearing my essence into the depth of my cells. I was left in a surreal state of amazed curiosity.

Had the fragment of stone been a key to open a portal? Was it a key that combined the energies of the two stones so that something within me could be aligned, transformed, or healed? Was the original intent that I had been called to the rock face to facilitate a transfer of information between the two stones, or between the three of us? What was the underlying reason I had been drawn to the teacher? I did not know, but whatever the reason may have been, or the end result, I expressed immense heartfelt gratitude to both.

Feeling much clearer and lighter on some deep inner levels I walked back to Maureen and told her of my experience.

As we arrived at the little island there was a feeling of sacredness that I had never noticed before. It felt welcoming, and it set the perfect atmosphere for the ceremony. We stood on the granite boulder and watched as dozens of dragonflies hummed in unison, weaving their way through the air. The arms of a beautiful large protective pine tree overlapped over our heads, and as we looked out over the pond we saw the abundance of water lotus resting gracefully atop their lily pads. Kneeling, we placed the Ilmenite in the sunlight on top of the granite and called in all four elements; fire, water, earth and air, asking if they could help with the clearing and re-balancing of the Ilmenite's energy. Thinking back to our arrival at the trailhead, maybe this was why we had been greeted and escorted by so many elementals. They had known our intent.

We placed our hands on the Ilmenite, and with Maureen's hand over mine we asked those within the Records, and the elementals to help us energetically channel what was to be our part in this healing. Emptying our minds, we opened our hearts and let be what would be.

As we felt the channeling finish, we looked at the Ilmenite with warmth, feeling its response. Satisfied, we expressed our gratitude to all that had assisted, and then quickly had to leave as another thunderhead rumbled ominously overhead. The Ilmenite felt energetically happier and lighter, and so did we. By the time we arrived back to the car the sky had cleared again so we decided to go for a swim. This was magical. In slightly different ways for each of us, it became the culmination of some deep inner clearing. It was for me, also a re-connection.

On and around the outcropping of rock the connection between the Earth, sun, water, and the goddess energies seemed powerfully enhanced. Under it, I sensed a nest of water snakes. A blue heron kept flying over us, adding its energy to set the stage for the experience, and the clearings that we were about to have.

I felt a deep inner need to swim off alone. Something was stirring within, compelling me to swim far out into the bay. I did not realize until I reached the spot that I had chosen why I had to. I was about to experience a profound transformation and it was important that I be alone, and totally within the Earth's watery embrace. I asked the Earth Goddess, Michael, and Rafael, to gift me with their healing and connecting energies, so that any lower energy that I held inside could be transmuted. Closing my eyes, I stretched out on my back and instantly became enveloped in swirling high vibrational energies. I asked to be cleared and that all doors into my Essence become fully opened and filled with joy. Before I had finished speaking these words, an image of a giant whirlpool, with pale green and murky brown colours flowing into it filled my vision. The colours, I knew, were being drawn out of me.

I swam below the surface and curled my body into a cannonball position, intent on experiencing myself inside the womb, asking to be re-born. I then visualized it. Seconds later, I opened my eyes and experienced a state of surreal awe. I was looking at my arms and hands floating as if seeing them for the first time, and then I looked at my legs and feet in some wonder. My limbs had become completely surrounded by a radiant glow. I visualized myself as a Light Essence merging into physical form inside the womb. All of my senses felt acute, as if this experience was actually happening.

Returning to the surface the world had changed, and I experienced myself on the surface of a primordial ocean. I felt creation happening around, and within me. I felt the undersea vegetation pulsing oxygen precursors into the water, and I had an inner knowing that the sea was the lifeblood of the planet. I witnessed as Celestial energies cascaded through the Earth's atmosphere and flowed into the water. I felt the creation of life happening around me, and I sensed the living entity that is the Earth responding with loving gratitude.

Suddenly, a giant serpent surfaced and swam towards me, raising its head. As it opened its mouth I told myself that regardless if it swallowed me or not, I would not be killed. My Light was eternal and I would re-manifest at my leisure. The serpent seemed to have heard, and understood, for it stopped for a minute to appraise me and then swam away. I wondered if it had anything to do with my serpent or kundalini pendant. I had called on the energies of the pendent to help re-balance the Ilmenite today, so perhaps this serpent in some peculiar way helped to re-balance me through re-enforcing a spiritual knowing. *We are infinite Beings within the Divine, living an experience in form.*

I was in an altered state as I stepped out of the water, and could see the shimmering, silvery translucent energies of my aura. I was glowing, and my body felt infinitely more alive. Lying down I placed my palm on the Ilmenite and serpent pendant, merging their energies into mine. As the sun showered its energy over me I became the Essence of the sun. I became the Essence of the rock. All that I was, was the Light of starry Essence within and outside of human form. I was physical and not physical. I was completely One with everything around me. Resting side by side with the Ilmenite I felt the energetic lightening continuing in both of us. I felt reborn into a world of Light, and I felt more wholeness than I had ever felt. I felt present and alive, and I felt as if my journey was just truly beginning.

Book Six

Deeper Understandings

What an exquisite feeling it was to be in that place, a pure oneness and connection of being, but it had not lasted more than a few hours. It was to become however, the first of many such experiences in the ensuing years. With each one, I would become immersed deeper into the Divine, and each was to last a little longer than the one before. Experience, integrate, grow, experience, integrate, grow, and so it continued. I think the hardest part of experiencing this cycle was feeling the frustration of not always moving as fast as I thought that I could. I was generally very patient, but not always with myself. It was all good though, because it was through my releasing of the attachments that became apparent with each deepening stage, healing each newly uncovered level that opened before me, and opening into deeper awareness of my heart and allowing my body the chance to fully integrate, that I have moved. It has all been in Divine timing as I become ready for the next step.

Within days of returning from Silent Lake the sky was filled once again with the same mysteriously wondrous colours that I had witnessed exactly two weeks before; perfectly parallel bands of vibrant colour, going beyond the rainbow spectrum. They flowed within a consistent pattern, perfectly north south from horizon to horizon; the same grouping of colours repeating itself. I asked the Lady for clarity and she verified that these streams of light reflected the next wave of transformational planetary awakening energies.

I found that part of the reason I had returned to Peterborough was to hold the space while the blanket of higher vibrations replaced the old energies, including those within me. I was told to breathe deep and to purposefully and with intent, exhale golden Consciousness, and to strengthen my essence by envisioning the energy flowing through my body, out my feet, and into the Heart of Creation.

I learned that on our path to becoming adults with God, we are to fully claim our lives from a state of calm knowing, love, the awareness of God's unconditional acceptance of our paths to learning, and joy. We are to embody and become this vibration. We are to feel it into our experience, feel it into our bodies and our hearts to become fuller co-creators. Through integrating the feeling of it, we are to return to the loving realization of the wealth of who we already are: the full completeness of all that we encompass within our human existence. This includes accumulated ancestral and karmic memories and experiences; of ourselves as a child, our teen selves, and our adult selves. We may have passed through the stages of life, but we still carry within us all that has passed before. We are to remember what we each, uniquely brought into this world, regardless of whether or not it was rejected, for that is our birthright and our gift to the world. Most of us have experienced rejection in one form or another, and to one degree or another throughout our lives. Be aware that it has not been other people alone that have rejected parts of who we innately are; we develop a pattern of rejecting certain aspects within ourselves in order to be accepted, to keep the status quo, or to maintain comfort levels. It is through our ability to fully know, honour, and love ourselves that we can claim with the spiritual authority of our Divine selves.

I was soon to meet Hira Ratan Manik. Meeting him was like meeting an aspect of my-self from eons ago. As he spoke to the gathered people of his experiences with Sun gazing, my body lit up with vivid remembrance. Part of me knew this; parts of me explicitly remembered gazing into the morning sun with ceremonial sacredness during other life times, and I felt tremendous joy. He reminded us that within the hour closest to sunrise and sunset it was perfectly safe for the human eye. Opening our essence to fully receive its benefits during these times, and offering our appreciation and love in return, becomes a powerful complement to our health and well-being as it rejuvenates our cells and organs. Opening our essence also boosts our vitality and sense of life. It becomes much more enhanced for people though, if they can be outdoors as they gaze, and if they can stand barefoot directly on the soil of the Earth.

Maureen and I felt it time to start new lives; start fresh with new beginnings, new hopes, and new dreams, so we opened a healing facility; The Centre for Integrated Healing. This was intended to be a healing centre for much more than met the eye. This was a healing centre for any and all beings that needed healings, whether in physical form, spirit, elemental, or the earth herself. As our intent radiated out into the universe I sensed word spreading, and I felt doors opening as many human spirits and other beings approached with curiosity. I found that there was no timeframe or dimensional barrier in the astral plain, and that nothing was linear or geographically restrained. Spirits that had been stuck in time loops from eons ago had become aware of us and were coming from wherever or whenever they resided. The glimmer of hope in their eyes told us all we needed to know, and was reward enough.

We could feel the joy of the building, the Celestial realm and the spirits, and we asked for their blessings to make our dream a success. We felt embraced by much love and anticipation, and felt deep fulfillment, feeling that we had aligned with our highest level of ability and service.

Shortly after, I received an insight on how lower vibrational energies were able to attach. '*We had consented to having the lower energies influence us.*' This phrase just flowed out of my mouth but I knew it was true.

Either we consented by default as we gave our power away during a state of fear, powerlessness, or self-recrimination, or we made spiritual agreements to set the stage for learning. Learning comes to us in many ways, but all of these are learning opportunities. Our discernment deepens, our understandings grow, we recognize scenarios that we do not need to walk into again, and we become stronger and wiser spiritually. Agreements that do not truly serve our highest good can be released though. I learned that all I had to say, out loud, was "I choose to release," followed by my intent centered within the calm, loving knowing of my own power as a spiritual essence.

To heal any consents that did not truly serve my highest good within myself, I set the intent to go to the point of origin in whatever times, places, lifetimes, or even between lifetimes that I made these consents or agreements, and I took full acceptance and responsibility for having made them. I honoured them for what they were, and I honoured myself within that moment in time, as that, for whatever reason, was the best that I could do at the time, but I set my intent to release them into the Light.

I felt the gratitude of connected awareness anchoring deeper within me as my intent was realized, and an energetic shift when the agreements were released to the Godhead. I sensed an inner feeling of freedom and lightness as my cells became free of their old energy programming, and I sensed my cells instantaneously radiating within a higher vibration. I felt that they could now truly begin regenerating with joy.

I later learned, that in verifying the source of information received within the Records, consciously, while in the state of being fully present, set your intent to connect into the Divine emanations first, and intend that only that which is for the highest good will come through. Specify, out loud, that any information offered to you, or the source of the information, be aligned with the highest vibrations of Light and the Christ consciousness. If you carry doubt, no matter how trivial it may appear to you, ask the highest Divine emanations to be present and offer the particular information, or source to them through your intent. In requesting this, their response will be automatic. Ask for clarity. If, after asking three times for verification, and it is not truly aligned for the highest good, it will not be able to maintain its form and will recede. This same way of verifying can be used to verify any information outside the Records as well. You may also ask yourself the question, "How does this information feel in my heart?"

The Lady Beatrice had been with me almost constantly since our first meeting, but now the Heart shaman had joined us and was drumming my scattered fragments back to me. As I felt these fragments re-integrate within my physical and non-physical bodies, the knowledge deepened to start co-creating my heart's desire from the vibration of the new soul world. This is the world that humanity now has the potential to move into, the world based on unconditional Love and Heart awareness. I found that the more fragments that re-integrated, the more I could sense dolphin and higher energy awareness. I realized that I could communicate through the Records with the collective consciousness of dolphins and whales, and I felt a rush of emotions and excitement as I anticipated a deepening connection.

Later, Maureen and I travelled to meet a small group of friends and held an impromptu ceremony to bring healing energies through for the Earth. As we stood in a circle holding hands, we combined our energies and instantly created a vortex. There were six of us and we were all surprised. We had not known what would happen after we set our combined focus, but we were not expecting to generate a vortex. There was energy circling clockwise through our group, but there was also a Light channeling from each of our chests into the vortex. We felt that there must have been higher being influences assisting in this, because as the energy swirled and amplified around us, a portal opened above the vortex and powerfully focused energies were brought through for the Earth. We were feeling dazed and in awe as the ceremony ended, as it had no longer been us alone involved in this healing intent. We had held the space and opened the door for the portal to emerge as we channeled through our hearts, but the majority of the energy had funneled through the vortex from the portal.

While I was walking on their land the next morning I became engulfed in a focused energy wave stemming from a pin point on the earth. I had been walking in deep reflection, my mind somewhere else, so I had just turned to it in acknowledgment and did not think anything more about it. I was so accustomed by now to feeling energy from the land that I thought it was just another occasion. However, when I re-entered their house Maureen grabbed my arm, wanting my assistance in finding something that had been insistently calling her.

I was about to be reminded how important it was to not assume anything. When an energetic awareness, or earth energy, reaches out to grab your attention, it is best not to take it superficially. This turned out to be the same energetic awareness that had just tried to get my attention, and it turned out to be very important, for this awareness was the forerunner of a portal surfacing. It was asking us to anchor this portal in and open it.

As we gathered everyone together, we had a sense that this was perhaps going to become the most significant portal yet on their property. While anchoring it in, and holding the space for it to open, I spoke a focused and determined intent from my soul, and then projected it outwards intending that the whole universe hear it. I intended that the energies radiating from this portal let the universe know that the original intent for the Earth was being brought back. The Earth, and all that had lived upon her, had at one time radiated pure heart energy. I could feel that knowledge seeping through this portal, and I was determined to bring it back.

Throughout this ceremony, an extremely large dragon lay observing us from the top of the hill. It seemed between realities, but it was obviously a guardian for the portal. Its calmly focused watchfulness led me to believe that it was fully aware of what we were doing and our intent behind it. This would turn out to be the beginning of a profound relationship for us. The date was October 7th 2008.

Within days this portal began calling out for stability and nurturing. It seemed more susceptible in a way to the pervading energies on our world, than the other portals on this property had been. I tuned in and found many higher beings around it, and realized with wonder that there were similar beings around everyone who had been involved in its opening. They, too, had come to assist in this emergence, and I felt we were all, in our own ways, midwives to what was being birthed.

I found that my intent alone assisted the portal to strengthen, and I realized that it and the energies starting to emerge were intricately connected to my own Divine self. Through this realization, I became more conscious and grateful for how this emergence was affecting me. I grew to understand that in order to become fully of service to it, it was important that I open to the childlikeness of Source. It was through the wonder, the joy, and the curiosity of my soul, not that of my head, that I would establish the greatest rapport. I sensed the Lady

Beatrice, whose essence I had found to be the Enlightenment of matter, was assisting me in these understandings.

Days later I watched as an Archangel exited a circle of Light and came towards me. I did not recognize this Archangel and he offered no name. He was approaching in a purposeful and serious manner, and as he drew close my mind went blank. I was not sure exactly what happened after this. However, I was aware that there was an aspect of my Essence that was moving through and experiencing the void, and this Archangel was leading me. Whatever happened throughout this experience, my energy had grounded more into my body, and my awareness had once again deepened and expanded.

Vivid dreams soon followed. I was sitting in front of a group of beings, perhaps some of my teachers, who kept stressing *"No matter how much a spiritual message may appear significant, or how much excitement it has generated in others, always, discern that it comes from the highest source."* This message was repeated continuously until it sank deeply into my psyche, so its importance seemed very real. They continued, *"If you are ever unsure whether or not it is from the highest source, you can call on Jesus, or set your intent that the highest being that is directly aligned with God consciousness be the one that comes to assist you."* You can add to this by lightly touching your main Grace point, as described earlier, to enhance greater clarity.

Another dream revolved around how our perceptions affect our experience of life, especially those perceptions that generated fear. In this dream, when the creature faced me and looked into my eyes, I started to scramble away in fear, but then a calm and confident Presence arose within me. I became a vessel of Light and the creature began to dissolve within the radiance. Once again I was reminded to be fully present within my own essence, and to open fully to allow the Divine Light to flow through me. Whether this creature symbolized a latent fear I did not know. What I did understand was that the confident and knowing Presence had recognized the creature for what it was. It had perceived the underlying energetic makeup and manifested fabrications, and had dissolved the power of its illusion. This dream re-enforced and re-emphasized the trust inherent with fully encompassing the place of oneness that is our innate spiritual essence. Apparently, this was a multi-layered lesson to me, for it kept coming back in ever deepening and inventive ways.

In the next dream I was native and two white men were trying to move me. They were doing their utmost to cause me pain and force a reaction, but

I prided myself on not giving them one. With growing insight, I realized that this dream was a mirror of how I had projected myself during this lifetime, and it was meant to enhance my spiritual understandings. I no longer had to prove to anybody, including myself, that I could portray myself as being beyond fear, pain, or outside intimidations. Many times throughout my life I had done just this. I had been gifted with the wisdom that I no longer had to hold myself rigid, energetically or otherwise, so I chose to set myself free. I had found a new source of strength: the unabashed expression of Heart energy; Love, Compassion, and Acceptance. I set myself free in all times, situations and dimensions of my experiences. I opened my spirit to move freely and completely within the flow of Divine Love and I was free. This facilitated a huge core release, and I felt immense gratitude to all those involved who had brought me to this place of awareness.

The power of gratitude, especially when the whole essence of the person lies behind its sincere expression, can be phenomenal. Maureen and I intuitively added the words Infinite Love and Light to this feeling, and inadvertently walked into another extraordinary experience.

We were guided to turn it into a mantra and our experience became profound. The energies started to shift rapidly as soon as we uttered the first word and we sensed movement. The Celestial realm it seemed had set this up, for we created a vortex and astral traveled much faster, and much further than we had ever traveled before. We had moved deep into the Celestial realm and became part of a circle of exceptionally high vibrational beings. Jesus, Quan Yin and Archangels were amongst them. Surrounding the circle we felt the awareness of the Lords of the Records, and the Lady's energy was immersing everything. Maureen and I felt like curious bystanders amongst these beings and were not really sure what was taking place, even though we played an integral part in the conversation. It was apparent that those who had gathered were regarding us as valued companions, and it felt as if we were being asked our perspectives on humanity; but the focus on humanity, was only part of a bigger universal picture that was being discussed. We were one piece only, but everything was inter-related. It can be a funny thing about astral projecting or merging into and experiencing other realities; you can be fully involved in something but totally clueless at the same time. We had no idea what was being said, or what we were saying in return. We had been the observers, as well as the participants, and it was the Divine that had gifted this experience to us.

In time, the circle spread apart and broke into small groups; then suddenly, all involved stopped chatting. We had become aware of a giant hand flowing towards us with its palm and fingers raised. The other participants understood that it was focusing on Maureen and I and stepped back to allow it clear passage. We stood entranced, held deep in the feeling of growing awe. As it closed around us we experienced an energetic shift that was timeless, embracing, nurturing, expansive, and freeing, but words alone cannot truly describe how surreal and completely encompassing our experience was. As the palm withdrew we became immersed in the deepest sense of inner peace and love that we had ever known. The lightness of the energy pulsed with pure joy, and there was a great deal of happiness and acceptance from those that had gathered. Whatever the awareness that had guided the hand was, or wherever we had been taken while it had immersed us within it, we could only imagine.

All too soon after this we were brought back into our bodies, and quietly lay side by side as we absorbed what had just happened. We had experienced two levels of consciousness at once. We had been fully alert in this reality as we continued to chant the words, yet at the same time we would occasionally interrupt the mantra to speak in awed whispers of what we were experiencing in our altered states.

What seemed to have lasted only minutes in our physical state seemed much longer in our altered state. We could not help feeling that this had been significant, and felt blessed and honoured. We also understood that while we had been immersed within the palm we were continuing to be cleared and refined. We felt swept up in anticipation, feeling that we were to play a major role in something imminently important.

Our vibrations had changed during this experience, but curiously, we never again experienced the same energetic power or Divine interactions as we had this first time, nor did we astral travel, which made our experience even more significant. We did have other experiences, though they were much more subtle.

If you find that you resonate with this mantra, or even parts of it, feel free to use, or refine it to make it uniquely yours; just maintain its essence. Allow its vibration to merge with the vibration of your own spiritual essence, and intend that it connect you to all that you are and to all that is. Imagine this connection deepening as it blossoms within your life. I found that an effective and powerful compliment to this was to hold the tips of your thumb and index finger lightly together as you are in the energy of the words. Connecting your fingers together in this way allows the vibration of the words to go deeper into your Essence. Realize that by going into your Essence, and into your heart, the energy of the words when directed by your awareness also goes beyond your Essence into the great what is. Your heart is a doorway that opens directly into the expansiveness of God.

Trust your heart. You will know by the feeling generated, when you have found the combination of words and repetitions that is right for you. Play with it and allow it to flow, for it will evolve as you evolve. If you want to broaden your experience, repeat each line three or more times as you go through this, and with your awareness, see what changes. Try bringing your breath into it, grounding yourself into God energy. What changes in your energy? What changes in your body? What changes in how you experience or perceive life? I found that repeating each line deepened my connection in a subtly yet powerfully different way. I also found that if I placed emphasis on the primary words as I chanted this mantra; I Am, Love, Light, Experiencing, choosing to Remember, Living Expression, Joy, Purpose, and Grateful, it anchored the energy of these words into my sub conscience and enhanced the power of their vibration as the words flowed into the Divine. I could feel my spiritual essence, and both my physical and energy bodies resonating, almost as if being stimulated by a Divine code, as the vibration of each word left my lips.

Infinite Love and Light
I Am Infinite Love and Light
I Am Infinite Love and Light Experiencing
Itself Within a Human Experience
And I Am choosing to Remember
I Am the Living Expression of Infinite Love and Light
Remembering Itself with Joy and Purpose
I Am Infinite Love and Light
And I Am Grateful

We had chanted it three times, and with each separate part we intended that the vibration of the words go deeper into our physical and energetic structures to anchor in the higher vibrations. We became the words as we spoke them.

Weeks later, I dreamed I was being confronted by an entity, and immediately remembered to go into the void. I had no conscious knowing of purposefully doing this before. Had this been what the Archangel was showing or instructing me on weeks before, when I sensed us passing through the void? I realized that I was entering it so that I could drop away pre-conceived illusions and attachments. As I observed myself within the void I could clearly see through the illusion this entity was projecting. I became a neutral observer, and as a result everything that it projected at me dissolved in my energy field and I was left unscathed. I felt that if I had retaliated or felt fear, or reacted in another way, I would have given it power over me. I would have been caught in its created illusion, and propelled into the veiled drama of my perceptions and reactions to it.

Offering our services through The Centre For Integrated Healing continued to be ongoing, but barely an iota of public interest was forthcoming. It was the spirits for the most part who sought me out. We could not understand it and questioned ourselves. We felt highly capable, and we had committed to following our hearts. We felt passion in offering our services through this centre. Were we being tested? Were we meant to be serving in a different way? Were we being blocked? Or were we somehow blocking ourselves? We had many questions, and a range of perplexed emotions.

During this time, I was called to focus once more on the portal. A friend that had assisted in its opening phoned to ask if I had gone through it yet. She had just astral travelled through it herself to see if she could, and her experience blew her away. I was intrigued, and curious about what my experience might be. After her call I set my intent and was immediately inside the portal. I saw myself riding a dragon, totally at ease, as if I had flown with them all of my life. We were flying fast through dark tunnels, and at one point I passed by several elementals over-looking an underground river. They acknowledged me as if they knew me.

After many minutes we reached a massive cavern where hundreds of dragons had gathered. The dragon I rode alighted in their midst, and I was let off in its centre. A pathway opened amongst them and I was respectfully guided towards a platform. They obviously knew me, or knew of something that I had done or was about to do, but I felt only the surreal gravity of the moment. Something about their attitude, and of my presence there, felt deeply meaningful. During the ceremony that followed a crown was placed on my head, and as I overlooked the dragons they bowed to me with honour.

I had felt a deep resonance with the idea that somehow I had once been a dragon rider since I was a teenager, so this was a powerful experience. I felt like Aragon in the Lord of the Rings trilogy returning into the full acceptance and empowerment of the part he was meant to play. What if in an alternate timeline this had been exactly my role and the dragons and portal were showing it to me?

I did not know what the universal purpose or purposes behind Chantal's timely phone call had been, but I had no doubt that the universe and the dragons had wanted me to remember this aspect of myself, and bring that energy into this lifetime's experience. I seemed to have been taken to a time before my shadows of illusion and fear set in. I was shown empowering and poignant visions that allowed me to see the gratitude, acknowledgement, and respect of beings that on some level, I was closely connected with. I was given a chance to remember how I stood, feeling my full power and authority anchoring into my body within another physical experience. It was to add another dimension to how I perceived myself.

The dragons adopted Maureen and our connection to them steadily increased. Many had become messengers between the Earth realms and us, and they were bringing messages of a powerful energy wave that was set to hit the earth. We were to be aware that deeply buried core stuff, especially karmic would be brought to the surface during this wave, and that this would cause a lot of humanity to feel unbalanced as these energies became opened to the Light.

We had found that these dragons were not the monsters of myth. They were respectful and loyal, and above all, they honoured truth and heart integrity. They had however, no tolerance for deceit, greed, or manipulative intent to dis-empower and control others, so in this regard they were fully capable of becoming the monster. It all depends on your perceptions and the energies you bring with you, as to how they will react to you.

Dragons live within their own reality, but they have the ability to transition through realities with uncanny perception. They have their own intelligence, their own code of honour, and their own unique way of being within the Divine. They are powerful friends, and they have much to teach us.

Days later a psychic scream was heard coming from the portal and at first it was thought to be a dragon, but I knew that it was not. There were many, many dragons associated with this portal but this was a being that had tried to emerge into our reality. As I tuned in I knew that it was very young, and that it had experienced a psychic shock as it came into contact with the erratic, collective harshness of the energy fields surrounding this planet.

It carried an energy that I can best relate to as the energy of rainbows, and as I tuned into it I realized how extremely sensitive and vulnerable it was to the undercurrents of our reality. It had been totally unprepared.

Now, as it began feeling my awareness it calmed down and became curious. The dragons were watching over this one, but it was a different dimension that had opened up within this portal. I felt that this was the first of many of these beings to emerge and I could feel the subtle energy of adults, though they were nowhere near this entrance to the portal. Although still a long way off, they too had heard the scream and were nervously grouping together as they approached.

This child stood about eight feet and I sensed that the adults were taller. A soft glow was radiating throughout the portal and I knew that it flowed from this child, and I could feel myself being immersed in its heart energy. In appearance, this child was translucent and slender, with shifting, spiraling colours of mostly blues and whites. I sensed that the adults radiated slightly different colours, and felt that they were possibly from an earlier period in Earth history, though perhaps of a higher dimensional Earth history.

The impact this young one felt as he hit our world had been startlingly intense. There was no one around the entrance to the portal when he emerged who carried the Light that could have cushioned its introduction into our collective energies. A message flowed into my awareness that a gathering of all who had assisted in opening the portal was being requested. This message held the same vibration and texture as the knowledge I had felt seeping through as we opened the portal; that of the Earth holding a radiance of pure heart energy, so I realized that it had flowed from these beings. The message resumed; *"More beings would emerge to communicate with you at that time."*

This gathering never did happen, even though it felt important that we did gather. I would eventually, even beyond this next moment in time, connect with them in my own way, for though it would take them a while, they eventually did come into the reality of our world. I would occasionally feel them around me and we communicated, though once again, on a level that was usually beyond my conscious mind. A framework is being laid between our worlds, little by little.

I sensed that I was being observed by many of these beings, both within the portal and on its far side, so without thought I automatically projected myself into their world. It was pristine and vibrant, and I knew with certainty that this was indeed a higher vibrational Earth; I could feel the heart-essence radiant within everything, the air, the ground, everything, and I could feel the Earth's awareness intermingling with all. I was standing amongst many of these beings, and was being immersed within the pure essence of grace that flowed from them. It felt majestically gentle, nurturing and loving. I know that we were communicating but I did not consciously understand. Seconds, or minutes later I came out of a dazed altered state, back home, not remembering anything more. I was curious where this was going to lead.

As more years passed I realized that they were assisting the energies of Heart consciousness to anchor into the earth's collective consciousness field.

Sometime later I experienced a dream that was unlike other dreams I had had, because this one occurred in stages. It started as I slept but finished hours later exactly from where it had left off. I was inside a native lodge and a shaman was explaining the rite of passage that we were about to pass through. A young woman was assisting him. Our journey was to travel underground, one at a time, from a hut a few hundred feet away and re-surface into the centre of our present group. Each of us in turn was to create the tunnel we used. We were given an instrument to assist us but all would be in blackness, and it was up to us to find and connect with the place inside where we could receive the shaman's guidance.

I was third in line and there was mounting concern for the young person who had been ahead of me. Time was dragging and the shaman was becoming agitated. After conferring with his assistant he shook his rattle and banged it on the ground, toning and chanting. Within a minute the person shot out of the earth, relieved and happy that she had made it.

My turn was next, but this was where the first segment of my dream ended. Hours later the flashback of my journey continued. The young assistant walked me to the entrance point where I was to start my tunnel and stayed with me until I descended. She radiated an inner beauty and compassionate knowing, and I felt that I had known her before.

In the tunnel I experienced myself as observer and in my body at the same time. I was slowly inching forward on my backside with my legs out front. Somehow I felt safer that way. The shaman's guidance was barely discernible and ebbed in and out; I felt some fear because of it. I changed my focus and transformed into a mole because moles' have no fear in dark places. I moved forward more easily after that, but then something happened to knock me out of my mole form and waves of intense fear enveloped and flowed through me. I forced myself back to the state of being where I could move into becoming fully present and grounded. I remembered a book I had read, and of how pertinent I felt Frank Herbert's perspective was when he had written the 'Litany against Fear,' from his book 'Dune'. I began reciting it now.

"I must not fear. Fear is the mind killer. Fear is the little death that brings total obliteration. I will face my fear. I will permit it to pass over me and through me. And when it has gone past I will turn the inner eye to see its path. Where the fear has gone there will be nothing. Only I will remain."

The fear dissolved and I felt a sudden deep peace. A blink of an eye later I was in the lodge being honoured and celebrated. I had no idea how I got there, I just was. Perhaps it was through my opening into a more relaxed state of being, after being jolted back into my human body with all the pre-conditioned hang ups that it carried, and allowing my awareness to take precedence over my emotions, beliefs and fears, that I was able to accomplish this task, because something obviously must have shifted.

What if the full significance of this vision was a reflection of our spiritual journey? Was this a journey through the layers of illusion and spiritual separation, and back to the trust and remembrance of how to fully open our awareness to Divine guidance? Was this a re-learning in how to listen, really listen, to Divine spirit within and around us as it guides us to become free from the limiting interpretations, and conditionings of our minds?

My dreams seemed to be taking precedence over waking experiences during this point; coming with greater focus and guided intent. Each dream became a teaching tool, assisting me to return to greater empowerment and awareness.

We returned to Silent Lake, and as we arrived at the rock outcropping I looked up and gasped in awe. An intensely shimmering silver translucent ring circled the sun, reflecting the vibrant rainbow colours of a second outer ring. It was beautifully surreal, and we stood entranced. The energy showering down upon us was vitally enlivening; it felt like a dimensional portal had opened.

We entered the water asking that the full combined impact of the sun and water integrate within us, and felt instantly cleansed, purified and completely alive. Hours later, we walked out of the park in a surreal state of peace. Returning to Peterborough, only an hour away, we were surprised to find that no one else had witnessed the rings.

Months later, under a crystal clear half-moon, I stood reflecting. Lessons in how to truly honour myself and claim my own value were deepening. There had been times when I had wondered if the universe was trying to see if I would fall back into the old work mold again. I would wonder if I was being tested to see if I was truly committed to moving deeper into the spiritual path, and honour the fullness of all that I was in the process.

I had found that the spiritual journey was not only about inner healing and opening oneself to receive and experience a greater encompassment and connection with Divinity, but it was also about learning how to honour and embrace our full truth within a human experience. I had to look deep within and ask myself, "Do I feel worthy enough to fully live, and express my truth in this world? Am I worthy enough, on my own, to be seen for who I truly am? Am I truly worthy enough, to unconditionally comprehend, believe, and experience that I am worthy enough? Am I truly worthy enough for God to love and accept me? Can I truly be free to be all that I am, and then to express all that I am as I search for deeper spiritual meaning, fulfillment, joy, and completion within my life?"

We are all innately worthy, and we are all loved beyond measure. I had been reminded of that time and time again by the Divine since I started this journey, yet I have continued to uncover more layers of karmic and generational fears and beliefs that undermine it. It is us, through conditioning or habit that has learned to judge and second-guess ourselves. I had opened into the awareness that humanities concept of worthiness was fabricated to enhance our feelings of separateness; from ourselves, from each other, and from God. Becoming whole includes redefining all that we know about ourselves. I found that my underlying uncertainties had influenced much that had held me back, and kept me from myself during my life.

Continuing to reflect, it was during these last months that I had realized that it was possible to heal on a much broader scope. As I focused inwardly to bring healing to myself, I found that I could project my awareness through time. I was able to connect and communicate with my other incarnations, both male and female from other lifetimes, as well as with aspects of myself from this lifetime, that had become stuck in time. I surrounded them with unconditional love and acceptance, thanking them for all that their life contained. They were curious at first, but eagerly embraced the higher understandings of the heart that I opened before them. I realized that it was through my honouring them that they opened to honouring themselves. I thanked them for living the experiences that they experienced, and thanked them for all that they had learned; for that had helped make me who I am. They found the self-acceptance, love and understandings they needed to heal and went freely into the Light, and as each one did, I felt myself becoming more whole. Missing pieces, fragments of my Essence that had become separated throughout time and space, were re-uniting once again into the completeness of my spirit.

As I brought healings to their experiences, especially those involving trauma, I projected my intent and awareness to also go beyond them. I radiated love and healing Light into concentric circles, and visualized them expanding into all times, places and dimensions of anyone that had been directly or indirectly involved. I then expanded my intent to include the earth and all other life, anything that carried the energetic residue of trauma, sadness, pain, grief, and more, anything that was ready to be healed within the Light. This allowed love and healing energies to circle through the timelines into our present moments from all involved. I found that the layers of pain that surfaced could be healed in a much more encompassing and far-reaching way. I also found that I could offer this to anyone who desired deeper healings, and realized that we all carried the ability within us to do this.

Anyone who could bring his or her awareness into encompassing the energy, with intent to heal could assist in making a very powerful difference in our world. People just had to understand that they could bring this ability forth. It made a powerful, yet subtle difference to my-self and others as layers of accumulated density left our energy bodies. The collective human and earth energies lightened as well each time I did this, though it was subtler to discern. Imagine the possibilities if more people came into their Light and understood that they could offer the same? Imagine how much people, collectively, could assist the human and Earth energy grids to release held density? Imagine how much more joy and light we would feel?

Beyond stemming my intent, using my own incarnations as the source, I projected my awareness to bring healings to collective battlefield traumas. I found that I could offer this to anything, or any event that I focused upon.

The immediate, and residual effects of trauma and suppressing unresolved experiences, affect not only how we perceive, but also our total state of well-being. There have been millions of accumulated lifelong experiences that make up who we are in this present moment. For those of you who believe in other incarnations, you can add their accumulated experiences to this as well. Now imagine these experiences continually overlapping one another, with each experience that we cannot fully deal with at the time leaving an energetic imprint that gets shoved deeper and deeper, further suppressing those that have come before.

Visualize if you can the very fine semi-transparent layers of an onion, with each overlapping layer making it more difficult to see its core with any degree of clarity. We are similar, with each of our accumulated layers further separating us from recognizing and experiencing our core spiritual Essence. Experiences that we have that are joyous and loving, and that we experience in an empowered and healthy way leave transparent layers, allowing us to experience full remembrance and connection with our core. As our semi-transparent, unresolved layers continue to interchange with the transparent layers in overlapping this core, they create increasing cloudiness. These layers become suppressed unintentionally into our subconscious, and eventually into our body's cellular memories.

Residual and ripple effects happen in many interlocking ways. Experiencing a situation where physical trauma occurs leaves physical energetic memory imprints that may get suppressed, but we also integrate any emotional 'feelings' that we experienced that may have been associated with this trauma; on top of that, any mental 'beliefs' that come into form from our perceptions of the experience may also get suppressed if they cannot be fully understood, healed and released at the time. In our human experience everything is holistically related; body, mind, emotions and spirit, and they all interplay. Spiritually, we may feel increasingly alienated the cloudier our connection to our core becomes, for this directly relates to our experience of Divine connection.

At our core, we have perfect clarity, and total connection with the Divine and with all that we truly are. We know the oneness and inter-connectedness of all life, for we are experiencing it. We exist in full Unity and Heart consciousness. However, there is no other way around what begins to happen as a result of our suppressing life experiences. Over time our perceptions become more and more distorted. We begin to forget our core Essence because we are slowly disconnecting ourselves from Source. Our egos, our pain bodies, and our survival mechanisms, in time, take over our sense of identity and begin to take over our reality. We become increasingly fragmented, disillusioned, dis-empowered, and empty.

As you may be beginning to understand, the amount we have suppressed in our lives is directly proportional to our state of being, our state of Health, and our sense of connection. The more we are separated from our true Essence and Divine Source, the more fear based thoughts, feelings of shame or guilt, victimization, confusion, anger, illness, unworthiness, and a multitude of other discomforting things take a hold on our lives. The basis of how we perceive and handle each new experience, as well as view past experiences, can also become increasingly distorted over time as we give our Hearts knowing and empowerment over to our egos, or to others that we perceive to be more self-contained and whole than we are.

What you may not be aware of is that it is not just the unresolved things in our lives that get suppressed, leading us to our sense of separation and disconnect. Some innate, very important and integrally empowered aspects of who we are can also inadvertently become suppressed or fragmented from our spiritual bodies, if we, or the outside world, view our aspects in question as fear or shame inducing because of lack of understandings or through a lack of acceptance of our Divine Essence.

Unlike how the unresolved issues affect us unconsciously, when these empowered aspects get suppressed or fragmented, we no longer have a realization of them in our daily experience. We have in effect allowed them to become alienated by unintentionally disowning them: Disowned because we have let others tell us how we should live, how we should believe, how we should feel, how we should absorb and integrate our environments or integrate what is handed to us, or how we should express ourselves; disowned because we have forgotten our own empowered birthright, and disowned because we could not anchor into our own fleeting sense of something deep within that we could grip onto as our core truth. These all affect our health, our joy of life, how we perceive each experience, and in how these perceptions affect our abilities to handle each experience.

Eventually we begin to seek for something spiritually, mentally, physically or emotionally nourishing outside of ourselves to fill the gaps created by our sense of disconnect or loneliness, and we sometimes give our power away in so doing. What we seek sometimes so earnestly is already within us, it has never left us; it is our core Essence, waiting for us to remember, and we have unimaginable numbers of beings who unconditionally Love and support us as we return to the knowing of it. Learning to trust our inner guidance and compassionately honouring all aspects of ourselves for what they are, is an integral part of the journey, so to, is empowering ourselves by taking responsibility and accountability for our own lives and healing.

Once we remember to observe and experience things outside of the influence of our egos, there is no good and bad, there just is. This is a journey about bringing all of who we are, and all of our self-concepts into wholeness and returning to the unconditional acceptance, Love, and beauty of our Divine nature.

You will find that the deeper you go within, the greater the energetic power of your intent becomes, and the greater the unlimited potential of your abilities move into the quantum realm of possibilities, where you can connect with All of who you are and the All of All that is.

In my own experience the more I have been able to bring those aspects, and more, into the Light of the God Source the more whole I become in the process. The potential of this is unlimited. When we can fully accept, honour and appreciate each of our experiences for what they offered us in the bigger picture of our growth, spiritually or in conscious awareness, and we are able to shine the Light of our unconditional Love onto them, it truly does free us and deep healings are effortless, joyful, and permanent. Our bodies remember and yearn for the openness of being that they are now sensing, however they are not used to it. For eons of time we have closed our bodies down and suppressed many things because that is how we learned how to survive.

You may wish to acknowledge these hesitancies within your body, but remember that your subconscious mind views and understands everything that it holds, without exception, as if it was actively occurring in the present moment. You may find it beneficial if you can be aware that your body and heart have highly developed innate awareness and intelligence of their own, and that they are more developed in many ways than your brain. They will joyfully work with you in harmonious co-operation if you ask them. When the time comes that you set your intent and embody your state of being to move inwards remember this; remember also that you are not jumping back into time, and these suppressed experiences are not separate from you.

This leads me into two more significant items that it is important that you remain aware of. The universe does not recognize the word 'not'. It only recognizes and responds to the emotional charge that we are holding inherently within, and to the duration of whatever we focus upon or are choosing to let stew inside. Ultimately though the universe responds to our choices or intent, and to the frequency of vibration that we are emitting. In setting a statement of intent, it is counter-productive to unintentionally draw more of what you do not want.

What I have found truly amazing is the power of the heart. You will find that the more you open to your heart, and the more you truly move into it, the more its resonance begins to align your energy structure and its frequencies of vibration, with the resonance of Divine Love. As this happens, you will find that everything begins to change. You will begin to raise your overall energetic frequency, and you will begin to encompass and attract to yourself, Divine awareness and energies that vibrate to the higher frequencies of Love. The same rules apply, but your experience of life will become much more uplifting and empowering. You will carry the energies of the heart as you learn to work in harmony with the universe. You will in many ways free yourself. This may seem abstract and easy to put into words, but your experience of its truth will deepen the more you move into it.

The second item to be aware of is, our subconscious mind does not specifically recognize, and the universe smiles at, our conceptions of the term 'my'. As far as our subconscious can relate to, which 'my' am I talking about? Which incarnation, or time period and stage of growth from within this life, personality aspect of 'my' am I talking about; remember that our unhealed fragmented aspects of ourselves are just as present within the consciousness field of our subconscious as our present moment self. They are all us, all sharing their own unique 'my' stage of personality and experience. If you take a moment to reflect on your own life, is your personality exactly the same as it was when you were younger? Is it exactly the same as it was before the last significant event in your life? There are subtle changes in our personalities through each stage of life that we go through.

All unhealed fragments or aspects can be caught up in their own created time loops. In my own experience of bringing healing to aspects that I have held within, they were not aware that time went beyond their perceptions until I held the space for them within the Light. Their realities remained just as real to them as ours does to us. Due to this overlap within our energy dynamics, the universe can sometimes be confused if your present moment self is requesting something that is focused towards 'my', if you carry an unhealed aspect that holds a greater energetic charge through its emotions or beliefs. A lot of times, what we are actually projecting out to the universe is unconsciously scattered or inconsistent, and we wonder why 'God' or the universe is not responding. The universe recognizes the I AM presence of our spiritual totality; our subconscious also has access to this expansiveness of awareness. You must remember that we are not our personalities or identities, they have been adopted by us to use in our current realities.

I have as well in these last months, been increasingly meeting and connecting with people, especially younger people, who possess heightened spiritual awareness, higher levels of Heart consciousness, and higher frequencies of energetic vibration. I sensed that many have come into this plane of existence, even though they do not always consciously know it, to assist the higher vibrations of heart energy and awareness to anchor into this reality. These people generally have a sense of something more; they may have a higher degree of intuitive observation and inner knowing, deeper emphatic receptivity, and resonate more with the energies that they are able to bring through, than with the paradigms that are established on the earth now. People who energetically vibrate higher are almost always sensitive to much greater extents than the population as a whole, usually in many different ways. They are quite often labeled, and they quite often have a little bit harder time fitting in.

Some of these people have been given, and have accepted a label to be an integral part of their identity; schizophrenia, ADD, ADHD, Autism, or hyper-reactive or sensitive in other ways. Labels in many regards have been applied through lack of broader spiritual understandings. There are times where a person feels or displays characteristics that align with a label, but no one can be boxed into one. There is so much more to what encompasses us, so much more to understand, and so much more that lay outside current perceptions. Getting assistance with, and attaining greater understandings of the reasons behind the characteristics and sensitivities can be beneficial, but accepting the label as part of your identity is something else again. Trust your instincts, your intuition, and your own hearts. You are not unusual. You may be resonating within a higher vibrational state of being and doing the best you can to adjust to living in the prevailing vibration and understandings on the earth now. There are many who are sharing similar characteristics and experiences, yet we are all unique, and we all have something to bring to this world.

This leads me to an observation concerning labels. People as a whole are highly influenced by suggestion, whether it be disempowering or empowering, which alone is worth repeating because it is so important to understand, for it becomes a powerful factor in how people's lives play out. We all know it but it is so insinuating in our global society that it has become second nature for us to accept it. What are people's automatic responses, especially when they are concerned about their, or a loved ones health or behavior? What are peoples automatic responses when they are told in a generalizing way, what their chances of surviving a health crises is, and what do they feel, when they are also told in a generalizing way, how long they can expect to live? For most people, they experience an initial feeling of fear, heightened stress, denial, self-hatred, and confusion about how and why it was brought on. They also feel, guilt, powerlessness, and finally, acceptance of the prognosis, diagnosis, and the resulting label. In a sense, they claim and anchor in the energy of belief and corresponding emotions, what they were told as an integral part of who they are and it becomes part of their identity. This becomes a self-defining trap.

We are not our identities; that is only something that we have assumed throughout our lives to fit in or to take on certain roles. We are far more encompassing, and we are all unique and cannot be boxed into a generalized label or assumption, for anything. There are so many different variables for each of us interplaying, and so many possibilities for outcome. How you respond to the situation in the moment that something is said or insinuated will determine the resulting life path that you will experience. This can change, but it is your initial reaction that will anchor the energy the deepest into your psyche. The deeper the belief is anchored, the more of whatever had begun to manifest into your life will be experienced. Go into your heart; what is your heart telling you? Ask yourself, do I accept this as my truth, or am I willing to become the neutral observer, the witness to it and see it from a place of higher heart awareness; from there, discern what is really asking to be healed or understood.

As I finished reflecting I started honouring the seven directions, north, south, east and west, above, below, and within. Turning to face the southwest, I experienced myself standing and looking at the sky in both Arizona and the park at the same time. I was not just astral projecting, I was there. This vision lasted a couple of minutes, and then a large meteor flew overhead in exactly the same direction that I was facing. The meteor had just finished burning when a UFO appeared in the exact spot that it disappeared. I watched it bouncing around for a few minutes, and then with amused delight I projected my thought to let it know that I was aware of it. When it reached a spot in the north by northwest it stopped for a few seconds, but then with a sudden trail of light that measured about a fingers width in the sky it disappeared. It did not seem to be moving away but it disappeared into nothingness. I stood there intrigued, wondering if it had projected itself into a portal.

As time flowed by, experiencing experiences that broadened my perceptions, understandings, or awareness had become a part of my life. These experiences would occur in spurts, with sometimes long interludes in between, but with each experience it would open my awareness enough to go further within to heal deeper layers of ancestral, karmic, and even this lifetimes unseen, or unresolved issues. I no longer felt a significant need to record everything and rarely did, but I will relate the experiences that I did record in the hope of opening your perceptions maybe just a little bit more.

In mid-summer we decided to tour the north shore of Lake Superior, and while we were still within miles of home we had the uncanny sensation of passing through a portal. It was hard to put into words but something was very different, even though it still appeared as if we were driving down the road. This seemed to last minutes before we came out of it and were fully back into our reality again. We looked at each other offering silent questions to the universe and continued on.

A short while later we were drawn to a set of hills. The radiating, high vibration energy was gentle and strong, and the closer we came to the hills the more I recognized the energy as Arcturian. We found their base fringing on our dimension, not seen, but very much there. My senses were perhaps, uncommonly tuned in in this way, and were becoming more enhanced as the years went on. We found it under a cow pasture and stood at the fence for many minutes absorbing the serenity of all that was around us. I sensed that there was, and is, a loving respectful connection between Arcturians' and cows, a sacredness.

On an energetic level we knew that we had been guided here and stood waiting. We did not wait long. Within minutes we felt ourselves leave our bodies and knew we were being guided through the base. In time we were taken to a room where we had an in depth conversation with many of them, but again, consciously understanding what was going on was not happening. It did not really feel important that we understand on our level of existence, I knew that an aspect of each of us understood fully. We were however, left curious. This had not been my first encounter with Arcturians'. I had felt an instant connection to them since first experiencing their presence during a healing session months earlier. They were the most heart centered Extra Terrestrial beings I had yet encountered. We left feeling deeply peaceful and calm, unsure of what or how any further forms of inter-actions occurred.

Hours later, as we approached Parry Sound, we sensed a powerful feminine awareness embracing us. She radiated an awareness that was of the earth but also not of it. We felt that she had purposefully sought out a connection with us because our connection deepened as she guided us towards her.

She had taken the form of an escarpment in the image of a reclining woman, and as we came alongside, it felt as if part of our consciousness was lifted out of our bodies and carried into her essence. These parts of our consciousness remained with her for days afterwards, but whatever transpired during that time did not register in our minds consciously. We sensed however, a deepening in our connection to the Earth as those parts re-integrated. Some form of integral link had been established, for I just had to think of re-establishing a connection and it was automatic. The location that she had chosen seemed perfect for her as she was overlooking the beauty of Georgian Bay. In part, I could almost describe her as a Celestial Goddess watching over and protecting the waters throughout this area.

The energy of the Lady Beatrice, and of what seemed creation energy soon surrounded us as we continued our drive, and later, two Arcturians' appeared and began scanning and re-configuring us. This journey was starting to feel as if it would become significant, and that the timing was not just coincidence. We could not help imagining that this trip to the shores of Lake Superior had no longer become just a trip, but that there had been a definite, but unknown, universal purpose behind it. Would something that we would encounter, be the fulfillment of what we had been so carefully prepared for since we had first met, and was it why we had met so powerfully in the first place?

Upon entering the boundaries of Bruce Peninsula National Park we became enveloped in an immense amount of ancestral native pain. The earth felt heavy with it and I was brought to tears. I opened to channel Love, Light and healing energies to these spirit memories, but I sensed that much more was needed.

Within minutes, a car passed us with its license plate reading 'IHELPUBE,' I help you be. It seemed magical how synchronistical events appeared to be falling into place now that we had hit the road together. Sign after sign after sign had opened before us since we started this journey. I felt that the universe was reminding us of how much we fit into all of this.

Exiting the harbour at Tobermory on the ferry MS Chi Cheemaun, which means big canoe in Ojibwa, I felt a huge presence alongside us and my eyes were drawn to look up, way up. Feeling silent surreal wonder I found myself looking at a Neptune or Poseidon like presence, half in the water and half out. He towered eight or more stories above the boat and stood calmly acknowledging us as we passed below. I realized that this particular being, described in ancient Mediterranean Sea faring stories, was real, and I felt honoured. Reflecting on all of my experiences, I wondered how much human myth really was myth. In these last few years I had met faeries, elves, leprechauns', dwarfs, gnomes, sprites, sylphs, unicorns, satyrs, dragons, and even the legendary Pan who I had found to be one and the same with the Green Man of Celtic lore, and, I had communicated with the trees, rocks and earth. Was I unusual? I did not think so. I was just lucky enough to have been given a chance to experience some overlapping realities that are just as relevant as ours. I wondered if the native communities on Manitoulin Island had any legends of this being watching over us now.

On the north shore of Lake Superior we felt a growing urge to have direct contact with Lake Nipigon, and the closer we came to it, the more we realized that it had become a necessity. The earth, Lake Superior, the elementals, native ancestral spirits and the mother energy of Lake Nipigon were all pulling at us to go.

We felt immensely connected to this land, and our deepening soul connection increased with each passing mile. We intuitively realized that Lake Nipigon was one of the places on the planet where the hearts blood of the Earth came closest to the surface. I had felt the Earth's Heart essence elsewhere, but this was a far deeper feeling and it was more intimate, seemingly closer to the source of her essence. We then passed the palisades and wondered if they were a signal that we were nearing the actual Heart of the mother. The land here felt sacred, precious. The mother energy felt very apparent, and she was holding an immense amount of pain that we empathically shared.

We drove through miles of burnt out land. A forest fire had ravaged through this area and only skeletons of the trees remained, but this was not the pain the mother was feeling, this seemed superficial. I felt that she was holding the pain and separation of the collective energy of not just humanity, but also of humanities pervading disregard and disrespect of other life on this planet, and the pain, bewilderment and confusion of their responses on their soul levels. *This is especially true of the soul energies projecting from mass slaughtering methods for food source animals and fish. The soul essence of these animals and fish came into this world agreeing to become food sources for humanity, but it was to be remembered that they were sentient Divine beings, all playing their own unique roles, and they were to be honoured and valued in the process of humanities desire for their sustenance. They respond to love, appreciation, and being honoured just as much as we do.* I also felt that she held the pain of not being seen, not being heard, and of not being appreciated. She held the pain of our dis-connection with her and she held the pain of her earth's children. She felt fragmented.

We now understood that this was what the Divine had been preparing us for, and that our being called here was the most significant reason for our journey. There was an energetic power, and uniqueness, within the combination of Maureen and my focused channeling of energies that we sensed, and hoped, could facilitate an integral part of the Earths healing here.

We set the stage for a healing ceremony, and then asked Lake Superior, the soul body of the Earth, and the Divine to channel their energies through us and into Lake Nipigon and all the area surrounding. Their awareness' immediately flowed about us, and we opened to channel all of the Love, Light and healing energies that the mother and this land needed.

As we finished we sensed the universe and earth continuing to work together. We were keys only but we felt the nurturing gratitude of all around us. Tuning into the Ilmenite I heard *"Continue going deep, expansion is from within."* I saw dragons, DNA strands, and the double helix. I felt galaxies forming as their energetic frequencies reverberated in harmony, and I experienced the radiantly comforting presence of Liam, an angelic being that was assisting and guiding me.

It really did seem that when humans choose to open themselves to assist another being from a place of wholeness and unconditional compassion, frequencies of healing energies that may not otherwise have been able to become integrated by the recipient, or channeled by the channel, can be, and, we were assisting in perfect harmony and cooperation with other aspects within the earths consciousness. Lake Superior and the Earths higher soul body had unconditionally offered their support, and each held their own distinct awareness.

Could another piece of the puzzle have just opened before us? What is the potential of humans working with the earth in ways that not only enhance healings, but that take us beyond ourselves? What if people just had to become aware enough, and grow into heart consciousness enough, to . . . well, perhaps I will just leave that to you to imagine.

Returning home we stopped into Pukaskwa National park and realized that we had had native lifetimes here, and I immediately felt a soul yearning. As I absorbed my surroundings, my inner being began drawing me specifically to the Horseshoe Bay area, and then with growing wonder,

I felt my staff coming increasingly alive with each step. It radiated an energetic Presence that was powerfully grounded and sure. I could feel the land around as it recognized its presence, and I could feel the living breath of the land as it breathed its welcome. Many spirits had begun gathering. My staff took on a personality of its own and spoke to them, and then let me know that it needed to be taken to the water. Many more spirits had now gathered and formed an honour guard around us as we walked. As I immersed the staff into the water, I knew we were home. Searching through my memory, all I could remember was that this staff had appeared in front of me on a path somewhere far from here, and I had known immediately that there was a connection and that I was meant to carry it. It had now returned to its full power and purpose, fully radiating the energy of this land, and I was part of it.

At dusk, we heard the hauntingly familiar sound of bagpipes wafting in on the breeze; the piper had picked a secluded spot way up on the cliff face to honour the sun setting over the water. As quietly as we could, we crept up behind him and sat in the bushes, silently mesmerized by the all-encompassing beauty of the moment. The setting sun, the perfect sunset, and the rolling white capped waves and steep rocky crags must have all reminded him of Scotland, for this tall Scotsman played on and on until the sun had disappeared over the horizon.

There was such an enveloping sense of peacefulness immersing us as the melodic voice of the bagpipes lifted our souls, that it made us feel as if we had indeed been transposed to Scotland in another time and place. The beauty and the sheer depth of soul connection I felt through these moments were just as spiritual to me as anything Divine, and I felt blessed to have become a part of it. To Doug MacKenzie of Thunder Bay, we will ever in debt and gratitude to you for that moment in time, for we will never forget it.

About a month later Kryon brought a high vibrational energy through that enveloped Maureen and I for minutes. We did not know what its purpose was and he did not speak. The Lady Beatrice held the space in the background, fully aware of what was being channeled, but she was not directly involved. The evening ended with us still not understanding, but we hoped it was leading us to our next stage of development and Divine purpose.

I slept well after that and then woke thinking about buffalo, and then one walked into my vision followed by White Buffalo Calf woman, a sacred Being in the lore of First Nations people's. I sat up fully aware, surprised, happy and honoured. She smiled and started talking, but I was only vaguely hearing her words so I focused on telepathy instead. Reading my heart, she understood, and with a smile in her eyes she continued talking; at the same time I started receiving visions telepathically. I was getting a sense that part of the teaching that she was offering me was to open to, and become aware that communications reflect perception and intent, and that clarity comes from the heart. I felt that there was more to this visit that I was not yet conscious of but I trusted that it would seep into my awareness at the right time.

During the late winter that followed my eyes flew open with amazement to find that I had walked into the perfect vantage point to receive a gift from the natural world. The angle and softened glow of the afternoon sun could not have been more perfect, as it brought everything into startling focus and vitality.

A hawk had landed on our garage roof with a freshly caught bird in its talons. I watched it feed and when it was about half way through a morning dove flew in from the east and landed on the wire about fifteen feet from the hawk. It was the calmness of the dove's stance that enhanced the feeling of significance, for it seemed as if it had come specifically to watch over the proceedings. They acknowledged each other and the hawk continued feeding. It seemed remarkably as if the dove had come to hold a sacred space for the hawk or the dead bird, and there was a sense of stillness in the air. Two thirds of the way through his meal the hawk left an offering, and then shimmied for a couple of minutes before flying south with the remainder of his prey. The dove remained for a few more minutes and then turned on the wire and flew back east along the same path he flew in on. This experience lasted about a half an hour, and with the setting sun, every detail and colour of the hawk was vibrantly alive.

I had never seen a hawk land anywhere near our house before, and our garage roof was certainly not the highest structure around, so I felt that this gifting was directly related to my time spent in the native elders conference earlier in the day. There had been a sense of grace throughout this experience and I felt honoured.

I later went to bed asking for a dream or a vision to give me greater clarity on the gifting, and as the waking/dream altered states are basically one and the same for me, this sequence of visions came as I was lying awake.

My vision was of a red-tailed hawk with a snake wrapped loosely around its legs, fully intact and still moving. My awareness leaped and I was in flight. I had become this red-tail. I was carrying the snake, unharmed, still loosely wrapped around my legs. I carried it in a sort of partnership over hills and forests, and landed in a den of similar snakes in the remains of a building. I saw large stone blocks and watched as the snake that I had carried moved towards the stairs. There was a powerful spiritual energy still remaining within the remnants of this building.

I began switching back and forth between human and hawk but I also felt a strong affinity to the snakes around me. I projected myself upwards and received an aerial view of where I was. I was in a South American jungle and overlooking an old pyramid. This area now appeared different than the hills and forests I had been flying over originally, and there was a feeling of significance about this place.

I transformed into the body of a bird again, though it no longer seemed to be the red-tail. I was flying over a mountain range and looking down on snowcaps, turquoise lakes and green valleys. I knew that I had a specific destination but was not sure where.

I was now inside one of the lakes and walking in human form towards submerged ruins. I might as well have been walking on land, as there was absolutely no resistance in my ability to move; breathing also, did not seem to matter to me. I sensed other presences around but it was the Earth that was calling me.

I removed a flat stone covering an entrance and walked down steps into a chamber. There were dragons and other beings, many of which seemed to be from another dimension. The Beings guided me to a place where I was no longer human or bird. I was within a semi solid form, and everything around me was semi solid as well. I could send my awareness anywhere and could see a tentacle of sorts trailing behind.

Once again my awareness shifted and I was amongst the stars. I had expanded in size, enough to easily embrace galaxies. I was pure energetic awareness and could feel the presence of others like me. I looked inside with my inner vision and saw myself as having returned to Earth. I was walking in a human body that I did not recognize. It was a beautiful day, blue sky, scattered clouds, hills, and I was walking beside a small river.

As I was re-reading this manuscript, I was blown away by what may be a profound insight. The following paragraph was what I wrote earlier, as I was reflecting on my visions during my sessions with Carolyn, the Psychotherapist that had opened my soul to working with energy.

'The last vision also held some resonance with me, but this time in a much more expanded way. I was a tentacle, or a feeler, in the awareness of a being

capable of being omnipresent at many levels and dimensions of existence. I sensed that it was not alone, and within seconds became aware of two more of its kind. I felt that they were more ancient than much of our known universe. I also sensed that every organism on Earth was attached by similar tentacles so that these beings would feel and learn from all of this planet's experiences. I later heard that I should read the Seth books by Jane Roberts, as they would offer greater clarity on this vision.'

This vision also seemed to reflect perfectly with the answer that came through the Akashic Records when I first learned how to enter them. I had asked the emanations of Light how they saw us, and I had experienced myself as being an energy imprint, with space and stars in the background. I was a thought pattern, a flow of swirling and spiraling inter-dimensional energies.

Were all of these visions reflecting one and the same being? Is that truly what we are as Divine beings? My soul is stirring, feeling as if I just stumbled into another level of possibilities, a much greater picture of understanding.

The visions continued; I began to feel the rhythmic heartbeat of the Earth and I transformed again. I now seemed to be shape-shifting into many things at once, living multiple experiences.

The vision shifted again and I had left the Earth and was now just awareness in empty space. I was not moving, and there was only a slight sense of minute movement around me. The movement stemmed from particles of a solar wind, but I could feel that each of these little particles held awareness and some form of consciousness.

The scene changed many times again, and each time it was a new experience. I experienced many incarnations, many forms of life on our planet. I connected to the dragons in snake form and relayed them a message. I experienced my spirit looking over my sleeping body, though I was up and writing these visions down as fast as I could. I was the sun, and felt the breath of my essence touching all, and then once again I was back to being the red-tail hawk flying with the snake, the same snake I had started with, though this time it was dangling from my talons.

These visions all happened within approximately twenty minutes, beginning to end, but even then still seemed to be happening from a greater distance, so the details kept fading until they eventually disappeared.

I felt that this series of visions demonstrated the full range of what all of us are. Could it be that we are all part of a Celestial awareness that could be anything that we focused our attention on, at any time or concurrently, anywhere in the universe? My experience seemed to demonstrate that we are, but reaching further than this, my heart awareness holds the feeling that we are.

Perhaps it was the arrival of spring that set the stage for what turned out to be another powerful day. A friend had just returned from a trip to Peru and was excitedly sharing his travels. As he showed us his photo of the Cathedral of Arequipa however, I snapped into a hyper state of focus. The knowing that a powerful and gentle feminine awareness, in the form of a giant snake, was trapped deep beneath the Cathedral against her will enveloped me.

My mind immediately flashed back to my own trip to Ireland and the release of the Essence trapped under the church in Clonmacnoise. Forming a circle, the three of us linked hands and Antun and Maureen added their focus to mine. A vortex formed quickly, grounding and magnifying our energies. I called in the dragons and projected my awareness to free the Essence. The dragons flew with the speed of the awareness and the combination of all of us, human and dragon blew in with sudden impact and the energetic walls that had been holding her prisoner dissipated. We could all feel her gratitude and joy as she flew free.

Antun shared an interesting postscript relating to this Cathedral. It had been, perhaps intentionally, built over the site of the entrapment, and since being built it had experienced major and sometimes specifically localized earthquakes and fires that had destroyed it completely. It had to be rebuilt many times. Was it perhaps the awareness that had been entrapped that had been squirming?

In the ensuing days I found out some information about this trapped awareness. It was the essence of the combined spirit of the local people. It had taken on the form of a snake because that was the form that the people chose to worship. The conquistadors and probably the knights' Templar or masons discovered how much she reflected the spiritual heart of the people when they arrived. Their purpose was to disempower the people to accomplish their own agendas, and in order to do this they had to find a way to remove her. As my friend Jennifer related it, another female could only have entrapped this essence, as only a female could truly understand the full extent of another female's power.

Jennifer had seer abilities, and as she continued I found out that there was a powerful local woman, an enchantress, who wanted and eventually demanded that she be acknowledged as a shaman, but the locals had for some reason refused. When the conquistadors arrived they recognized how powerful she was and a trade was arranged. In exchange for their acknowledgment and gold, this woman would entrap the spiritual Heart of the people so that they would become more easily manipulated and dis-heartened. Until Antun had with such synchronicity, taken the photo he did, followed by the spiritual realm's focusing my attention to it, she had succeeded.

A few days after the release the enchantress involved came to me and I found out that after her physical body died she too became entrapped. The Spanish conquerors had manipulated her ego just as thoroughly as they suppressed the local people, though she thought she had become all-powerful and free. She told me that she had come into greater understandings and had changed, but then her energy started coming into my body with a manipulative intent. I told her that I would not allow it, and gave her a choice of either going into the Light or journeying along paths that I saw opening up to her.

She chose to journey and I followed her into other portals of existence beyond the earth. Her spirit, still influenced by ego and lower vibration, felt excitement, joy and anticipation as she directly entered one of these worlds and abruptly plummeted into a life-form within that existence. Whether or not she knocked out the spiritual essence that had inhabited that body, I did not know, but I felt her gloating with satisfaction.

Jennifer had offered another message as well, and as I felt its truth, I learned my next important lesson. I ask the people of Peru for your understanding as I was to learn that even in coming from good intent, and channeling beneficial energies, that if they were re-introduced too rapidly they could cause equal disruption or confusion as things re-aligned, especially if the people had been separated from them too long.

Her message had been, "*The Spiritual Heart of the People is a very powerful, but compassionate energy. Its release has caused some misunderstanding and confusion among the People on the spiritual level. With the entrance of Heart energy, coming from those outside, the People will be able to assimilate this powerful energy into their everyday thoughts and actions.*"

I projected my thoughts to the South American shaman, asking that they assist the people to more easily re-anchor it in. It was a healing or change energy and needed to be embraced and tempered by the People. By allowing it to remain rampant, without the people fully realizing it was theirs once more and understanding to re-embrace it would only bring about more fear and confusion. The People must take control of it and bring it into their dream of the future. They must allow it to work with them in creating the new world of their souls.

This had been a poignant reminder. The extent of the responsibility that my abilities were leading me to is heightening, and I must always remain aware that as I am moving into ever deepening levels, I am also moving into ever deepening levels of accountability.

Shortly after, Antun and I were involved in another experience. Occurrences that would have once caused my eyes to fly open in shocked wonder now rarely even caused me to bat an eye. Perhaps I was already primed for this, for it seemed as if I was subconsciously anticipating what was about to happen.

We walked into a hologram. The feeling was odd and subtly uncomfortable, even though visually it appeared exactly as this part of the path should have looked. There was just a slight shimmer in the air. I could feel the awareness of the beings that were projecting it and knew that they were not holding any ill intent, but I could feel a dissonance between their resonances and mine and knew that our vibrations were not totally compatible.

I told them that they could observe but not interfere, and we started walking again. The sensation dissipated and then disappeared so I acknowledged and thanked them. Since entering the hologram I had been tutoring Antun about all of the intricacies of it, and of our observers. It felt totally natural for me as if being consciously within a hologram and communicating with its operators happened all of the time. That in itself was the most surreal thing about this experience, because I had not consciously done this before. In another sense I was left wondering if this scenario had been purposely set up to increase our awareness, and that these beings were actually teachers of some sort. Was it coincidence that we walked into this experience at this particular time? It seemed to tie in quite nicely with the conversation we were having about perceptions and discernment.

This also tied into a broader perspective. I had been learning deepening levels of awareness relating to what we magnetize into our experience. Whatever we give our focused emphasis to, especially if combined with an emotional charge, will be what manifests before us. This can be undermined by what we hold in our subconscious if that holds more energetic power, but it will be true whether it carries dissonance or life enhancing heart energy. What manifests before us also occurs through default; by not making decisions because we do not care, or we are afraid of the repercussions if we do make a decision. We maintain our spiritual power and birthright, or we give it over to others in the hopes that they will make a decision for us. Whichever of the above holds true for us, in each moment, will determine what manifests into our lives.

Antun and I appeared to have drawn this into our experience, and we must have been deemed ready by the Divine to receive the insights offered. I wondered how much more of humanities everyday realities might have holographic content. It seemed that the Matrix movies portrayal of how realities can be programmed might hold some relevance in our world.

Our perceptions are perceived by how we have learned to interpret the world. If we allow ourselves to 'unlearn' what does not truly serve, and open ourselves to how our own instincts, and our own hearts, guide us to interpret what we perceive, we may begin living in a way that enhances much more of our empowered potential. This may be worth thinking about.

Ultimately our experiences of life will be dependent on the vibration we carry and what we 'allow' into our space; everything that we have seen, read, or heard, in other words experienced and anchored into our lives, whether it is subconscious or conscious creates our vibration, and it is always being influenced.

How much have we healed what lay inside? How many layers of fear, or beliefs that may not hold total spiritual and heart resonance with us do we carry? How much have we learned to unconditionally love, honour and accept ourselves? How much are we choosing to move consciously toward God? How much are we willing to accept responsibility and accountability for every aspect of our lives? What are we choosing to focus our thoughts on? Are we choosing to perceive and react to whatever situations we are experiencing from the awareness of the heart? Are we willing to bring the awareness of the heart to past experiences, beliefs or perceptions? And so on. Look deep inside, be totally, gently and lovingly honest with yourself, and ask the questions that pertain to your life. Only you, have the final say. Sometimes the hardest part of my journey has been really gaining the clarity on aligning with the truth of my humanity as a spiritual being, and then narrowing down and releasing what does not truly serve.

We draw to ourselves whatever holds the same energetic resonance as what we reflect from within. This is why healing what we hold within and aligning to our essence is so important. Most of what we reflect stems from unresolved experiences that we had buried over this and other lifetimes. Suppressing our identities, our truth, our beliefs, pain, or our emotions will eventually adversely affect our lives personally, always, be it subtly or more traumatically. It was not the optimal response to bury things but it was not bad, so try not to judge how you may have handled it. We all dealt with whatever our situation was in the best way we could, or knew how at the time. Generally there were a multitude of beliefs or emotions involved, some of which would anchor into our energy fields or psyches' to eventually become patterns within our lives. Everything reflects upon, and compounds everything else.

Life becomes easier once we can view ourselves with gentleness and bring loving compassion to whatever we have trapped or suppressed, or to whatever we automatically try to suppress in the future because it became our pattern of being. I have mentioned this before but it is worth repeating, it is not just that our emotions or beliefs get suppressed, but with each tiny thing that does get suppressed, little fragments of our spiritual essence become separated from us. The more whole we become, and the more we open to our hearts, the clearer and higher our vibration becomes.

My understandings have been deepening in other ways. The more we can immerse ourselves into the 'feeling' of gratitude, the more we can literally become the living embodiment of it. In my own life I have been continually amazed at how just being in this state of being has accelerated and magnified the life enhancing experiences, and healings that I experience. I have not always managed to maintain it, but the difference in my life is noticeable when I have. Everything flows with more joyful ease and playfulness.

The time of relating my experiences has come to an end. It had been my intent, and hope through the writing of this book that you absorb the essence of why it was written. It was to inspire you to remember that regardless of what you may have experienced throughout your life, your innate essence is Divine and you can come back into the full embracing empowered experiencing of it. You can return to greater states of health, inner love, and alignment with who you innately are. You can free the binds that have bound you. You have the ability to open your experience of life to whatever you set your intent and focus upon. Follow the stirrings of your heart, for it will lead you to an expansiveness and fulfillment that your mind just cannot reach. Experience a lightness of being that becomes lighter and lighter the further you go. Believe that it is possible! You have followed my journey; I came from a place of total separation, pain, and disconnection. This is past; it is no longer my experience. As I have walked closer into the Light of God, the Divine's all-encompassing Love just grows.

I will share one last experience, for it is the one that allowed me to move fully into my heart and into the realm of God.

First though, perhaps it would be relevant to relate an experience that led into it. I began by projecting my awareness into my throat chakra. From there I asked my heart consciousness to come into my throat chakra to embrace my conscious 'mind.' I asked it to nurture my mind and bring it into my physical heart, allowing the consciousness of my mind to first experience the energy of my heart chakra. Our mind holds a structured linear energy and I sensed that moving it directly into my heart might be too much of a shock. The energy of the heart is pure spiritual awareness and love. It has no bounds, no structure, as we know it. It holds and radiates a field of infinite God consciousness.

My mind was only in my physical heart for a minute before it jumped back into my head, afraid of losing its identity. I brought my heart awareness back into my head to hold the space for my mind, and then called upon the earth mother for assistance. As my mind settled and calmed, back in its comfort zone, we told it that all was OK and that it would maintain its essence; it would be a re-birth. Feeling somewhat eased, my mind started back, but needing to experience structure in order to feel secure, it created stairs before it could begin the descent. The voice of a higher Presence told my mind that the stairs were illusion but my mind could not comprehend it; its worldview was physical, analytical, and it needed to physically walk down the stairs.

I began envisioning my mind walking both down a flight of stairs and up a flight of stairs at the same time. Physically down towards my human heart but inter-dimensionally, spiritually and vibrationally up. With each step, my heart and mind began to return more integrally to Divine balance and cohesion. I felt that it was in combination with listening to Tom Kenyon's Heart Dimensional attunement that I was able to focus so precisely into uniting my mind/heart connection.

What turned out to be the most profound experience I have experienced yet began as a dream but quickly moved into fully conscious and focused attention. I was able to enter the presence of my heart and experience God.

Although this dream and subsequent experience were powerfully, and intimately profound for me on a very personal level, I ask you to reflect on your own lives and the world around you as you read these last couple of pages. It was only later that I realized that what I experienced, along with the choices and decisions that I passed through, are played out every day in our daily lives on a global level. The clues are there, lying both before and within us, in everything that we do, in every experience that we experience. It is our choices in each moment, and our free will, that reflects the script we ultimately play out. Each choice gives us the chance to unfold deeper into the knowing of ourselves within the all-embracing experience of the Divine; each choice gives us the option of remaining where we feel most at ease, or where we are most afraid to move out of. It is all good and it is all Divine timing as we are individually ready to take another step. Either way we are loved more than we can ever realize.

With this experience, but more specifically how I responded to it, my life once again underwent a major change and I became firmly committed to walking deeper into the Divine path.

The dream began in a house with a garden in the back, and it included about ten people that I have known. It seemed we were playing a sort of game, with somebody leaving little clues; opportunities for learning, opportunities for growth. Some people totally disregarded them but most of us were playfully looking for the next clue.

Initially I was just curious, but after a while I began to feel that Jesus was leaving these clues. One by one people began falling away, losing interest. As each new clue was discovered the lessons were going deeper and we had to look deeper within. I began to understand with the clarity of my inner self, that with each opportunity that we were being presented, we were being given the choice of remaining in the old familiar reality or moving into something totally unknown but closer to God.

Eventually I was the last person, and I was feeling a lot of uncertainty about whether or not I truly wanted to leave all that I knew behind. My emotions were pulling this way and that and I could feel the contortions within my abdomen.

I watched as the people around me congratulated the last person to fall away for choosing to remain behind. I could not understand why they were congratulating him and not me, so when I asked, they told me that they could relate to the other person but they could not relate to me. A transparent window now appeared between us but it was not yet solid. I was still questioning myself, and the feeling of loneliness from being separated was sweeping over me. I was separated now whether I went back or not. I could no longer return to the reality I saw them in. Their lives appeared superficial to me now, as if they were only shadows living a pretense. My emotions and all that had been programmed into me were still pulling me though.

The voice, and the yearning of my heart outweighed my anxiety and regret at leaving, and I made my final commitment to fully move forward. Once I did, I found myself outside of a moving train, though it seemed an enchanted train in an enchanted realm. It was travelling through vibrating, flowing waves of vibrant gold and white light, and the light shining from its passing windows shone forth with an even more intense radiance of white Light.

I could feel the presence of a being beside me. At the time, I did not know who it was but months later I realized who; it was Gabriel. I was asked numerous more times if I was sure I was ready to commit myself. Each time, the question would carry more intensity, and each time I would feel the qualms in my stomach stir deeper. There was no la-di-da spiritual lightness here. The foundation of my fortitude was being tested.

As I said the final yes I felt an immense rush of vibrant energy flow into my physical body and could see its shimmer around me. I knew that I had now been given the gift of merging with the fullness of all that was my Light body. While experiencing this, I was spontaneously moved into one of the passenger cars. Divine, radiant Light essence was all around me. I could not see the physical presence of the few people that shared this car, but I could feel their Light essence.

I sensed that I was about six passenger cars back from the engine on this train, and I could feel about four more cars behind me.

I recognized the person sitting in the engine and operating the train. She was a dear friend of mine who has journeyed much further along the path than I yet have. In many ways as I had watched her journey, she had opened my eyes, and my heart with inspiration. It was her example that had helped solidify my resolve. Jesus stood by her side and was helping to guide the way. A beam of golden white Light, much more intense and focused than the golden white light permeating everything outside, flowed in direct line from a point ahead of the train, through the engine and through the aisle of every box car. I could feel the inner pulsing of it. It was immensely powerful and I could feel, no, what I was experiencing in this moment went beyond feeling; it was the focused expression of God guiding the train, and it was a homing beacon for all who walked this path.

My heart and soul were swelling with pent up emotion; thankfulness, joy, love, and surrender. I was going Home. I was on the train of God. There is no real end to this story; I know that now. My heart will always be one with God. I have returned.

I was a little stunned when I was gifted the ah ha perspective about how this moment in time reflected our living reality so pertinently; it stood out so stunningly, and beautifully obvious to me now that I became awash in amusement for not having seen it before. Oh I had heard it from different people and felt some truth in it, but experiencing the seeing of it so vividly really took this knowing to a different level; it was no longer just a mental or abstract curiosity. It leaves me wondering what else is right in front of our eyes, if only we could open into our hearts enough to see it.

I know there are more steps to go, and I do not know what truly lies ahead, but I know that I am serving from a much deeper place, a place where I can feel the Presence of God through me. I could not fully feel this Presence until now.

I felt vitally alive after this experience, but I asked that with each new step that leads me further into God, I be re-tested so that the further I progress, the purer I am walking in truth. After having progressed through this experience, the awareness that I could no longer compromise myself in any way anchored in, because now even the thought of it hurt. Living in truth as I walk the path of God, means that I live in truth in all ways. That may be my biggest challenge, filtering through every aspect of my life and narrowing it down to clear myself of all distortion; my thoughts, my beliefs, my choices, my security blankets, my fears, my hang ups, the foods I eat, my actions and re-actions, everything. Now I truly understood the message I received long ago on my journey when my guides said, *"You must work on becoming clear in all ways."* At that time I had no idea that there would become so much depth of meaning to those words.

This experience reflected the many layers of intent and focused direction that had encompassed this journey. I had continually reaffirmed and deepened my intent, and had uncompromisingly committed to come fully into my heart. I had reconnected with the fullness of my essence through healing what I held inside. My connection to Christ and the Divine continues to deepen exponentially, and, as I began to experience the realization that the existence of God was indeed truth, I opened to allow the essence that is God to unfold within me. I do not feel that I would have achieved what I did without going through these steps.

We are all aspects, little filaments as it were, of the creative field of energy we know as God, all of us on our own unique individual journey of experience within this field of consciousness. Time has no meaning. In the higher realm of the totality of our spiritual essence, there is only the joy and the curiosity of experience.

Each of our life experiences ebbs and flows within this bringer of life, yet we all move within an oscillating spiral of God consciousness. It is us that have learned to react in ways that make us separate; conditioned teachings, conditioned perceptions, and conditioned responses. By going back into our hearts and reconnecting with our own Divinity, and the Divine Essence that is God, we can find our way.

The layers of separation and disconnection, emptiness and pain, will begin to fade away as we begin to recognize, honour, and playfully sing our own hearts song.

It is time now to consider your own life, your own path, your own healing and spiritual journey, and the experiences that may open you to a fuller sense of joy and connection. If you were to sit quietly and remain still for one moment more, and open your chest and your lungs to take a breath right now, can you begin to feel the magic, and the blessing that your life truly is.

So much has opened before me, so much that I know that I have known before, and so much that I know is opening to me for the first time, that I feel immersed in the sheer immensity and gratitude of it all. This, I offer to you.

A Few Closing Words

On this journey there can be no comparisons to the current stages of any other person's journey. Re-discovering our spiritual connection to the Light, the Divine Light of God, in a deeply personal manner, will be a reflection of who we are. Individual perceptions and understandings of our life experiences have shaped the paths we are on and they are uniquely ours. Therefore, though many people are on the spiritual path, no two paths will ever be exactly the same . . . and no two ways of reaching each stage will be the same.

In time, I stood before God, and it was an experience of opening and surrender that words cannot encompass, but my journey was not finished. In a sense it had only deepened into another level; a level that is compelling me to focus on the masks that I have, and continue to wear. It is a level where I am being asked to no longer hide the full truth and the full expression of my own being. It is a level where movement into Divine honesty becomes paramount. Hiding behind illusion or distortion in any way, consciously or subconsciously, limiting myself behind beliefs or fears that do not truly serve the highest good, radiating a projection that is not inherent with my true self, or by not fully encompassing my full integrity at all times, I know, that I will move no further. To fully open to, and allow the God Essence to flow through this body, I must be a clear and pure conduit on a level that I had not previously comprehended. I remember this place, in a sense, the birthplace of my spirit, and it is a vitalizing, fulfilling and joyful memory, but it is the light at the end of the tunnel, and for me to become re-aligned with the vibrancy of that light myself while still within this body, I must return to it from the pureness of my being.

This book has been a reflection of my life experiences and spiritual awakening, though I know more awakenings are yet to come. You will have your own as you continue opening on your path. What is so beautiful about our journeys of reconnection is that we truly learn to honour and love ourselves for who we are. By opening to and allowing our own Light to shine, we learn to perceive with the eyes of the Soul, and see more clearly the Divine Light within all else. We begin to realize how we truly are all inter-connected within a field of unconditional Love and acceptance.

Can you allow yourself to believe that who you truly are, lies beneath your assumed identities and roles, behind your social masks? Can you imagine that you are not your personality, your ego, or your experiences? What would your life be like if you knew you were not only your mind, and not only your body? These are only partial reflections and aspects of the totality of who we are within Divine essence. Can you feel what it would be like to live on this planet if humanity as a whole found the joyful beauty that resides within?

You are the one you came into this world to remember; you are the one you came into this world to find. That is your purpose. That is why you are here, to find your way back to becoming the living embodiment of your Light on earth, and then to share the grace of God flowing through, for God always has, and always will shine through you as you honour and express the uniqueness of you throughout this world. It is through this remembrance that we return to the divine knowing of God, and to the divine knowing of ourselves within God.

In many ways during the writing of this book I became an observer to it, even though I was the participant. A deep seated yearning to open, and connect with the energy of the heart, and with something deeply spiritual both within and outside of myself has consistently become a theme throughout my life. I always felt the knowing that there was something much more, but it was not until I had grown in heart awareness enough, and opened to Divine Love enough, that I could anchor the Light of its understanding conclusively into my life. It was through connecting with my Essence and allowing it to grow and blossom within me that I was able to unfold. It was through healing the many layers that needed healing, and awakening to the knowledge and love offered, that nourished the transformation that became my life. It was the culmination of all of this that opened the door of discovery, leading me to what I had been yearning for.

If you are willing, allow yourself to ease into your own spiritual and healing journey with sincere commitment, compassion and focused intent; embrace yourself within the love, joy, and anticipation of it. Believe that all is possible; believe that the answers to all that you seek will flow from within you. Open yourself to experience a vibration of love and Divine connection that may surpass anything that you could have dreamed.

Can you sense the reflection of God radiating from within your own life? Can you feel the reflection of your own Light? Can you believe in yourself and your right to be? Can you imagine what it could be like? I value you, I love you, and I feel the Light of your Heart within you. Believe, as you embrace the creative and joyful passion of discovering and honouring the full embracing encompassment that is you. Imagine what it could be like.

Look deep inside and allow yourselves to remember, for you are the ones who will make the difference. We all have our own stories. We all have much to share. It is through us that Heaven, or whatever our concepts of this may be, that the unconditional Love and Joy that is our innate nature, will blossom so beautifully into this world once more.

It is OK to allow yourself to believe.
It is OK to accept that you are worthy.
It is OK to open your Heart in this world.

You are loved more than you will ever know. I Love you.
Reach out your hand if you will, and when you are ready, know that the universe will catch you as you truly remember how to shine the Light of your own essence into this world.
The Invitation lies open before you.
Happiness lies within you.
Love surrounds you.
Remember.

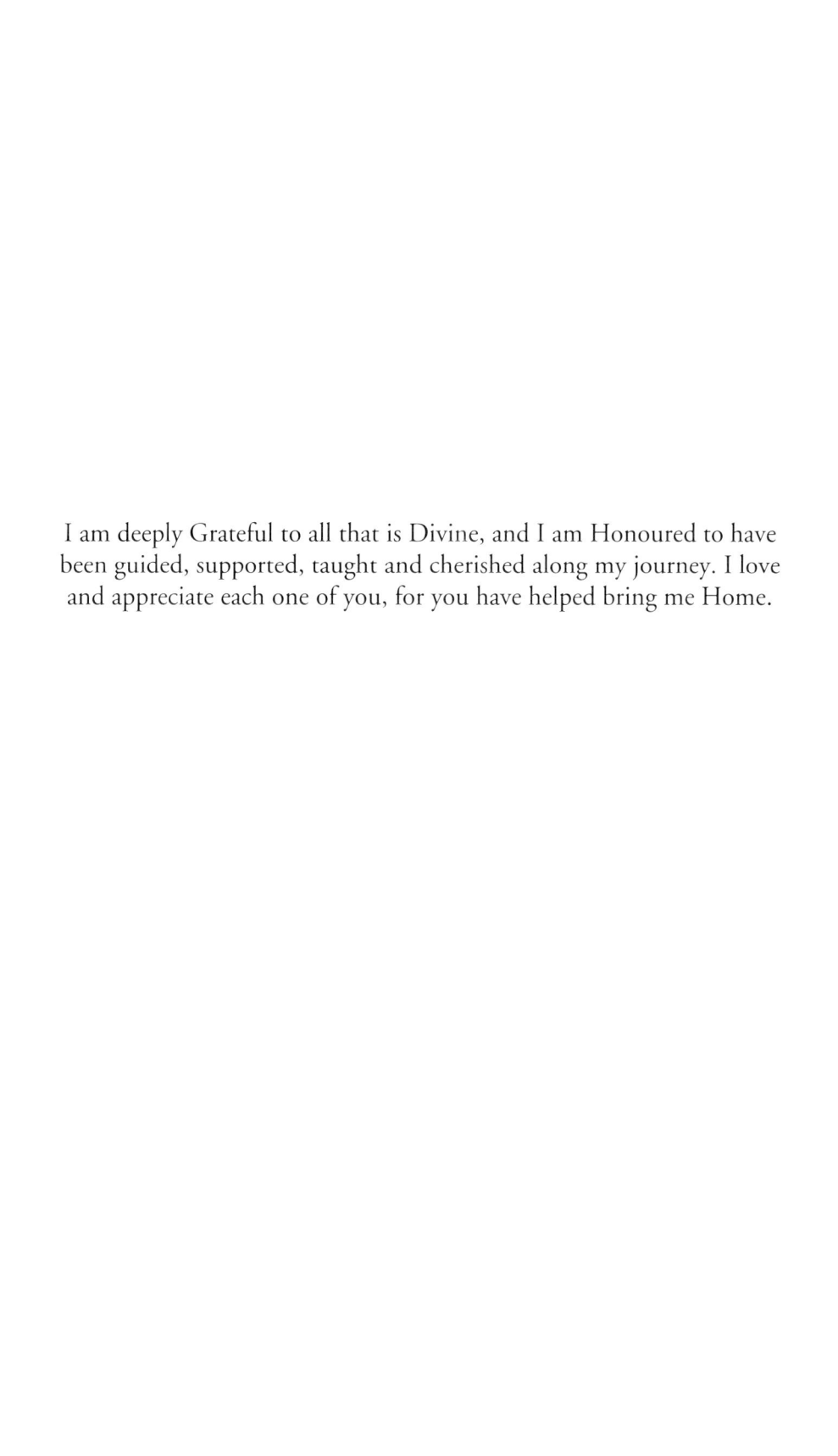

I am deeply Grateful to all that is Divine, and I am Honoured to have been guided, supported, taught and cherished along my journey. I love and appreciate each one of you, for you have helped bring me Home.

John offers his services as a holistic practitioner, workshop and course facilitator, and spiritual guide to those sincerely on the spiritual and healing path. He has opened his heart and soul to full service of the One Divine Heart, and is a conduit and anchor of Light. His own journey continues.

You can contact John through his web site

johnstevenalbin.com

I honour you, with the greatest respect

Wishing you Infinite Love, Light and Blessings

John Steven Albin

Edwards Brothers Malloy
Thorofare, NJ USA
December 21, 2012